DATE DUE

DEMCO 38-296

Children of the Dark House

Cartoon by A. E. Fisher, published in *The Bookman,* about the time of the publication of *Light in August.*

Children of the Dark House

Text and Context in Faulkner

Noel Polk

University Press of Mississippi
Jackson

he family at
knapatawpha Conferences
pecially for
Evans and Betty

"Children of the Dark House" is a heavily revised and expanded essay combining three essays in which I initially began exploring Oedipal themes in the early years of Faulkner's greatness: " 'The Dungeon Was Mother Herself': William Faulkner: 1927–1931," "The Space Between *Sanctuary*," and "Law in Faulkner's *Sanctuary*." These three, along with "Trying Not to Say: A Primer on the Language of *The Sound and the Fury*," "Man in the Middle," "Woman and the Feminine in *A Fable*," and "Faulkner at Midcentury," were originally published as listed in the Works Cited list.

I thank the University of Michigan Press for permission to reprint "Trying Not to Say" and the *Mississippi College Law Review* for permission to reprint "Law in Faulkner's *Sanctuary*." "The Artist as Cuckold" was originally delivered as a lecture at the 1995 Faulkner and Yokna-patawpha conference, and will be published in Kartiganer and Abadie, ed., *Faulkner and Gender*. Jackson: UP of Mississippi, due 1996. I thank Ann Abadie and Donald Kartiganer for permission to publish it here. "Ratliff's Buggies," published here for the first time, will be included in *Haunted Bodies: Gender and Southern Texts*, edited by Susan V. Donaldson and Anne Goodwyn Jones. Charlottesville: UP of Virginia, due 1996. I thank the editors for permission to publish here.

Copyright © 1996 by the University Press of Mississippi
All rights reserved
Manufactured in the United States of America
99 98 97 96 4 3 2 1
The paper in this book meets the guidelines for permanence and durability of the Committee on Production Guidelines for Book Longevity of the Council on Library Resources.

Library of Congress Cataloging-in-Publication Data

Polk, Noel.
    Children of the dark house : text and context in Faulkner / Noel
Polk.
        p. cm.
    Includes bibliographical references and index.
    ISBN 0-87805-867-2 (cloth : alk. paper)
        1. Faulkner, William, 1897–1962—Criticism and interpretation.
    2. Southern States—In literature. I. Title.
    PS3511.A86Z94635 1996
    813'.52—dc20   95-39505
                                                                    CIP

British Library Cataloging-in-Publication data available

Contents

Introduction: Pleasure of the Texts

I don't know anything about inspiration because I don't know what inspiration is—I've heard about it, but I never saw it.

LG 248

I received a copy of the printed book and I found that I didn't even want to see what kind of jacket Smith had put on it. I seemed to have a vision of it and the other ones subsequent to The Sound and the Fury *ranked in order upon a shelf while I looked at the titled backs of them with a flagging attention which was almost distaste, and upon which each succeeding title registered less and less, until at last Attention itself seemed to say, Thank God I shall never need to open any one of them again.*

"Introduction" 708

The essays in this collection derive from an abiding interest in the intense reciprocities between William Faulkner's life and his work, between his lived and his imaginative lives. Most of them explore his engagement with his psychic life, the last two his more public social and political selves. The first concerns the specific site of that reciprocity, the manuscript and typescript pages on to which he translated, transmuted, one life into the other—through what conscious or unconscious processes of refraction, repression, or sheer exploitation we are only now beginning to understand.

The first essay thus signals where, for me, things begin in literary criticism, the encounter with the text at the level of its most basic components: the words the author put on the paper, the conditions under which they got there, the mechanical means by which they were altered or left alone in the typing, editing, and printing processes. A good deal of my critical work, here and elsewhere, turns upon things I have learned during my ongoing encounter with Faulkner's texts through editorial labors, which involves multiple comparisons of the published and unpublished forms of each work, multiple proofreadings of the so-called "New, Corrected Texts," and untold hours trying to parse out fine Faulknerian distinctions between "diningroom," "dining room," and "dining-room." It's not *all* fun.

I am far from claiming, however, or believing, that encounters of an editorial kind give me a special advantage in "close" readings. Indeed, the constant concentration on the microcosmic elements of spelling, punctuation, and syntax have often dulled my eyes to macrocosmic issues, and I am regularly stopped cold by students or neophyte readers, not to say other Faulkner scholars, who point to a passage, a word, in a "New, Corrected Text," which I do not recognize even though I am responsible for its presence on the page—and which, seen, makes the entire text crackle again with the newness of a first reading. Even so, it is one of my great privileges and pleasures to have worked so closely with Faulkner's manuscripts and typescripts, to have studied the texts as they evolved through the visions and re-visions of his writing.

Nor am I confessing to the sort of bardolatry that sanctifies everything the Great Man signed or touched or wore. I'm not really moved by those mass-produced "limited, signed" editions of Faulkner's later career, by which time it had become standard publishing practice to supply authors not with the books themselves but with statement of limitation sheets which were then tipped in to specially-bound books; he hated the ordeal of signing 1,000 or more of these sheets. Nor am I even particularly moved by those actual books he signed because they got stuck in his face in situations where he could not refuse to sign; these books had no meaning for him, and no particular relevance to him as a writer (though to be sure, of course, I would buy one if I could afford it).

I am not speaking of academic pleasures in the scholarly evidence the manuscripts provide, though I have been endlessly fascinated and provoked by this evidence. The fact that certain pages of the manuscript of *Absalom, Absalom!* are written in the same green ink that he used to write the entire *Pylon* manuscript suggests that even though he put his problems with *Absalom* aside long enough to write *Pylon*, he didn't completely abandon the former. And it is stunning to note that his first impulse, in *The Sound and the Fury*, was to have *Father* kick and abuse T.P. during Caddy's wedding: in each instance (WFMS 6:8-9) Faulkner originally wrote "Father," then at some later moment, after completing the entire passage, went back, deleted "Father" and interlined "Quentin" above the deletion. Other, more subtle transformations take place in *The Sound and the Fury* manuscript, as when Faulkner's handwriting changes on the final pages from the crisp block lettering of its early pages to a slanted, almost cursive writing—a sign, I will have it, of a joyous quickening in the pace of composition, of Faulkner's ecstatic race to keep up with a novel that had taken over and was writing itself: these final pages are comparatively free of revision. For me, it's magic.

Nor do I speak of my tactile, visual, pleasure in the manuscripts' physical qualities, though they provide such pleasures in abundance. Few things in my scholarly life have given me the kind of personal pleasure that I got from showing the manuscript of *The Sound and the Fury* to a friend late one cluttered Friday afternoon at the Alderman Library. You who have held it know that it is, simply, gorgeous. It and the manuscripts of *Sanctuary*, *As I Lay Dying*, and *Absalom, Absalom!*, are almost *objets d'arts*, each individual page a canvas sensual to the fingers and pleasing to the eye: rule-straight lines of highly stylized handwriting forming a visual counterpoint to the scope and power, the psychological chaos, of the world the handwriting is creating. The pages thus speak eloquently of a shoring up against that chaos, of compression, of control.

They also speak of the discipline to which Faulkner subjected his lived life, virtually every day. For all the speed with which at his most productive he produced nearly a novel a year, not to mention numerous short stories and screenplays, he was by no means a hasty and careless writer (his smart-aleck claims to the contrary notwithstanding): the manuscripts, which preserve tens of thousands of major and minor revisions, pages with more than twenty different pagination numbers, demonstrate just how careful and deliberate he was, how persistent and patient with his own methods for getting what he wanted. Writing *Absalom* in Hollywood, he was up well before the crack of dawn to get in a stint on his own work before heading to the studio to work on filmscripts.

Faulkner's manuscripts and typescripts are therefore of a completely different order of signification for me than the grist for editorial mills that they provide. He kept thousands of pages. Garland's 44-volume *William Faulkner Manuscripts* prints in facsimile nearly 20,000 pages of the fiction manuscripts at the University of Virginia and the New York Public Library; several thousand more pages of filmscript, fiction, and poetry are in other collections. He kept holograph manuscripts for most stories and for each novel from *Flags in the Dust* to roughly Book IV of *The Hamlet*, at which point he generally began composing at the typewriter; he kept ribbon and/or carbon typescripts for each novel and most stories. Even when he stuck them in a box in the back of the closet under the front stairs, he kept them. He gave the carbon typescript of *The Hamlet* to his godson, Philip Alston Stone, the son of his old Oxford friend and sometime mentor, but he kept the ribbon copy. The only original manuscripts of his mature productivity that he gave away were the holograph manuscripts of *Absalom, Absalom!*, donated in the late thirties to a group trying to raise money to support the freedom fighters of the Spanish Civil War, and the manuscript of *The Sound and the Fury* to Joan Williams in the early fifties. These gifts, and their recipients, are perhaps the best measure of the value he placed upon those manuscripts he kept. These manuscripts comprise an astonishingly rich and complete record of Faulkner's activity as a writer. Moreover, the evidence suggests that these extant thousands are but the tip of the iceberg, the pages he kept after discarding those he had written through and past.

He didn't just keep them, however: he preserved them. Doubtless his reasons were at one level very practical: they might form a financial legacy of some sort for his family to sell if they needed to. But it seems to me more complex than that. There is an almost ritualistic quality to the way he hand-bound the carbon typescripts of each novel through *Sanctuary*, just as there is something ritualistic in the way he would often sculpt one page of manuscript by scissoring a passage from a previous page and pasting it to the current one; numerous manuscript pages contain more than one such paste-on. Frequently these passages are only a few lines long, so that it would have been easier, even more efficient, to have re-written the passage onto the new page. The scissors and paste, then, seem to have allowed him a hands-on, a tactile engagement with his imaginative life through an almost finicking preciosity: as though there was something inexpressibly fragile about his imagination, about the entire enterprise, that required a more intimate touch than even his fine-nibbed pen and the spidery-delicate neatness and order of the individual pages could give him.

The post-*Go Down, Moses* manuscripts and typescripts are, quite to the contrary, sprawling and vigorous in their comparative disarray. When he wrote in ink he used a pen with a thicker nib to write a hand less deliberate, less finely chiselled than the earlier hand, and lots harder to read, perhaps even for himself. Whereas the earlier typescripts are neat and generally clean, even when containing holograph or typed revisions, the later ones preserve the kinds of revisions he made on the earlier manuscripts: thousands of words, lines, paragraphs cancelled in ink or grease pencil or typed over. Moreover, an increasingly parsimonious Faulkner by and large typed these pages on the versos of earlier versions of those same pages, indiscriminately typing sections of *A Fable*, for example, on versos of superseded pages of *Requiem for a Nun*, too, as well as on those of *A Fable*. These typescripts probably represent a stage in the composition process that in the earlier works would have been the stage just prior to the final typing, which he himself would have done. In these later books he saved himself the extra typing job by sending this complete penultimate version directly to his Random House editor, who made corrections (for good or for ill) and sent it on to the printer.

It may be easy to understand why Faulkner would preserve those beautifully-crafted early manuscripts and typescripts, not so easy, perhaps, to understand why he would have kept the hundreds of pages of foul papers from *Requiem* and *A Fable*. But these pages, like the early ones, are, I have come to believe, all part of the ritualized significance the act of writing had for him. Though he did no scissoring and pasting on these late typescripts, they contain evidence of similar rituals of composition: among the *A Fable* typescripts, for example, are numerous passages which he retyped several times—not revising each time, but just retyping, perhaps priming the pump, as it were, during spells when the writing was going badly, perhaps merely incanting passages that pleased him.

Perhaps the manuscripts are a record of his accomplishment as a single individual working alone, as opposed to the collaborative processes of editing and publishing, during which he necessarily had to surrender some of his autonomy. Indeed, he took almost no interest in the printed forms of his books: he occasionally fought losing battles with editors over their alterations, but he *never* restored his original intentions back to what had been editorially altered. And he never revised a novel after it was published; for all we know, he never even re-read his novels (except, of course, those passages he read in public). For all intents and purposes, when he gave a typescript to his publishers he lost interest in it and proceeded immediately to the next blank page; what proofing he did he did with some obeisance to his professional duty, but he took no pleasure or interest in these more mechanical stages of literary production. His preservation of these sites of his actual work, then, is not a talismanic clinging, but rather an act of reverence, perhaps, of homage, to the agony and sweat that he so often associated with the act of writing.

In thinking about the reciprocities between Faulkner's lived and imaginative lives, I am in some ways making a formal distinction that Faulkner didn't necessarily have to make (and in writing "Mississippi" in 1953 he simply dismissed the distinction out of hand). I am not particularly interested, in the essays reprinted here, to discuss how he appropriated the details of his life as citizen Faulkner to his fiction. Others have done superb jobs of noting such details, though they have mostly assumed that the exchange between life and fiction runs only in one direction, from the life to the work. I am not sure that this need be the only direction that reciprocity can flow—indeed, it is not reciprocity unless it flows equally in both directions. I believe, for example, that Faulkner's political activity in the 1950s was a direct and noble and courageous response to the racial morality of *Light in August, Absalom, Absalom!, Go Down, Moses* and *Intruder in the Dust*, a recognition of the relationship between politics and art that many of his more doctrinaire southern New Critical contemporaries and critics simply denied, or escaped, by claiming to believe that art can be hermetically sealed away from the moral processes of the lived life. For me, one of the loveliest minor effects of his political engagement can be traced in the fiction: in the early works he nearly always wrote "negro," with a lower case "n"; in *The Town*, his first novel after the years of political turmoil, he invariably capitalized it. *Go Down, Moses* contains a mixture of "N" and "n," especially in the final chapter; it is perhaps a conscious, perhaps an unconscious, distinction Faulkner was beginning to make, even in 1942. For an editor of *Go Down, Moses*, this is an "inconsistency," an "irregularity" that presents a problem; for one interested in Faulkner's life, it signals a moment of transition in the development of his political consciousness. A small thing, you will say, and I will agree; yet it is there, in the typescripts, a subtle marker of that reciprocity between life and works.

Though Faulkner didn't revise his books after they were published, he was nevertheless constantly revising, rewriting, the work of Yoknapatawpha, each new character, each new vision, forcing itself back upon and into his life, moving him toward implicit questions about the meaning of his own experience which in turn asked new questions for the fiction to explore. None of the reciprocity of the earlier fiction is as dramatic as his political activity of the 1950s, of course, but it seems clear that during the early stages of his career he was working through certain of his own psychic problems. His revision of *Sanctuary* was, I believe, to a large extent a result of his conscious recognition of those problems, and one of the reasons *Light in August* is so much cooler and more formal a novel than its predecessors is that Joe

Christmas is less autobiographical than Quentin Compson and Horace Benbow and Elmer had been, though beset by the same demons.

Indeed, for all its astonishing variety, Faulkner's work returns constantly, compulsively, to certain powerful images that form a sort of ground zero in Yoknapatawpha, images based in family pathologies and the terror that is childhood in Faulkner: seductive mothers, weak fathers; iron-haired bespectacled repressive grandmothers; dark houses from which children must escape through windows instead of doors; windows that separate characters from a fecund world that beckons and terrifies. The list is a long and almost infinitely varied one, and I've tried to identify them in all their similarities and differences in "Children of the Dark House." Though they occur most frequently, most obsessively, in the fiction up through *Light in August*, they are very much a part of the rest of his fiction, too: so much a part that together they form a considerable part of the language, the signifying gestures, of Faulkner's fiction. They are all rooted in the Oedipus complex and mostly understandable by reference to the works of Sigmund Freud; I believe that they are all likewise rooted in Faulkner's own family pathologies and that a good deal of the specific energy of his fiction, especially the early works, is autobiographical.

Five of the essays reprinted here began in the attempt to understand his revisions of *Sanctuary*, and in the simultaneous discovery of curious triangulations between Faulkner's life, his works, and the works of Freud. Most of them explore the resonances created throughout the fiction by his compulsive use and re-use of the images described above. The final two essays look at him as a man engaged with his outer world as well as his inner. "Man in the Middle" explores his entry into the nation's civil rights struggles in the 1950s, and "Faulkner at Midcentury" examines the relationship between his increasing personal despair during the years of his public success as a lionized, indeed revered, certifiably immortal Nobel laureate.

I have gladly taken the occasion of reprinting to revise and update these essays; the encounter with my prose of 20 years ago has been, to say the least, a chastening experience. I cannot adequately thank all the friends who in one way or another have contributed to the contents of this book. Many more people than I can name who have heard some of these essays given as lectures or read various versions of them have made useful suggestions for revisions, additions, and rethinking. I've not always had the grace to accept their suggestions, but I've never failed to appreciate their time and trouble in making them.

I am particularly grateful to Elisabeth Muhlenfeld, Dawn Trouard, Edwin T. Arnold, and James G. Watson for reading and commenting extensively on *Children of the Dark House*, and to Seetha Srinivasan, of the University Press of Mississippi, for believing that these essays are worth collecting in this volume.

I am no less grateful for the friendship and wisdom and good advice of Ann J. Abadie, André Bleikasten, Joseph Blotner, George Bornstein, James B. Carothers, Susan V. Donaldson, Doreen Fowler, Richard Gray, Richard Godden, Michel Gresset, Evans Harrington, Stanley Hauer, Dan Hise, Lothar Hönnighausen, Anne Goodwyn Jones, Donald M. Kartiganer, John T. Matthews, Thomas L. Mc-Haney, Neil R. McMillen, Michael Millgate, Peter Nicolaisen, François Pitavy, Stephen M. Ross, Hans Skei, and Theresa Towner; there's a special place in my heart and my work for the late Jim Hinkle, the late Albert Erskine, and the late Cleanth Brooks.

At the University of Southern Mississippi I have always had the unfailing cooperation and encouragement of President Aubrey K. Lucas, and of the Chair of the English Department, David Wheeler. I also thank Jesse Stevens, Denise Tanyol, and Robyn Preston for various other necessary editorial labors.

Children of the Dark House

Where the Comma Goes

Editing William Faulkner

*Although those who concern themselves with details are re-
garded as folk of limited intelligence, it seems to me that this
part is essential, because it is the foundation, and it is impossible to erect any building or establish any method without
understanding its principles. It is not enough to have a liking
for architecture. One must also know stone-cutting.*

Saxe, qtd in Foucault, *Discipline & Punish*

Scholarly editing is the ultimate act of criticism, because
it involves a wider range of issues than interpretation alone does, from
macrocosmic ones like the author's *meaning*, to more mundane and
practical microcosmic ones like *where does the comma go?* Dealing with
all these issues responsibly requires extensive knowledge of publishing history and of publishing techniques and procedures, of standard
usage in the author's period, of the author's preferences at any period
of his or her career, of the author's relationship to commercial editors, to financial considerations, and to the political and cultural
times, and of the author's practices in composing, revising, and proofreading. The editor must be sensitive to an author's most subtle nu-
ances of style, punctuation, and spelling, as well as to larger issues in
the work, but also constantly aware of the complex interaction between his or her own aesthetic sense and the author's, because in
order to determine where the comma goes the editor must constantly
differentiate between authorial *error* and authorial *intention*. Finally,
the editorial act is central to the critical enterprise because editorial

decisions impinge directly upon questions of canon and literary history.

This is not just an apologia for editors, but rather to suggest the variety of complex issues involved in editing any text. And if these issues impinge on the editing of works up through the nineteenth century, during which time grammar and punctuation usage was at least thought to be evolving toward some theoretical point of "correctness," they are much more central to the editing of the works of the high moderns, who merely demanded that readers re-think the entire semiotic systems by which they had read the precedent literary generations.

Thus the immediate problem in editing a modernist text is that the editor can no longer usefully call on W. W. Greg's distinctions between "substantives" and "accidentals" (those variations that affect meaning directly and those that do not; in practice the distinction has come to be that between words and punctuation) because Greg assumed a stability in language that it was precisely the purpose of many modernists to challenge. How useful would Greg be to the editor of e. e. cummings, for example, who must decide whether an unpaired close-parenthesis, or a comma or a colon, in the middle of a word is correctly placed or whether its placement is a compositorial, editorial, or even authorial error? The gap between "substantives" and "accidentals," never a very large one, virtually disappears in modernist texts, especially in radically modernist ones like *Ulysses* and *The Sound and the Fury* and *As I Lay Dying*, wherein *every* jot and tittle is at least potentially substantive.

Cummings is, of course, the most extreme example of an author at odds with the conventions of written language, at play with the relationship between the signifier and the signified; he indeed uses that relationship as the absolute meat and meaning of some of his poems. Of fiction writers, William Faulkner was clearly the most radical experimenter with the visual representation of language, more radical, in some ways, than Joyce; a great deal of Faulkner's fiction is intimately concerned with the inadequacy of words, written and spoken, and some of his most memorable passages articulate this inadequacy, as in Addie Bundren's poignant complaint that "words are no good; that words dont ever fit even what they are trying to say at" (AILD 115).

Doomed by his craft to deal with inadequate words, Faulkner perforce resorted to an inventive array of other visual devices—italics, double and single quotation marks, flush left paragraph margins; dialogue separated by dashes; uncapitalized and unpunctuated and ungrammatical passages in characters' speeches and thoughts; extremely long compound-complex sentences (which, however, always parse); spaces, gaps in the text; and line drawings of a coffin and of an eyeball as part of the text—to try to communicate what words by themselves could not. Even though there are large issues in editing Faulkner's texts, nearly all of the most perplexing editorial problems center around the regularity, or irregularity, of Faulkner's manipulation of these textual devices, the extent to which either regularity or irregularity is part of the texture of his intention; the problems of that "intention" anyway; the extent to which any editor can hope to differentiate those things that should be emended from those that should be left alone; the ways in which any editor's aesthetic sensibilities—his or her sense of what literary art *is*—affect editorial decisions. Applied to all authors, solutions to these problems cannot but force us to consider the effect such decisions eventually have on literary history and on the canon.

In this essay I'd like to lay out some of the problems I have faced in editing the texts of William Faulkner, but I must note at the beginning that none of the texts I have edited[1] can be considered "definitive"—whatever that means—by any of the general standards accepted over the years by followers of W. W. Greg and Fredson Bowers and promoted by the Modern Language Association's Center for Editions of American Authors (CEAA) and its successor, the

1. *Sanctuary: The Original Text* (1981); *The Sound and the Fury* (1984); *Absalom, Absalom!* (1986); *As I Lay Dying, Sanctuary, Light in August,* and *Pylon* (1985); *Absalom, Absalom!, The Unvanquished, If I Forget Thee, Jerusalem [The Wild Palms],* and *The Hamlet* (1990); *Go Down, Moses, Intruder in the Dust, Requiem for a Nun,* and *A Fable* (1994). All have been or will be published in Vintage International paperback form.

Committee on Scholarly Editions (CSE). Although I have been the grateful beneficiary of lots of help and advice from colleagues and friends in Faulkner studies, these new texts are essentially a one-man show, for which I happily take credit where due and, less happily, blame. I've made extensive use of the available holographs and galleys, letters and other evidence, but my procedure for the "New, Corrected Texts," as they are called, has been essentially to trust Faulkner and his typescripts, documents he himself prepared, and, where possible, to restore his typescript readings in preference to editorial and, occasionally, even authorial revision. A "definitive" edition of Faulkner will have to await a more extensive project which will more thoroughly examine all the available evidence; the new texts are intended to restore Faulkner's typescripts, to *de-edit* them, to use James B. Meriwether's excellent term, in order to get into print texts as close to Faulkner's typescripts as possible.

But accepting the typescripts as *expressing* Faulkner's intentions begs several questions about how well they actually *contain* them. The typescripts are very clear, generally, but they are marred by a number of typos, revisions, irregularities in patterns of narration and punctuation, and perhaps by outright misreadings of his own handwriting![2] Some of the differences between the published texts and these typescripts prove that Faulkner or somebody did some revising or polishing or changing on now lost galley or page proofs—the only places where such changes could have occurred. Likewise, there are some problems caused by Faulkner's acquiescence to editorial emendation and the extent to which he, in James West's phrase, delegated his intentions to editors who were expected to divine those intentions through the typescript, through correspondence or conversation, and then to execute them in places where Faulkner failed to.

Except for the well-known instances of *Sanctuary* and *Requiem for a Nun*, Faulkner but rarely initiated revisions in galleys; such revisions

2. Faulkner once told a group at the University of Virginia he wrote so fast "that somebody said my handwriting looks like a caterpillar that crawled through a ink well and out on to a piece of paper. If I leave it until tomorrow I can't read it myself, so it's got to be put down quick and then typed quick" (FU 194).

as he did make in proof normally were to correct typos, to respond to editorial queries with a correction, a minor revision, a *leave as is* or, occasionally, to repair damage that editorial intervention had caused. The evidence suggests that Faulkner did not normally get terribly exercised at editorial intervention; he did, of course, object to Ben Wasson's editing of *The Sound and the Fury*, and he insisted that his typescript readings as regards italics be restored (Polk, *Handbook*, 3–6); and with *Pylon* he repaired one problem by adding a bridge between two scenes. In no instance did he insist that editors leave his apostrophe- and period-less contractions and abbreviations alone, and I don't recall a case in which he restored edited material to short stories as he collected them.[3] It is true that he objected to Random House editors' wholesale revision of *Absalom, Absalom!*, and to their bowdlerization and retitling of *If I Forget Thee, Jerusalem*; but it is also true that he never made any effort, even in the fifties, as a powerful Nobel laureate, to have those alterations corrected in new editions. How close, then, is it possible to get to Faulkner's *intentions*, in large or small matters, even as they express themselves on typescripts he prepared, when he himself did not often protest editorial intervention? That is, does his acquiescence to editorial intervention imply a preference for editorial changes? It would be, I think, naive to assume so.

To a large extent, of course, *all* authorial intentions are delegated intentions—to the extent, that is, to which any author must entrust the work to other hands to bring it to publication, and nearly all do; even writers who publish or revise themselves are in effect delegating their intentions to another self, a self different even if only older and so having different intentions about the text in hand than when she or he originally submitted it. I now think, for example, that Faulkner eviscerated a superior novel when he revised *Sanctuary* in galleys; Hershel Parker and Brian Higgins have argued that Fitzgerald was

3. As with the stories collected in *The Unvanquished*, he probably sent to book editors tearsheets of inconsistently *Post-* and *Scribner's-* and *Collier's*-edited stories pasted to his typing paper, without bothering to correct their bowdlerizations, their re-punctuation or re-paragraphing of his prose, or their normalization of his dialect.

well on his way to doing the same thing when he revised *Tender Is the Night* after its publication. Parker continues to argue that authorial revision is not necessarily improvement (*Flawed Texts*), and I believe we have to admit the corollary, that not all editorial changes are necessarily bad ones. If we insist upon the primacy of what authors actually put on paper, at the expense of their intentions, we may as well publish all literary works in typescript and manuscript facsimiles; if we accept the author's agreement with or acquiescence to editors' or collaborators' alterations, we have little choice but to stick with the work's first published edition; in either case we, as editors, have unintentionally theorized ourselves out of work. Taken to one extreme, answers to questions about authorial intention aid and abet those who want to see texts as cultural documents, products not of an author alone but of a time and a place, which should therefore be studied only as they were originally *published*, not as they were written. Taken to the other extreme, answers that insist upon the absolute primacy of what the author wrote, instead of on what he or she intended, may in some cases actually diminish the perceived aesthetic or artistic value of a work, a consequence that could have profound effects on the canon.

Thus the editorial enterprise raises several crucial questions about complex relationships among author, editor, art, and salable artifacts. Could we? should we? knowingly downgrade a work back to an author's "intentions" if an editor's emendations had somehow made the work demonstrably superior to what the author had written, superior even to what the author had *intended*, whether the author had delegated that intention or not? The question is not just one of correcting error; indeed, the larger questions address themselves directly, perhaps even antagonistically, to aesthetic considerations: simply, what makes one work or one author "better" than another? What are the standards—aesthetic or commercial or political—that make such judgments necessary, or possible? Most of the debate about James West's edition of Dreiser's *Sister Carrie* and about Henry Binder's edition of Crane's *The Red Badge of Courage*, both of which audaciously claimed to restore what the author wrote, has centered less on the finer points of editorial theory than on whether the new texts are "better" than the ones we have grown comfortable with (Parker, *Flawed Texts*, 147–180 and *passim).*

Try as we must to keep them at bay, aesthetic considerations, always highly subjective and personal, can never be very far from an editor's decisions. More than one friend has argued with me that Faulkner's editors at Random House did him a *big* favor in editing *Absalom, Absalom!* so heavily. Saxe Commins and company rewrote significant portions of that novel by deleting many passages, by drastically altering the punctuation, and by "clarifying" many of Faulkner's deliberately ambiguous pronoun references. Questioned whether I was going to restore one particular passage, I was able to respond with an enthusiastic Yes, partly because I do not think it my job to *improve* Faulkner or to impose my editorial powers on his aesthetic prerogatives, although obviously an editor cannot escape doing so. But since my own aesthetic sensibilities have largely been shaped by Faulkner, I am forced to confess to a profound, perhaps even blind, confidence in Faulkner's sense of himself as an artist (he told a friend that he thought *Absalom* was "the best novel yet written by an American" [Blotner (1984), 364]) and in his attention to the details of his text.

I readily grant that such special arguments for Faulkner allow me to slip off the theoretical hook as regards other authors. For me, in editing Faulkner there is hardly ever a conflict between aesthetics and intention, or between intention and accomplishment; and so when possible, as I say, I trust him, allow him to stand, dingdongs of doom and all, and I seriously doubt that there are enough dings in any of the "New, Corrected Texts" to cause a general lowering of our estimates of them. With other authors whose self-confidence, not to say achievement, was not so great as Faulkner's, the gulf between intention and accomplishment might be wide indeed, and how I might edit them is another question altogether.

Discussions of complex aesthetic issues can be enhanced by access to as many different "versions," as many different stages of composition of any work, as are available, so that we can contemplate the novel as a *process* rather than as a completed *object*. I have, for example, argued that we ought not think of a single *Sanctuary*, that we should think of the two versions[4] as "forming a single literary text that is far more significant than either of the versions taken singly" ("Children of the Dark House"). But the critic's understandable desire to have many versions of a text is precisely the problem for the editor, who must deal in particulars—particular texts, particular commas and semicolons, particular paragraphs. This is partly why the CEAA and CSE have expended so much energy on apparatuses for their editions: the historical collations and the tables of variants and emendations seek to provide access to as many different reconstructions of the in-process text as possible. Not many editors will have the luxury that I fortunately have had of editing and publishing multiple versions of the same novel;[5] most editors will have to choose what to do, line by line, comma by comma, and readers will be stuck with these choices for some time to come, especially if Norton, say, in its canonical (marketplace) wisdom, decides to transubstantiate our meagre bread into the actual living body of its literature anthologies.

Generally speaking, for the Faulkner texts up through *Go Down, Moses* in 1942, there are relatively few problems figuring out who,

4. *Sanctuary: The Original Text* (1981) reproduces the typescript text of that novel's original version, the text Faulkner submitted to Cape & Smith, then revised when he saw it in galleys. The Library of America text (1985), published as a Vintage International paperback (1990) as *Sanctuary: The Corrected Text* is a new text of his revisions, published originally in 1931.

5. I have been able to edit *The Sound and the Fury*, to make corrections for the Vintage paperback, and will be able to make other corrections as necessary. I have overseen publication of that novel's manuscript and carbon typescript in facsimile—four different versions of a single novel. I have edited the two different versions of *Sanctuary* and have overseen facsimile reproductions of Faulkner's typescript, a third version, and of his holograph manuscript, from which can be reconstructed, I suspect, a large number of other "versions" of the original text of *Sanctuary*. *William Faulkner Manuscripts*, Garland's 44-volume facsimile edition of the most important of the extant Faulkner manuscripts at the Alderman Library of the University of Virginia and at the New York Public Library in fact make available for reconstruction *all* versions of Faulkner's texts; Garland and other publishers are also publishing facsimiles of other authors' manuscripts and typescripts.

Faulkner or editor, did what to which texts, and it is nearly always possible to speculate intelligently about what Faulkner *wanted*—and what he wanted is usually contained pretty plainly in the typescripts, despite my previous disclaimers. Nor does his seeming acquiescence to editorial collaboration make it necessary to accept those editorial alterations.

Editing the novels of Faulkner's late career, however, is complicated considerably by Faulkner's desire to enforce some uniformity between the last two novels of the Snopes Trilogy, *The Town* (1957) and *The Mansion* (1959), and the first, *The Hamlet* (1940), and by his failing memory and apparent refusal to reread the earlier works. In *The Hamlet*, for example, Mink Snopes' ambush victim is Jack Houston; in *The Mansion* (1959) Faulkner called Jack Zack. Albert Erskine, Faulkner's last editor at Random House, with Faulkner's full approval, changed Zack to Jack throughout; and, again with Faulkner's apparent approval, altered other minor ingredients of the narrative to give the entire trilogy more consistency. Clearly, at one level at least, it was Faulkner's intention that the submitted typescript be revised toward conformity with the other novels of the trilogy. Should a modern editor, discovering *other* discrepancies, then feel free to impose total consistency?

Editing his later novels is problematic indeed. Faulkner's practice upon completing *A Fable* (1954), *The Town*, *The Mansion*, and *The Reivers* (1962) was to send a complete or nearly complete typescript to Random House, then follow it to New York after Saxe Commins and then Erskine had had a chance to work through it. Commins, then Erskine, and Faulkner would sit in the editor's office at Random House, the text between them, Faulkner sometimes fully engaged in the work, sometimes not. They would go over it together, working through editorial questions, Faulkner initiating some changes and directing Erskine to make them, Erskine asking questions or making suggestions, and Faulkner would either revise the text himself or get Erskine to. In short, there seems to have been not only delegated (negotiated, at any rate) intention, but absolute collaboration on certain details of the text of the late novels—for Faulkner an efficient merging of composition with editing—and, since Faulkner and editor frequently used the same grease pencil to mark the text, it is sometimes impossible to tell who made a particular mark, much less who originated it.

How *is* an editor to determine "intention" where the evidence is so inconclusive? Not to accept the edited typescript is to deny Faulkner certain kinds of consistencies and regularities he seems to have wanted, and it is an act of scholarly supererogation to try to second-guess either Faulkner or the editor who worked directly with him on the typescript. On the other hand, to emend toward any form of regularization is to valorize regularity, control, *neatness* as an aesthetic standard, and to work against the manifest and deliberate untidiness, even tastelessness, of such writers as Faulkner and Thomas Wolfe.[6] But to accept *every* emendation on one of these typescripts is to accept a lot of readings that were made by the editor acting alone and that are in my judgment demonstrably wrong or inferior to what Faulkner typed, no matter who altered it. Yet to accept some emendations, selectively, is to impose my own aesthetic judgments upon the author's, which all editors—and critics too—ought to be loath to do, even though, I repeat, the editor finally has nothing else to fall back on; to think otherwise is simply to be hamstrung by editorial theory.

But here we are back at the question of how to determine the difference between authorial error and authorial intention: can one always tell the difference between a misspelling or misuse and a neologism or coinage? Faulkner had an exceptionally large vocabulary, but there were some words he misused—he didn't always get the difference between "arrogate" and "abrogate" right, for example—and several he misspelled, or used archaic forms of: for example, "knowlege," "penetentiary," "rythm," "irreconciliable," and "indefatiguable" are listed in the *Oxford English Dictionary* as historic, and there-

6. Faulkner wrote to Warren Beck in 1941: "I discovered then that I had rather read Shakespeare, bad puns, bad history, taste and all, than Pater, and that I had a damn sight rather fail at trying to write Shakespeare than to write all of Pater over again so he couldn't have told it himself if you fired it point blank at him through an amplifier" (SL 142). See Parker, "Regularizing Accidentals."

fore presumably legitimate,[7] forms of these words, which Faulkner may have encountered in the OED itself or in his vast reading. Did he *really* prefer "rythm," as Meriwether implicitly argues in his edition of *Father Abraham*? Editing Faulkner, I am forced to walk the very *very* fine line between protecting him from error and allowing him his archaisms and idiosyncracies.

My not entirely satisfactory approach to solving such problems is to look at the context in which such words appear, and to treat those words whose unconventional spellings seem to affect the sentence's rhythms somewhat differently from those which are simply spelled phonetically. Thus "indefa*tigu*able" and "irrecon*cili*able" do affect the prose's rhythms, and may well be the way Faulkner *heard* or pronounced those words; in contrast, "rythm" and "knowlege" do not affect pronunciation or rhythm and, further, as unmodern spellings, seem to call attention to themselves in ways which I do not believe Faulkner intended; they thus can detract from other, more important things going on in the text. Obviously, Faulkner sometimes intended to call very specific attention to certain words, and on those occasions it is crucial to allow him his own usages and idiosyncracies. But, again, what's the difference between an allowable idiosyncracy and an error?

I can suggest how these considerations work to affect the editing of particular texts by paying some attention to *The Sound and the Fury* (1929) and *Absalom, Absalom!* (1936), two quintessentially modernist texts. Faulkner submitted the typescript of *The Sound and the Fury* to Cape & Smith in the late fall of 1928. The publisher turned it over for editing to Ben Wasson, who decided that the text's many intricate time shifts could be more efficiently indicated with extra line spacing than with Faulkner's own system of alternating italic and roman passages. When Faulkner saw the galleys, he was sufficiently moved to write Wasson the well-known letter in which he declared, "I know

7. Editors commonly rely on the OED as a final authority for many of their editorial decisions. This may be a mistake: since the OED is based on printed, not manuscript, sources, a bow to its authority in usage may in fact merely perpetuate housestyling or printing conventions or typographical errors rather than actual *usage*.

you mean well, Bud, but so do I. Put it back." He went on, in that letter, to say that he was going to add a few more italic passages, and directed Wasson to oversee both the restoration of the original italic passages and the installation of the new ones (Polk, *Handbook* 5–8). How else Wasson or any other editor at Cape & Smith tampered with the text of *The Sound and the Fury*, much less what changes Faulkner made on the ribbon typescript or galleys, we do not know, since neither document is known to exist. What we do have are: 1) a holograph manuscript, which differs from the carbon typescript so extensively as to be of little use as a representation of *final* intentions; 2) a carbon typescript, the major document for any new edition, on which Faulkner inked several experimental changes from the typed text; 3) a sample gathering of the first few pages, which preserve the text as Wasson edited it; and 4) about 40 pages of a preliminary version of the Quentin section—a ribbon typescript copyedited at Cape & Smith and sent back to Faulkner—which, unfortunately, don't tell us what we need to know to edit the rest of the novel.

In editing *The Sound and the Fury* I made every effort to follow Greg whenever it was reasonable to do so. Given the extant documents, it would normally be proper to choose the carbon typescript as copytext, and to adopt its accidentals unless there was good reason not to. But to accept all of the carbon typescript's accidentals would mean throwing out many changes Faulkner made himself, or instructed somebody else to make. For example, he seems to have typed portions of the Benjy section at least three times, using three different systems of punctuation. He finally evolved a system which called for a period at the end of all quotations, whether a comma, question mark, or exclamation mark should normally have been there; this method of punctuation brilliantly conveys Benjy's limited perception of emotion or tone. But Faulkner came to this method only after considerable experimentation. The holograph manuscript is not heavily underlined for italicization and is punctuated normally. The first typed version of the Benjy section is also punctuated normally: commas, question marks, and exclamation points come inside the quotation marks. He tried again, however, and retyped, removing all end punctuation from direct quotations. The fact that no more than one method of punctuation appears on any single page, however, makes it clear that the carbon typescript is really a composite of at least three different whole or partial typings of the Benjy section. We do not know whether the ribbon typescript setting copy was also a composite or a completely new typing. If it matched the carbon typescript, we have to assume that Faulkner made the punctuation changes himself, in ink, before submitting it or instructed Wasson or some other editor to make the changes.

I can discover no pattern in the carbon typescript's punctuation of the Benjy section that would justify retaining the three different methods in the new edition; that is, there are no punctuation distinctions between black and white speech, for example, or between past and present time. Clearly, then, we have to accept the regularized punctuation of the published book's Benjy section as more nearly representing Faulkner's intention than the carbon typescript does. But doing so raises questions about the Quentin section. Faulkner read galleys at least for italics in the Benjy section, but there is no evidence that he ever saw proof of the other three sections. In the Quentin section, he typed two important passages—Quentin's recollection of his fireplace conversation with Caddy's fiancé, Sidney Herbert Head, and his painful memory of his encounters with Dalton Ames and with Caddy in the well-known suicide/incest scene—with no paragraph indentations: all paragraphs in these passages begin flush with the left margin. This device calls visual attention to these passages, which erupt out of similar stimuli to Quentin's consciousness, and which Faulkner seems to have wanted readers to see as thematically related to each other. They were printed, however, with normalized paragraph indentation, no doubt because editors and compositors worried about how confusing a paragraph that ended flush with the right margin might be. Did Faulkner ink these paragraphing changes on his ribbon typescript? Did he instruct Cape & Smith to make these changes? Did Wasson or another editor take it upon himself to change this, too, while altering the Benjy section? Faulkner in fact revised the typescript of the Quentin section some time after it was copyedited. Did he see galleys for the Quentin section? If so, did he accept the altered typescript "intentions" as a *fait accompli* when he saw galleys? We have no evidence that he saw galleys for any but the Benjy section. For the "New, Corrected Edition" of *The Sound and the Fury* (107–111, 149–164) I restored the flush left readings of the carbon typescript, not with a great deal of confidence that Faulkner did not make or order the changes himself, but only with the evidence that the flush left paragraphs indicate a pattern in the section's visual apparatus that is demonstrably part of Faulkner's intention at the time he submitted the typescript to the publisher. The carbon typescript of the Benjy section does not *contain* Faulkner's intention, but does seem to point toward it clearly enough to make it possible to reconstruct it. The carbon typescript of the Quentin section contains *one* intention demonstrably Faulkner's; there is no evidence to indicate whose intention the published text might represent.

Absalom, Absalom! poses very few problems in its accidentals, largely because preserved among Faulkner's papers are the copyedited typescript setting copy at the University of Virginia, and a set of corrected galleys at the University of Texas, which record the editorial process that made the 1936 published text so different from the typescript that Faulkner submitted. A rough estimate suggests that there are some 2000 variants, accidental and substantive, between the typescript and the published book. Three editorial hands delete and add punctuation; replace deliberately ambiguous pronominal references with their proper name referents (Faulkner caught one change on galley and irritably chastised the editor for getting the antecedent wrong!); shorten Faulkner's lengthy sentences and lengthen his short ones; make regular sentences out of passages Faulkner enclosed in parentheses; shift and, worse, even delete entire passages, sometimes as much as ten lines at a time. The 1936 Random House *Absalom*, then, is the most heavily- and worst-edited of any of Faulkner's novels, saving perhaps only *Flags in the Dust*. The new text will make it necessary to reconsider the novel's stylistic complexities; whether we shall be more or less pleased with those complexities, I am not prepared to say.

In most cases, there was no question for me but to restore Faulkner's typescript readings. Only one major problem editing *Absalom* required some care not to impose meaning where there was none or, by the same token, to deny it if it were there; but, of course, *all* editorial decisions involve an imposition of meaning on a text. As published in the 1936 first edition, the chronology contains several discrepancies from the novel proper: for example, Ellen, according to the chronology, was born in 1818, but the tombstone in the novel gives her birth as 1817; in the chronology Charles Bon was born in 1829, the evidence of the novel suggests 1831. There is an early manuscript and an early typescript version of the chronology; nothing remains of the genealogy but the published version, and neither chronology nor genealogy is connected to the extant manuscript, typescript, or galley proofs of the novel. Given Faulkner's many experiments with novelistic structure, it is certainly possible that discrepancies between the chronology and the narrative proper are deliberate, that these appendices are part of the modernist technique of *Absalom* and in fact are as much a part of the novel proper as the concluding newspaper account of the incident on board the *HMS Bellipotent* is a part of *Billy Budd*. This is a bellipotent argument against correcting the chronology to agree with the "facts" of the novel; indeed, in a novel full of (and even built around) interpretive voices, each positing a set of "facts" designed to make its own case about Thomas Sutpen, in a novel full of disquieting ambiguities about the nature of historical truth, one might well see those appendices as yet another voice, more or less external to the novel proper.

Yet I was persuaded to make the chronology's "facts" agree with the "facts" of the novel, when it was possible to do so; the evidence persuaded me to treat these appendices as aids to the reader of a very complex novel. Two pieces of information decided the issue for me. First is the outright error in the chronology which lists the fall of 1910 as the date on which Quentin and Rosa Coldfield go out to the Sutpen house and find Henry there: this is an absolute, glaring error. Second, perhaps more telling, is that according to the novel proper, Judith Sutpen and Charles E. St. Valery Bon die, in 1884, of yellow fever; according to the 1936 published chronology, they die of small-pox. The manuscript version of the chronology says simply that they "died." In the holograph manuscript of the novel, they die of small-pox, as in the published chronology. Page 258 of the typescript setting copy, however, shows that Faulkner, following the manuscript, origi-nally typed "smallpox" and at least the next word, then went back, x-ed out "smallpox," and typed in "yellow fever" above. He did *not*, however, go back and change the manuscript or the chronology to agree with his revised thinking.

The evidence, then, suggests, though of course does not prove, that Faulkner got confused about relationships among events in this very complex novel, and manufactured the chronology for himself—perhaps after he came back to it from his brief interlude of work on *Pylon*—to help him keep straight all the dates and relationships; then he discarded it, for his own purposes, as he wrote past a particular date. Someone, perhaps at Random House, suggested that it be ap-pended to the book, and Faulkner allowed this to happen, without correcting or updating it; and apparently none of the original editors, for all their wholesale revision, had read it or the novel closely enough to be aware of the discrepancies. The evidence thus suggested that the appendices were not modernist adjuncts to the novel, but merely aids to the reader, and so I treated them as appendicular material, separate documents with separate if related purposes; I corrected their dates, where possible, to conform with the "facts" of the novel, and so confirmed them in what the evidence testified about their orig-inal "intention."

The editorial enterprise, then, is uncertain at best, and editors who claim to have produced a "definitive" text may well spend eternity in a special circle of hell proofreading new editions of *Finnegans Wake*, and they would deserve no less. No fewer than a dozen proofreadings by at least four different pairs of eyes left me with at least one glaring typo in *The Sound and the Fury*: "treees" (6) which had persistently hidden itself from us in *all* stages of proof. So much for "definitive," much less for "final intentions," which can, probably must, change from day to day for any writer engaged with his or her material. The whole notion of a "final intention" is at bottom an intensely romantic one which assumes that at some point, any point, in the composition process, a writer is in full and complete control of *every* aspect of the work, from comma placement to large and profound themes; I doubt seriously that this *ever* happens except as an illusion, even though I cling to the oldfashioned notion that authors are essentially smarter than we are, or at least better-informed about the work they are writing, and that what we perceive as problematic in any text may simply be our own blindness.

To conclude, I'd like to detour slightly from Faulkner to report an instructive exchange with Eudora Welty regarding the text of her first collection of stories, *A Curtain of Green*. For years the most available text of this important collection was that of the Modern Library's *Selected Stories* (1954), a plate reprint of the 1947 Harcourt Brace second edition. But its textual antecedents are quite problematic. The first edition (Doubleday Doran, 1941) was set from Welty's typescript, which shows numerous and, to my eye, injurious editorial interventions in matters of style and punctuation. When Harcourt asked her for printer's copy, she sent them, curiously, a copy of the 1943 first British edition, which had been set from the Doubleday text after its editing toward British usage and house-styling. The Harcourt Brace text was, then, with numerous changes from the original (among which were four completely dropped lines, including a whole paragraph of dialogue), even further distant from those typescript intentions, and the popular Modern Library text perpetuated those differences. Nearly thirty years later Welty apparently used the Modern Library text, dropped paragraphs and all, to revise from when preparing the *Collected Stories* (1980).

In 1984, Michel Gresset, translating *A Curtain of Green* for the first time into French, wrote asking for some help on some Southern idioms and for advice on what to title the translation (*A Curtain of Green*, he said, did not translate meaningfully into French; he proposed *L'Homme Petrifié*. I noted that his queries were keyed to the Modern Library text and wrote back proposing that he use the Doubleday first edition for his translation. Gresset counterproposed that, in view of Welty's revisions for the *Collected Stories*, we ask her.

I wrote her, proudly enclosing a copy of my learned essay on the text of *A Curtain of Green* (Polk, "The Text of the Modern Library *A Curtain of Green*"). She wrote back as follows:

> Thank you for your interesting letter. I appreciate your being of good assistance to M. Gresset, of the University of Paris. In regard to your questions, I think *Petrified Man and Other Stories* is a good title and perfectly acceptable as a substitute one for *A Curtain of Green* (which was the editors' choice in the first place only because nobody had anything special against it, out of all the titles in the collection). About the translation text and my own preference, it is of course that text I most recently provided, for *The Collected Stories*. As you saw, I had made changes, and my reason was in every instance toward clarity, I believed—clarity was my object. I don't see much use in retaining something cloudy or confusing just because it was earlier, though I am not of the scholarly persuasion and I expect you demur. Anyway, while of course I respect you and am grateful to you as the bibliographer, I feel as I do from the author's wish to get the meaning across, which is probably undying, don't you imagine? Thank you for your aid.[8]

I have no doubt that James, Irving, Whitman and other late revisers of their works would have responded similarly. There are, or should be, lessons for us all in such completely understandable authorial attitudes, even if some of them are painful and even if none is particularly helpful to an editor. The lessons are multiple, and contradictory, and for critics involve such considerations as the meaning of "clarity" in Welty's letter. Creators do not stand still in time, and neither do their works. Neither, in painful fact, do critics. But editors and texts *must*. Editors are by definition charged to produce *a text*, to make pedestrian decisions about where the comma goes and to make sure it gets where it's supposed to be. The *ideal* of scholarly editing is to make all possible forms of a text available to the reader, since that is the only way to bridge the gap, the abyss, between and among any set of authorial

8. Eudora Welty to author, 26 November 1984. I am grateful to Miss Welty for allowing me to use this letter.

"intentions" and outside influences on any given work of art; but that is only an ideal, and most editors will have to choose one version or text to produce; most will have only one comma to wrestle with, and that comma may well be the still point of a turning critical world.

The sheer impossibility of the task, then, makes the editorial enterprise an awesome, sobering responsibility. At the same time, and paradoxically, of course, that very impossibility relieves us of some measure of that responsibility, and perhaps ought to give us enough distance from comma placement to consider some of the larger implications of editorial responsibility. That is, if the texts we edit are as close as some of us will ever come to justifying the ways of God to *man*, it cannot be lost on anybody that the greater part of our editorial energy is being expended by white men working to establish—or, rather, to *re*-establish, *re*-canonize—the already canonized texts of other, already established white men; we are therefore in effect mostly justifying the ways of white men to each other. This is an understandable result of the forces which have shaped the canon, and it may be that the editorial enterprise is the most effective way to address the problems at the heart of the canon. Serious discussion of the arduous and particular process of making large and small editorial choices (where a comma goes, where an author goes) and, especially, of the cultural and aesthetic training that influences those choices, will, I think, eventually, inevitably, give a voice to the legitimate claims that female and black and other minority writers and readers have on the canon.

We obviously need to take our editorial responsibilities seriously, and to get all those commas where they ought to be, but we ought at the same time always keep in mind that our texts—even those of Faulkner, Joyce, Shakespeare—are *not* the Graven Tablets nor the Pentateuch, no matter who is justifying what to whom, no matter what tradition is being reified in the editorial process. Perhaps in fact we should all do well to remember that the Father/author of the Ten Commandments delegated a good deal of his intention to a male editor who with a good deal of editorial supererogation proceeded to destroy the original hand-printed plates and then reconstruct the text from memory, no doubt making the author's meaning clear with some accidentals of his own.

Children of the Dark House

Extracts

We ran up the steps and out of the bright cold, into the dark cold. (SF 7)

The stairs went down into the dark and T. P. took my hand, and we went out the door, out of the dark. (SF 34)

The clock tick-tocked, solemn and profound. It might have been the dry pulse of the decaying house itself. . . . (SF 285)

They were set in small grassless plots littered with broken things, bricks, planks, crockery, things of a once utilitarian value. What growth there was consisted of rank weeds and the trees were mulberries and locusts and syca-mores—trees that partook also of the foul desiccation which surrounded the houses; trees whose very burgeoning seemed to be the sad and stubborn rem-nant of September, as if even spring had passed them by. . . . (SF 291)

They reached the gate and entered. Immediately Ben began to whimper again, and for a while all of them looked up the drive at the square, paintless house with its rotting portico. (SF 298)

He looks up at the gaunt face framed by the window in the twilight. It is a composite picture of all time since he was a child. . . . For a while still she looks down at him from the composite picture, neither with censure nor appro-bation. Then the face disappears. (AILD 32)

The house came into sight, above the cedar grove beyond whose black inter-stices an apple orchard flaunted in the sunny afternoon. It was set in a ruined lawn, surrounded by abandoned grounds and fallen outbuildings. But nowhere was any sign of husbandry—plow or tool; in no direction was a planted field in sight—only a gaunt weather-stained ruin in a sombre grove. . . . (S 206)

. . . looking down at the child, at its bluish eyelids showing a faint crescent of bluish white against its lead-colored cheeks, the moist shadow of hair capping

its skull, its hands uplifted, curl-palmed, sweating too, thinking Good God. Good God. (S 262)

The woman drew the box out from behind the stove and stood above it, her hands still hidden in her shapeless garment. "I have to keep him in this so the rats cant get to him," she said. (S 262–63)

The child wailed, a thin, whimpering, distressful cry. (S 271)

The woman sat on the edge of the bed, looking down at the child. It lay beneath the faded, clean blanket, its hands upflung beside its head, as though it had died in the presence of an unbearable agony which had not had time to touch it. Its eyes were half open, the balls rolled back into the skull so that only the white showed, in color like weak milk. Its face was still damp with perspiration, but its breathing was easier. It no longer breathed in those weak, whistling gasps. . . . (S 290)

He walked quietly up the drive, beginning to smell the honeysuckle from the fence. The house was dark, still, as though it were marooned in space by the ebb of all time. (S 332)

Just as they began to descend the hill he looked back at the gaunt ruin of the house rising above the once-formal cedar grove. The trees were massed and matted now with long abandonment; above the jagged mass the stark shape of the house rose squarely like an imperishable and battered landmark above an extinct world. There was no light in it. . . . (SO 26)

He spoke a single word, pointing up the lane with a mittened fist which clutched the whip, toward a single light which shown in the dusk. "Home," he said. . . . "I said, there is your home." Still the child didn't answer. He had never seen a home, so there was nothing for him to say about it. (LA 505)

The house squatted in the moonlight, dark, profound, a little treacherous. It was as though in the moonlight the house had acquired personality: threatful, deceptive. (LA 524)

Before him the house bulked square and huge from its mass of trees. There was a light in one window upstairs. The shades were not drawn and he could see that the light was a kerosene lamp, and now and then he saw through the window the shadow of a moving person cross the further wall. But he never saw the person at all. (LA 567)

As they recrossed the lawn, a window that had been dark was lighted and Miss Emily sat in it, the light behind her, and her upright torso motionless as that of an idol. (CS 123)

We had long thought of them as a tableau, Miss Emily a slender figure in white in the background, her father a spraddled silhouette in the foreground, his back to her and clutching a horsewhip, the two of them framed by the back-flung front door. (CS 123)

. . . and your grandfather said, 'Suffer little children to come unto Me': and what did He mean by that? how, if He meant that little children should need to be *suffered to approach Him, what sort of earth had He created; that if they had to* suffer *in order to approach Him, what sort of heaven did He have?* (AA 164)

1. Dark Houses

Faulkner's original title for both *Absalom, Absalom!* and *Light in August* was "Dark House."[1] Why he abandoned the title, twice, is impossible to know. Perhaps its oblique allusion to Dickens' *Bleak House* was a different kind of weight than he wanted either novel to bear, and perhaps he wanted to downplay that title's deliberate appropriation of the Gothic tradition, even if the novels themselves do not. Perhaps he thought *"Absalom, Absalom!"* more richly allusive than "Dark House," but there are ways in which the rejected title seems more appropriate and thematically functional for the earlier novel than *Light in August*, which, for all its provocative suggestiveness, does not, in my judgment, bear the profound dialectical relationship to the novel that Faulkner's best titles do.

1. He used title in February of 1934, describing to Bob Haas, his editor at Random House, the book he was putting aside for a while; it would become *Absalom, Absalom!* two years later (SL 78–79). "Dark House" actually appears on the title page of the manuscript of the novel, deleted and replaced by "Light in August" (WFMS 10:1,1).

Faulkner drew this portrait in ink, probably in the mid to late teens, on a sheet of paper also containing one of his early poems. Original in the Harry Ransom Humanities Research Center, University of Texas at Austin. Used by permission of Jill Faulkner Summers.

The twice-rejected title calls riveting attention to rich reciprocities between *Light in August* and *Absalom, Absalom!*, in each of which an antebellum house is destroyed by fire. The fires that destroy the physical structure also effectively destroy dark and deeply ingrained familial and cultural structures that contain the seeds of the novels' major crises: they are dark houses indeed, given the secrets they contain and what those secrets do to the families that live in them.

Faulkner's fiction is a house-haunted landscape, a terrain marked by structures ranging from shotgun sharecropper shacks, ephemeral and poisonous as mushrooms, to antebellum mansions, both dilapidated (the Old Frenchman place) and pristine (Major de Spain's), whose permanence, whose economic hold over Yoknapatawpha, is as secure as their long deep roots in Mississippi's historical and cultural power structures. They are a pervasive, symbolic presence too, inscribing on Faulkner's North Mississippi landscape the class structures of the plantation system.

At least two narratives central to the entire work of Yoknapatawpha cluster around a desire for the Big House: Thomas Sutpen's blitz-creation of his mansion out of the primal ooze of the north Mississippi wilderness and Flem Snopes's more patient step-by-step path to local eminence almost by osmosis through a series of structures that he owns but does not build. For him everything turns on his possession of the ruins of a mansion, the Old Frenchman place, of a sort that Sutpen might have built. It is significant, and fitting, that the final novel of the Snopes trilogy is titled *The Mansion*, because in that title are crystallized so many of Faulkner's major concerns.

In *The Mansion*—and in the mansion—Flem confronts the emptiness of the American dream, which he has so masterfully succeeded in realizing. But its emptiness is necessarily lost on Yoknapatawpha's Have-not population, who live in economic bondage to those structures, and whose culture insists that they see the mansions not as symbols of their oppression but, quite the contrary, as symbols of lives to which they might realistically aspire. The American dream gets written in to the language of mansions so strongly that Sarty Snopes, confronting Major de Spain's gleaming mansion in "Barn Burning," equates such structures not just with money and success, but with justice, safety: "*Hit's big as a courthouse* he thought quietly, with a surge of peace and joy whose reason he could not have thought into words, being too young for that" (CS 10). Major de Spain's mansion symbolizes something quite different to Sarty's father, of course, who does have at least rudimentary language for understanding how his own poverty is directly related to Major de Spain's wealth: not justice here, but disfranchisement; not for him the American dream but the American nightmare.

But what Sarty wants from the mansion/courthouse is not social or economic equity. He wants, rather, a sanctuary from the depredations of his barn-burning father, whom he both loves and fears. "*They are safe from him,*" he thinks:

> *People whose lives are a part of this peace and dignity are beyond his touch, he no more to them than a buzzing wasp: capable of stinging for a little moment but that's all; the spell of this peace and dignity rendering even the*

barns and stable and cribs which belong to it impervious to the puny flames
he might contrive. . . . (CS 100)

As he contemplates the De Spain mansion, he becomes aware of his
father's presence beside him, an intrusion into his reverie of sanctuary, a shadow presiding over this mansion as ominously as, in Horace
Benbow's mind, Popeye's shadow looms over *Sanctuary's* Old
Frenchman place, and in the same language:

> this, the peace and joy, ebbing for an instant as he looked again at the
> stiff black back, the stiff and implacable limp of the figure which was
> not dwarfed by the house, for the reason that it had never looked big
> anywhere and which now, against the serene columned backdrop, had
> more than ever that impervious quality of something cut ruthlessly from
> tin, depthless, as though, sidewise to the sun, it would cast no shadow.
> . . . But it ebbed only for a moment, though he could not have thought
> this into words either, walking on in the spell of the house, which he
> could even want but without envy, without sorrow, certainly never with
> that ravening and jealous rage which unknown to him walked in that
> ironlike black coat before him: *Maybe he will feel it too. Maybe it will even*
> *change him now from what maybe he couldn't help but be.* (CS 10–11)

Sarty is wrong, of course, to think that his father might be moved by
the majesty of that mansion to change himself "from what maybe he
couldn't help but be." He is also wrong to believe that the De Spains
are beyond his father's touch, as subsequent events prove. And he is
crucially wrong to believe that his emotional investment in De Spain's
social order can protect him from his father's terrorizing hold over
him and his family. In fact, then, courthouse and mansion, political
and economic bastions of the symbolic order, are much more likely
to conspire to maintain his father in his familial place of localized
dominance over Sarty than to free him from them.

To be sure, the justice of the peace who tries Ab in the story's
opening pages compassionately arranges for Sarty not to have to testify against his father, but he does not, finally, save Sarty from Ab's
retribution. In fact, by allowing Sarty not to testify, the "justice," even
with his manifest good intentions, inadvertently insures that Ab will

be found innocent of the charge and restored to his place within the system. Sarty then receives the same punishment from Ab for not testifying and telling the truth as he would have gotten if he had actually done so. Moreover, it is not certain that Sarty would have told the truth to the justice; but his father's mere accusation that he was going to is enough to justify the punishment. His own family, then, denies Sarty the resources of the law that Ab has outside the family. It is worse for Sarty, because if he had testified, one assumes that Ab would have been taken to jail and he, Sarty, would not have been punished at all—at least not physically. For all practical purposes, for Sarty and his family, Ab *is* the law.

Thus courthouse and mansion—legal structures and domestic structures—always work to reify each other, to confirm the other in their mutually-reinforcing hegemonic positions as arbiters of law, power, and order. "Barn Burning" provides a perfect example of the way in which family structures are both nested in and mirrored by legal and economic structures, figured in these semiotically powerful buildings. It is no accident that Faulkner sets the opening scene of "Barn Burning" in a general store, a local economic center: political, social, familial, and moral principles intersect where money changes hands.

Sarty must choose between two value systems that are in conflict over the particular but in complete agreement over the general. He must choose between an abstract principle of social justice that favors property over people and a more immediate, concrete principle that insists upon family loyalty above all else. Each system has its hold over him, and each asks—nay, demands—that he martyr himself in its name. Whichever choice he makes, he suffers, in the abstract or in the particular. And choose he eventually must.

Sarty's dilemma thus crystallizes and encapsulates the dilemma of nearly all children in Faulkner—certainly up to 1938 when "Barn Burning" was written—who in their own ways also get caught in the crossfire between contending but mutually reifying structures that demand their obedience. Even so, Sarty differs immensely from those children in the early fiction because for all the intensity with which he wrestles with his dilemma, his choices are based in a developing social consciousness, not in the deep sexual psychoses of so many of his earlier cousins. Indeed, Faulkner completely removes the sexual as a component in Sarty's family problem, but it is absolutely central to the children in the earlier works; and nearly all adults in Faulkner were children whose families provided no sanctuary, but quite the contrary.

Sarty at least *has* options, his cousins do not. "Barn Burning"'s larger, social, context allows him a certain autonomy to negotiate between the power structures of mansion and courthouse that Faulkner's earlier children do not have: each option has its own dire consequences, but at least he can choose which consequence he will bear. Children in the earlier fiction do not have such clearly defined options precisely because, enchained in their parents' houses, they have no commerce with the courthouse except as it stands beyond and validates the power of the father—or, more specifically, of Lacan's "Name-of-the-father." Children in Faulkner's work of the period 1927–1932 are prisoners in the dark house of family dysfunction, houses whose darkness is rooted in fear and loathing of the life processes of sex and death, in denial and repression of desire. The dysfunction is Oedipal in its origins and in its more particular manifestations.

The dark houses of Faulkner's early fiction bear many and obvious relationships to the Gothic mansions of Poe and the British and American literary traditions, the conventions of which are well known, and have frequently been discussed in Faulkner criticism (Kerr, Pitavy). There is no reason to rehearse them here except to note, briefly, the dark "House" of Usher, to invoke it as the embodiment of its inhabitants' mental states. In "The Haunted Palace," the poem almost at the absolute center of the story, that stands as the story's interpretive key, Poe depicts the "house," the haunted palace, as a human head—the palace door a mouth, the hair unfurled banners, the windows eyes through which travellers passing by can see into the disturbed psyche of "monarch Thought's dominion":

> And travellers now within that valley,
> Through the red-litten windows, see

> Vast forms that move fantastically
>   To a discordant melody;
> While, like a rapid ghastly river,
>   Through the pale door,
> A hideous throng rush out forever,
>   And laugh—but smile no more. (327)

Faulkner's houses are never quite so bluntly allegorical, but they frequently partake of that quality of Poe's "Palace" in representing the lives of those who build them, of those who live in them. Rosa Coldfield believes that Thomas Sutpen's mansion has "accepted and retained" its builder, "as though houses actually possess a sentience, a personality and character acquired not from the people who breathe or have breathed in them so much as rather inherent in the wood and brick or begotten upon the wood and brick by the man or men who conceived and built them" (AA 70). And as Joe Christmas escapes one evening from his McEachern foster home, he sees it "squatted in the moonlight, dark, profound, a little treacherous. It was as though in the moonlight the house had acquired personality: threatful, deceptive" (LA 524). In Faulkner as in the Gothic tradition, the two meanings of the term "house" are combined: the building itself and the family that inhabits it are one.

Throughout Faulkner, but especially in the 1927–1932 period, houses play a particularly significant symbolic role in the lives of his children. He does not specifically represent the Compson house as a head, as Poe does his Palace (though to be sure Quentin's sister becomes a "Head"), Faulkner nevertheless depicts the Compson children as always acutely aware of the windows of Benjy's and their mother's rooms; especially when lights are on in these rooms, they experience those windows as inescapable eyes that monitor their every activity. When they are outside, like Poe's travellers, they have to climb trees to see what dark secrets lurk inside; when they are inside, those windows become eyes to the burgeoning life going on outside, which the "house" itself, the family's repression, denies them; they allow the children to see what they cannot be permitted to have. In "Miss Zilphia Gant" Faulkner makes the symbol explicit; Zilphia's mother literally puts bars on the windows of their little house to keep Zilphia in, and to keep suitors — experience — out. But she is no more a prisoner in a home with barred windows than Emily Grierson is in a home with an imperious father and a whip. Though the Name-of-the-father rules, the house is frequently, as we shall see, and significantly, the mother's body, and just as frequently it is a mother or grandmother and not the father who works the repression in the name of the father.

Time and time again, often at crucial moments in their lives, characters in Faulkner stand at windows looking out, immobilized in that frame, an icon of impotence and frustration. Some escape *through* those windows into sexual experience (Caddy, Miss Quentin, Joe Christmas, Lena Grove), others feel a certain comfort and security being on the inside and not having to face the life outside (Quentin and Gail Hightower). But those who do escape feel ambivalent because leaving and returning through the window is a transgressive act that puts them at odds with all that the "house" represents of law and moral prohibition. To transgress, to be free, is to inflict guilt upon yourself and to deny yourself the relative stability of life within the house; to stay inside is no better because you want to be, but cannot stand to be, outside, untethered from the security that the house provides. Those who escape through the windows do so because doors are closed and not transparent: they cannot see through them but must be content with merely hearing what transpires in the next room. Doors, then, are points of entry to the house's labyrinthine dark secrets, and, significantly, they are in Faulkner mostly closed; when open, the frames are likely to be filled with figures of authority that bar passage or block the view within. Quentin and Rosa, for example, are characteristically constrained by the closed doors at Sutpen's Hundred, behind which lurk the mysteries of sex and death.

I am concerned here with those mysteries in this early period of Faulkner's achievement, with their impact on the children who live in the dark houses where those mysteries are hidden, and with the emotional and psychic baggage that they create for the children to carry with them for the rest of their lives. In this essay, I will concentrate primarily on the miraculous years 1927–1932 and on the two versions of *Sanctuary*, though I will also range rather freely throughout Faulkner's work, to try to give some sense of how firmly a part of Faulkner's entire career these concerns are. The differences between the two versions of *Sanctuary*—the revised version that Faulkner published in 1931, and the unrevised typescript version that he originally presented to Hal Smith in 1929, but was not published until 1981— reveal a good deal about Faulkner's aims and methods during this formative creative period, and the works he wrote before, between, and after the two versions bear astonishing resonances with the two *Sanctuary*s that are very much worth our attention.

I will view this fiction primarily through a Freudian lens. I do not want to reduce these works to Freudian paradigms, or to suggest that the Freudian approach is the only way to make sense of these works: years of criticism from other approaches demonstrate that these complex works cannot be easily reduced to any single "meaning." Nor do I intend to engage in any arguments about whether or how much Freud Faulkner read, for the evidence of *Sanctuary* and *Light in August* seems overwhelming, and the short story "A Courtship" provides plenty of parodical evidence (Polk, "The Artist as Cuckold"). Given what we now know about how omnivorously he read, it seems much safer to assume that he did read Freud rather than that he did not. It seems to me demonstrable that the Oedipus complex is fundamental to Faulkner's work of this period and that *Sanctuary* and *Light in August* in particular are direct and powerful specific responses to Freud's Wolf Man case history, and I approach the Freudian material that I evoke not as a way to psychoanalyze the author—though I in fact believe that the fictional materials of this period are immensely autobiographical—but merely as one of the sources Faulkner mined, as he mined the Bible, Homer, Shakespeare, and Dostoyevsky.

2. A Child Is Being Beaten

In the heartbreaking final few pages of Quentin Compson's monologue in *The Sound and the Fury*, Quentin returns from his outing in the countryside in order to make sure that at least his physical life is in order before he commits himself to the peaceful bottom of the Charles River. After he has washed and changed shirts he turns out the light and goes to the window for a final moment of meditation—the same symbolic window through which the shining sun had, that morning, created the shadow on the sash that put him in time again. The curtains brush against his face, reminding him of "someone breathing asleep, breathing slow into the darkness again" (173). But what he sees through the window at this crucial point in his life, moments before his death, is not Harvard Yard, but home: three members of his family, in characteristic modes. Several things in this scene deserve attention, both for their immediate impact on Quentin and for their resonances throughout Faulkner's fiction:

> *After they had gone up stairs Mother lay back in her chair, the camphor handkerchief to her mouth. Father hadn't moved he still sat beside her holding her hand the bellowing hammering away like no place for it in silence.*

In direct response to this family portrait, he elides into fragments of a childhood conversation with Caddy, which alternates their quite different responses to another family portrait, a picture in a book with which they are equally fascinated:

> When I was little there was a picture in one of our books, a dark place into which a single weak ray of light came slanting upon two faces lifted out of the shadow. *You know what I'd do if I were King?* she never was a queen or a fairy she was always a king or a giant or a general *I'd break that place open and drag them out and I'd whip them good* It was torn out, jagged out. I was glad. I'd have to turn back to it until the dungeon was Mother herself she and Father upward into weak light holding hands and us lost somewhere below even them without even a ray of light. Then the honeysuckle got into it. As soon as I turned off the light and tried to go to sleep it would begin to come into the room in waves building and building up until I would have to pant to get any air at all out of it until I would have to get up and feel my way like when I was a little boy. . . . (173)

The phrasing—I'd *have to* turn back—suggests a near obsession with the picture, a compulsiveness whose goal is to convert the dungeon into his mother, into a dark, enclosed maternal space: *the* dungeon. Quentin's image of Mother as dungeon, well-known and mostly mis-understood, is brutally reinforced in the novel's final section by a narrator who describes her as carrying "a huge bunch of rusted keys on an iron ring like a mediaeval jailer's" (281), and it is an image perfectly consonant with Jason's and Benjy's descriptions of her. But for the moment I'm less interested in Mother as entrapment, as medi-aeval jailor, than in Quentin's compulsion to identify her with the dungeon, his *desire* that they be the same.

Since Quentin has suicide on his mind, it is easy enough to understand his association between death and the enclosed maternal space of his desire, and to extend those associations to include the caverns and grottoes of the oceanic waters of his ultimate desire. Clearly, for Quentin, this dungeon is a desirable place, a womb or tomb in which he can find peace. Irwin suggests that Quentin's suicide results from what Freud calls a "fixation in secondary narcissism" (42), that is an

> attempt to make the subject the sole object of its own love, to merge the subject and the object in an internal love union [which] reveals the ultimate goal of all infantile, regressive tendencies, narcissism in-cluded: it is the attempt to return to a state in which subject and object did not yet exist, to a time before that division occurred out of which the ego sprang—in short, to return to the womb, to reenter the waters of birth. But the desire to return to the womb is the desire for incest. (43)

The dungeon Quentin seeks is his mother's womb, then: a place of safety, a sanctuary; but because it so clearly represents the incest he desires, it also represents the punishment for that desire that he needs and abhors. He forces the association between "mother" and dun-geon in the picture because he cannot force the relationship between mother and security in his real life, a fact that continually frustrates him: "*If I could say Mother. Mother*" he says, later (SF 95). So desper-ately does he need his mother-dungeon's sanctuary that when the fecund odors of honeysuckle come wafting through the window into his room he runs from it, from the window, deeper and deeper into his own dark house, down the stairs, to the bathroom, seeking a drink of water.

In Quentin's memory, Benjy bellows uncontrollably and his father sits helplessly by while his constantly-ailing mother presides over the Compson household. If she is the jailer, the house is a prison and the grounds a fenced compound. The children can escape this dark house only by dying or by climbing through the curtained window and down that well-known tree; Caddy and her daughter do so regularly into sexual experience. Quentin can only gaze out the window, any symbolic window, and watch life from the dungeon in which he wants to be enclosed.

Quentin "interprets" the picture, then, until it becomes an expression of his desire for his mother. Caddy, by contrast, wants to "drag" the two faces in that picture book out of the shadows of their dungeon not to free them, but rather in order to "whip them good." It is not clear whom the faces belong to, though Quentin seems to locate his parents there, in the weak light, he and Caddy lost "below even them" in the darkest reaches of the dungeon. Since we are in Quentin's memory we may question whether it is Caddy or, more likely, Quentin who wants to whip the prisoners. Caddy does not seem likely to beat anybody, and it is Quentin who, at Caddy's wedding, kicks poor T. P. so cruelly.

Caddy's and Quentin's desire to whip those shadow-bound prisoners, to punish someone, is of a piece with and directly related to Addie Bundren's confession of a sadistic pleasure in whipping her pupils: "I would look forward to the times when they faulted," she tells us, "so I could whip them" (AILD 114). Addie and Caddy have much in common besides their rhyming names: Addie's father's dictum that "the reason for living (is) to get ready to stay dead a long time" (AILD 114) is a pithy summation of Jason Compson's more discursive nihilism. They share a certain masochistic urge. Addie admits that when whipping her students she is really whipping herself: "When the switch fell I could feel it upon my flesh; when it welted and ridged it was my blood that ran" (AILD 114), and it seems clear from a number of passages in *The Sound and the Fury* that Caddy's sexual activity, at least as Quentin recounts it, emerges not at all from a rampant sexual appetite but rather from some deep dissatisfaction within herself, from a desire to punish herself for something she cannot name: *"There was something terrible in me,"* Quentin reports her saying; *"sometimes at night I could see it grinning at me I could see it through them grinning at me through their faces"* (SF 112); we don't know whether the *them* through whom she sees that *something* are her parents or the conglomerate faces of her lovers, or something even other than these two possibilities (SF 112). Again, we should not forget the possibility that Quentin is projecting here, that he is attributing to Caddy things that he himself feels, because he *wants* Caddy to feel remorse, guilt, for the pain that her sexual life is causing him.

In a similarly remarkable passage in *Sanctuary*, Temple Drake describes to Horace Benbow her incredible night at the Old Frenchman place. She is at the time of the telling a prisoner in Miss Reba's whorehouse; she is in an upstairs room whose curtained window she spends a lot of time looking out of; she is also lying in a bed to which she ran, for security, immediately after being brought to Miss Reba's; and while still bleeding from her rape, she wears a towel wrapped around her loins, unmistakably like a diaper; thus it is worth recalling that she was raped in a "crib," and that the citizens of Jefferson who lynch Lee Goodwin call her a "baby" on whom they would not have used "no cob" (S 383). Temple describes to Horace her fantasy as she lay on the cornshuck mattress at the Old Frenchman place listening to all the shadowy comings and goings of the mysterious world moiling behind the doors and windows of the old house, just outside her vision: "I hadn't breathed in a long time," she tells him. "So I thought I was dead." Her fantasy gets very specific: "I could see myself in the coffin. I looked sweet—you know: all in white. I had on a veil like a bride." Then she describes her encounter with Popeye, whom she more than once during the novel calls "daddy," and who violates her so grotesquely in that crib:

> And I'd lie there with the shucks laughing at me and me jerking away
> in front of his hand and I'd think what I'd say to him. I'd talk to him

like the teacher does in school, and then I was a teacher in school and it was a little black thing like a nigger boy, kind of, and I was the teacher. Because I'd say How old am I? and I'd say I'm forty-five years old. I had iron-gray hair and spectacles and I was all big up here like women get. . . . And I was telling it what I'd do, and it kind of drawing up and drawing up like it could already see the switch.

Then I said That wont do. I ought to be a man. So I was an old man, with a long white beard, and then the little black man got littler and littler and I was saying Now. You see now. I'm a man now. (S 330–31; SO 217)

In this astonishing passage Temple Drake *becomes* Addie Bundren, the teacher, right down to the white wedding-dress shroud, the coffin-bed of mattress-shucks, and the veil. (We may here remind ourselves of how often Quentin and Benjy remember Caddy in her veil and in her flowing white wedding gown; neither can we overlook the fact that Narcissa Benbow, Horace's sister, almost always wears white.) Temple becomes Addie Bundren out of an immediate need to be invulnerable to her outrageous misfortune; significantly, in her fantasy she is not just an older lady, but, also like Addie, a school teacher. Like Caddy and Addie, Temple wants to strike out, to hit something, to punish someone; as a teacher she can do this legally and with impunity. It is, I suggest, the same impulse that makes Caddy think of being a king or a giant or a general.

In ways that we will discover, Caddy and Addie and Temple are also structural cousins of *Sanctuary*'s Ruby Lamar. Claiming that she might compromise Horace in Jefferson if she is seen too often with him, but more likely fearing that in her desperation she will betray Lee by telling Horace about Temple, Ruby tells Horace just to let them be: "You've been kind. You mean all right, but . . . I guess I've got just what was coming to me. There's no use fighting it" (SO 11). *I've got just what was coming to me.* The phrase stops one: it is very puritan of the seemingly unpuritan Ruby to feel that she somehow deserves to be left alone with her baby after Lee is executed, either by Popeye or by the state of Mississippi. What has she done to *deserve* her punishment? And why indeed would she consider it a punishment to be free of a man like Lee Goodwin, much less need to cling to him, no matter what the cost to her dignity or her physical well-being? Certainly by the text's standards, Ruby has done nothing sufficiently "evil" to deserve such punishment—at least in a world that is as just as Lee believes Jefferson's legal system to be. But it is precisely the point of *Sanctuary* that morality, legality, and justice have nothing to do with each other, except incidentally, and by no design of the system itself. By *Sanctuary*'s standards, Ruby, the least self-serving, the least exploitative character in the novel, is very nearly the saint that criticism has long held her to be. Why, then, should she feel that she *deserves* to suffer as she does? Her feelings spring from nothing rational, any more than Caddy's and Addie's do.

Robert J. Kloss has suggested that Addie's monologue can be understood by reference to Freud's essay, "A Child Is Being Beaten." This important essay is as well a useful starting point for understanding Ruby and for much else of what goes on in *Sanctuary*, indeed for understanding much of Faulkner's work during the period between 1927 and 1932, and beyond that period as well.

Fantasies of child-beating are, Freud reported, very common even among people who were not themselves beaten as children; they are invariably related to incestuous fantasies arising from the Oedipus complex and from the subsequent and mostly unconscious feelings of guilt that are the psychological legacies of our sexual attachments, as infants, to our parents. Thus in one phase of the child-beating fantasy, the child being beaten is a competitor for the love of a parent, probably a sibling or perhaps the other parent; the beating confirms that that parent does not love the other, but only the fantasist. In the most crucial phase, the one at the core of the fantasy, the child being beaten is in fact the person having the fantasy; the fantasy is a response to guilt over having wanted, as an infant, to slay the parent of the same sex in order to have complete sexual and emotional possession of the parent of the opposite sex. Most infants outgrow the Oedipal stage in the normal course of development, but in others the Oedipus complex remains well into adulthood, a vestige of that infantile sexual compulsion. Thus the person who fantasizes about children being beaten is in effect expressing an unconscious need to be punished; a need to be punished not for a sin or sins actually committed, but for sins he or she *desired to commit*; so far as the functioning of guilt is concerned, the desire and the deed are one and the same.

Whence the *need* to be punished? Freud is not able to say with any certainty in this 1919 essay. But he speculates about its relationship to the human personality in terms that will make it possible to go immediately back to *Sanctuary*: guilt, he writes,

> seems to correspond to a scar-like formation which is similar to the sense of inferiority. According to our present orientation in the structure of the ego, which is as yet uncertain, we should assign it to the agency in the mind which sets itself up as a critical conscience over against the rest of the ego . . . which cuts itself loose from the ego in delusions of being watched. (194)

Guilt is that part of the personality that Freud was later to call the super-ego, the policeman of the personality, that forces it toward some ideal standard of behavior: a relative standard, to be sure, based upon some notion of right and wrong imposed on the personality by an agency or circumstance *outside* the personality, and which reminds the ego, constantly, how far short of perfection it falls. Guilt, then, the need to be punished, derives directly from the sexual and emotional conflicts that constitute the Oedipus complex.

I propose that the problems of all of these women are neuroses rooted in a family pathology, a sexual pathology, that *Sanctuary* very clearly delineates, and that fugues significantly throughout Faulkner's fiction of the period from 1927 to 1932. For Horace and Temple and, I believe, for Caddy and Quentin, the neurosis is clearly based in Oedipal tensions; for Ruby not so clearly, though to be sure she has been raised by a father who calls her a whore for having sexual urges and who murders her lover as she watches (S 218).

Oedipal tensions dominate Faulkner's male characters too, Horace Benbow no less than Quentin Compson. We will have occasion, then, to suggest that Horace's mother is in fact much more akin to Caroline Compson than to the frail, helpless wraith of a woman he insists upon remembering. Given many other relationships between Horace and Quentin Compson, and between the novels in which they appear, we might well look backward to the relationship between Caroline and Jason Compson for some sense of the nature of Horace's parents' relationship, and of their effect on their children; or to Addie Bundren and Anse. Indeed, John Irwin might better have explored the similarities between Horace and Quentin in *The Sound and the Fury* and the original *Sanctuary*, which seem to me far more intimately related than *The Sound and the Fury* and *Absalom, Absalom!*

3. The Space Between Sanctuary

Faulkner wrote *Sanctuary* in the spring of 1929, according to his own dates on the holograph manuscript. He gave the typescript to Hal Smith who, according to Faulkner in his infamous and deliberately misleading introduction to the Modern Library issue of the novel in 1932 (Cohen), told him it was too outrageous a novel to be published: "we'd both be in jail." So he forgot about it, he claimed, until eighteen months later, when Smith suddenly sent him the galleys, preparatory to publication. Reading *Sanctuary* in proof, Faulkner said, he found it to be so bad that he had to revise it into something that would not shame *The Sound and the Fury* and *As I Lay Dying* too much; in fact, he revised the novel extensively, and paid for the cost of resetting those passages that he revised.

Perhaps, of course, his reasons for revising were purely artistic. Between 1927 and 1932 Faulkner wrote *Flags in the Dust*; wrote *The Sound and the Fury*; wrote *Sanctuary*; wrote *As I Lay Dying*; revised *Sanctuary*; revised the Quentin section of *The Sound and the Fury*; wrote *Light in August*; and wrote and/or revised about thirty short stories, some of them among the best he would ever write. In quantity alone, this record is astounding; in quality, it is perhaps unparalleled in the literature of the English language. What he accomplished in the eighteen months between the two versions of *Sanctuary* is easily equal to what many major writers produce in a decade, even in a career. It should not be too difficult, then, to believe that what Faulkner taught himself about his craft during that year and a half is enough to account for his dissatisfaction with the early version.

But we cannot account for the two *Sanctuary*s simply by chronology of composition, because in spite of a lot of factual information from this period, we still are not sure exactly when he wrote what. The dates on the sending schedule could not possibly represent the order of composition; they are rather clearly the dates Faulkner sent them out to magazines: even with his speed, he did not write "Mistral," "Pennsylvania Station," and "The Leg" on November 3, 1928 (WFMS 9:1–2; Meriwether, *Literary Career*, 167–80).[2] There is no evidence to indicate when these and other stories were written, although it possible that he wrote many of them, at least early versions, in Europe or in the months immediately following his return to Mississippi.

We can, however, with some certainty trace the origins of *Sanctuary* to his time in Paris. In one letter home he described having written something that most readers have taken to be related to *Sanctuary*'s final scene; he reported having "written such a beautiful thing that I am about to bust—2000 words about the Luxembourg gardens and death," and he spoke of having done 20,000 words on his novel (SL 17). The description of Temple Drake in the Luxembourg Gardens as it appears in *Sanctuary*, however, is a mere 344 words long. Assuming that Faulkner was counting accurately, we may well ask what became of the other portions. It is not clear whether the 20,000 words and the 2,000 words are part of the same work, but even if the novel he is referring to is *Elmer*, which he had been working on since leaving New Orleans (McHaney), it is almost impossible to believe that they are not somehow intimately related, especially given the ways in which *Elmer* is thematically related to the later works. Did any of those 20,000 words become part of *Sanctuary*?

Other fictions he worked on in Paris—*Elmer* (1925; published

2. See Putzel. For other significant discussions of Faulkner's short story career, see Meriwether, "The Short Fiction of William Faulkner: A Bibliography"; Meriwether, "Faulkner's Correspondence with *Scribner's Magazine*"; Carothers; and Skei, especially Chapters 2 and 3.

1983) and a pseudo-mediæval allegory entitled *Mayday* (1926; published 1978)—have significant and specific affinities of theme, character, and *mise-en-scène* with *Sanctuary*, *The Sound and the Fury*, and *Flags in the Dust* (Gresset, *Fascination*, parts 3 and 4). Moreover, Faulkner completed *Sanctuary* in the spring of 1929, while Cape and Smith copyedited *The Sound and the Fury*. At some point during that spring Faulkner put *Sanctuary* aside long enough to revise extensively and retype 41 pages of the Quentin section of *The Sound and the Fury*, so that in important ways *Sanctuary* and *The Sound and the Fury* are practically simultaneous. I have suggested in the "Afterword" to *Sanctuary: The Original Text* that Horace Benbow, the Prufrockian hero of *Sanctuary* and *Flags*, is a 43-year-old Quentin Compson—what Quentin would have become if he had lived that long (299).

The order of their publication would argue that after he abandoned *Elmer*, Faulkner wrote *Flags in the Dust*, had it shortened for publication as *Sartoris* in 1929, then incorporated into the ongoing *Sanctuary* some of the Benbow material that was cut from *Flags*. It is more interesting, however, to speculate that *Sanctuary* is the prior work, the matrix in which the great explosion of 1927–1932 was born. The holograph manuscript of *Sanctuary*—recording Faulkner's thousands of revisions, his constant shifting of passage after passage, page after page—and the revised galleys, characterized by the same restless shifting of large blocks of material, demonstrate how very difficult *Sanctuary* was to write. Clearly he conceived of *Sanctuary* as a highly experimental novel, and seems to have had a lot of trouble getting its chaotic and troublesome materials to coalesce. The extant materials, then, make it possible to speculate that Faulkner worked on *Sanctuary* sporadically through the mid-to-late twenties, then defaulted into *Flags*, a much more traditional novel. After *Flags*, something magical moved him into *The Sound and the Fury*. The experience of writing *The Sound and the Fury* then released him to complete work on the Benbow-Temple Drake book, which in its "original version" was exclusively about Horace Benbow.

The revised *Sanctuary* is more nearly Temple's book than Horace's, and Temple is less clearly an aspect of Horace's psyche than in the first version. Critics may well argue that the revised *Sanctuary* is a "better" work than the early one; there is much to support such a position, but I am not interested in such arguments. What seems indisputably true to me is that the first *Sanctuary* is in myriad ways a more interesting book than the second, and that taken together, in their inter- and intratextual relationships with each other and with the other novels and stories in the space between, the two versions form a single text that is far more significant than either of the versions taken singly. We cannot now, I believe, pretend to understand either *Sanctuary* without also coming to terms with the other. The novels and stories of 1927–32 thus form a veritable spider's web of intimate connections, a fascinating web of intertexts: to touch the web at one point is to send thrilling little vibrations into nearly all the other parts.

Faulkner's major revisions of *Sanctuary* involved cutting or altering those passages that dealt most explicitly with Horace Benbow's childhood, his parents, his nightmare visions, and the looming presence of Popeye in his waking imagination. In the revision Faulkner removes us from Horace's sometimes cloyingly introspective mind; he recasts the early version's stream of consciousness as direct quotations from Horace as narrator. It is very much to our purposes here to stress the fact that while he deleted all the material about Horace's childhood in the revision, he also added the long passage about Popeye's childhood, a short biography that inversely reflects Horace's early years, involving an "invalid" mother, an itinerant absent father, and a crazy pyromaniac grandmother who burns down Popeye's dark house. A sickly child, Popeye becomes in revision very much the equivalent of Ruby's nearly-dead baby. In this extended addition, then, Faulkner inscribes into Popeye's childhood the very pathologies that he had just deleted from Horace's. In Popeye's childhood they at least *seem* more appropriate, but these similarities demonstrate a powerful kinship between Popeye and Horace that other scenes in both versions merely suggest.

The early *Sanctuary* is Horace's book entirely: his profoundest anxieties and insecurities, his deepest fears, his darkest fantasies lurking everywhere inside his uneventful, bourgeois existence are all projected outward into the grotesque shapes of those characters from the Memphis underworld who inhabit his nightmare—for nightmare it surely is. A good deal of *Sanctuary* takes place in darkness, in halls dimly lighted or completely dark, in houses hiding dark secrets and shameful acts shamefully spied upon, in corridors formed by trees and hedges; faces appear and disappear in and out of windows and frames, blur in and out of focus, and combine in crucial passages, such as the one in which Temple and Ruby and Narcissa and Horace's mother and Popeye all become one in Horace's mind. *Sanctuary*'s nightmarish qualities are a defining part of its meaning.

Perhaps, then, Faulkner's reasons for revising were more personal than artistic. The intensity with which he portrays family dynamics during this period and the compulsive frequency with which themes related to problematic parent-child relationships appear in the fiction invite speculation about their sources, their significance in Faulkner's life and in his work. Clearly *Sanctuary* cost him a great deal to write— much more, the evidence of the manuscript suggests, in the original writing than in the revising; just as clearly, the materials of *Sanctuary* were far more significant to him than his smart-aleck indictment of it—"the most horrific tale I could imagine" (ESPL 177)—allows.

After Smith postponed publication of *Sanctuary*, Faulkner was left holding not just an unpublished novel, but a nightmarish world which he could not exorcise, a myriad of images, doubtless from his own psychological preoccupations, that he returned to obsessively in the months that followed. By the fall of 1930, he had worked his way through many of those preoccupations, or at least brought them under some artistic control. Looking at those galleys, he must have felt himself looking at a self he thought he had long since abandoned—or escaped. The works in the space between the two *Sanctuary*s form a kind of filter through which Faulkner pushed the nightmare phantasms of the first version of *Sanctuary*, with the result, even if not the intended one, of exorcising them completely or at least of rendering them so obvious that he perhaps had to suppress them. I am not concerned, here, to explore the autobiographical content of these fictions, though obviously the possibilities for biographical and psychobiographical study are enormous (Wittenberg, Minter, Martin) though. I in fact believe that Faulkner is never very far from autobiography during this early period. Indeed, I believe that what Faulkner meant when he said *Sanctuary* was *bad* was that it was actually worse than bad: it was intolerably *close*.

4. Nightmare Shapes

That *Sanctuary* is Horace's nightmare is rendered explicitly a number of times. The following passage occurs during Horace's return to Jefferson after he has been in Memphis listening to Temple's story at Miss Reba's whorehouse. He had caught the predawn train to Memphis earlier in the day; as he walks back home away from the station he has the sensation that between morning and evening

> there had not been any elapsed time between: the same gesture of the lighted clock-face, the same vulture-like shadows in the doorways; it might be the same morning and he had merely crossed the square, about-faced and was returning; all between a dream filled with all the nightmare shapes it had taken him forty-three years to invent. (SO 219; S 332)

This is a highly charged passage, since after all Horace has been to a brothel hearing stories of rape and murder and sexual fantasy. All of these "nightmare shapes" become "concentrated" in the "hot, hard lump" of undigested coffee in his stomach, which in turn becomes the immediate physical cause of the nausea that overtakes him only minutes later when he returns to his home and sees the blurring face of Little Belle in the photograph.

In the spectacular conclusion to the scene, Horace vomits. As he does so *he* "plunged forward and struck the lavatory and leaned upon *his* braced arms while the shucks set up a terrific uproar beneath *her* thighs." The passage's gender slippage reflects Temple's at Miss Reba's earlier in the day when she had told Horace her fantasy of first becoming a middle-aged schoolteacher and then a man. The ambiguity of the slippage here allows Horace the widest range of transformations: at the moment of vomiting he is either Temple Drake, the violated, or Popeye, the violator; or he is both simultaneously: the coffee he vomits is something "*she* watched . . . black and furious go roaring out of *her* pale body" (SO 220, my italics). He identifies with Popeye, who smells black, "like that black stuff that ran out of Bovary's mouth" (SO 25), and so with Emma Bovary, the old arch-adulterer herself. The passage also connects him to other characters in the novel who vomit, Gowan at the Shack, Temple's Ole Miss co-ed friend, and Uncle Bud (Bleikasten, "Terror and Nausea"). In the nightmarish recapitulation of all that Temple has told him, in a dreamwork condensation of its materials, Horace thus identifies himself completely with Temple, Little Belle, Popeye, and Bovary. In another important scene that Faulkner deleted in revising, Horace yet again fuses Bovary and Popeye and the repulsive black emission from their mouths—surely death and menstrual blood—with all the women in his life: all, including Popeye, in turn fuse with his invalid mother (SO 60). Horace's identity is thus diffused centrifugally among the novel's major characters. He is at one and the same time male, female, androgynous; the seducer and the seduced; the violator and the violated; father, brother, sister; son and lover; protector and destroyer.

All characters, male and female, in the original *Sanctuary* are Horace, emanations from his haunted mind, projections of his unconscious. As Lawrence Kubie pointed out in 1934, *Sanctuary* contains all the distortions of reality one associates with dreams in general and with nightmares in particular (224–25; Freud, *The Interpretation of Dreams*). *Sanctuary* partakes of the peculiar quality of dreams described by August Strindberg in his preface to *A Dream Play*:

> [T]he author has . . . attempted to reproduce the detached and disunited—although apparently logical—form of dreams. Anything is apt to happen, anything seems possible and probable. Time and space do not exist. On a flimsy foundation of actual happenings, imagination spins, and weaves in new patterns: an intermingling of remembrances, experiences, whims, fancies, ideas, fantastic absurdities and improvisations, and original inventions of the mind.

The personalities split, take on duality, multiply, vanish, intensify, diffuse and disperse, and are brought into a focus. There is, however, one single-minded consciousness that exercises a dominance over the characters: the dreamer's. (Strindberg 1111)

Strindberg's description of *A Dream Play* describes *Sanctuary* very well indeed, but a more immediate and familiar source for *Sanctuary* is *The Waste Land*, a poem whose influence on Faulkner, specifically on *Sanctuary*, has been demonstrated over and over again. In one of the notes to his poem, Eliot explains his use of Tiresias, the blind seer of ancient literature, who announces catastrophe to so many of the ancient nobles and who presides over the events of section III of *The Waste Land*. Having been first a male, Tiresias was then female for seven years before becoming a man again. Jove and Juno, arguing about whether men or women got greater pleasure from sex, asked Tiresias to arbitrate. He took sides with Jove and testified that women indeed knew more of sexual pleasure, whereupon Juno blinded him; Jove, to compensate for his loss of sight, gave him the ability to know the future. Tiresias, Eliot explains,

> [a]lthough a mere spectator and not indeed a "character," is yet the most important personage in the poem, uniting all the rest. Just as the one-eyed merchant, seller of currants, melts into the Phoenician Sailor, and the latter is not wholly distinct from Ferdinand Prince of Naples, so all the women are one woman, and the two sexes meet in Tiresias. What Tiresias *sees*, in fact, is the substance of the poem. (Eliot 72)

Likewise, what Horace sees is the substance of *Sanctuary*. All characters in *Sanctuary* are Horace; all women his mother, all men his father, and in him the two sexes meet. All characters are eventually the same character, then: that is why one can melt into another, why Ruby and Temple and Narcissa and Belle and Little Belle and Horace's mother and Popeye become fused in Horace's imagination. They are all the same person, they are all Horace. Tiresias knows the secret of Oedipus's misfortunate life, and all the characters in *Sanctuary* are the nightmare formulations of Horace's repressed sexual life. Although he is not blind, he is the Tiresias figure nevertheless, the hermaphroditic, the sexless. He is also Oedipus, as we shall see, since like Horace Oedipus is both offending son and punishing father: he, like Horace, is the self-punishing, self-mutilating son.

Thus Horace waking is not the center of *Sanctuary*, but rather Horace sleeping, offstage; his nightmare features himself performing a series of frantic movements, none of which extricate him from the sexual and emotional morass of those nightmares. Faulkner had used this device before, in one of his earliest works, *Marionettes* (1920), which features two avatars of the central male character, Pierrot: a drunken one situated to one side of the stage, slumped over a table in a stupor, and another, who plays out on stage the fantasy of the drunken one.[3]

Why does Temple's tale—his own nightmare—affect him so physically? There is no answer in the revised *Sanctuary*, in which this scene survives intact, but there are clues in the original version. The first describes Horace as he passes the jail and looks up at the window in which lie the hands of a condemned Negro murderer. The barred jail window and the Negro murderer are important points of reference for Horace, as for us, much more important in the original text than in the revised version. *Sanctuary: The Original Text* in fact begins with the description of that window and of the Negro murderer's hands lying peacefully between the bars. The Negro had "slashed his [wife's] throat with a razor so that, her whole head tossing further and further backward from the bloody regurgitation of her bubbling throat, she ran out the cabin door and for six or seven steps up the quiet moonlit lane" (SO 3).

The fascinated, almost loving detail with which Horace reconstructs the moonlit scene suggests that he has rehearsed it many times; it thus stands as a kind of paradigm for something in his fantasies, some opposition to his anemic response to the complications of his life. Part of Horace, it seems clear, is fascinated with the Negro's simple solution to his marital troubles. Doubtless he wishes he were passionate enough, *masculine* enough, to solve his own problems so

3. See Pamela E. Knights' interesting discussion of other relationships between *Sanctuary* and *Marionettes*.

easily; he must be troubled by the murderer's capacity for decisive action, an implicit reproach to his own impotence. Moreover, he may be attracted to what he believes to be the Negro's safe incarceration in the sanctuary of the jail. He may feel, as Gavin Stevens and Temple Drake believe of Nancy Mannigoe in *Requiem*, that the Negro is free of trouble and worry; he has nothing more troublesome to do than wait to die. Further, there may be in Horace's mind some relationship between the Negro murderer and Popeye—that "black man"—who, at the book's end, is also in jail, waiting to die. Finally, Horace may identify with the Negro because of the impending finality of his deserved punishment. The Jefferson jail, then, is Horace's equivalent of Quentin's mother-dungeon, to which he is attracted and by which he is simultaneously repulsed. Hence his fascination.

Faulkner excised this passage when he revised *Sanctuary*:

> Each time he passed the jail he would find himself looking up at the window, to see the hand or the wisp of tobacco smoke blowing along the sunshine. The wall was now in sunlight, the hand lying there in sunlight too, looking dingier, smaller, more tragic than ever, yet he turned his head quickly away. It was as though from that tiny clot of knuckles he was about to reconstruct an edifice upon which he would not dare to look, like an archaeologist who, from a meagre sifting of vertebrae, reconstructs a shape out of the nightmares of his own childhood, and he looked quickly away as the car went smoothly on and the jail, the shabby purlieus of the square gave way to shady lawns and houses—all the stability which he had known always—a stage upon which tragedy kept to a certain predictableness, decorum. (SO 141–42)

This is a very important passage in the early text, equally for the way it reveals the nightmares that haunt Horace as for the way it reveals his strategies for evading those things he doesn't want to confront directly.[4] What he sees through that jail window, the hands lying between the bars, touches the quick of some childhood experience so

4. See John T. Matthews' provocative readings of this and several other passages in *Sanctuary: The Original Text* with which I am dealing ("The Elliptical Nature of *Sanctuary*"). His discussion maps a terrain related to, but slightly different from, my own.

powerful that he looks away immediately, self-protectively, directing his eyes and his body toward home, back toward what he consciously remembers as "all the stability which he had known always." Yet the original version of *Sanctuary* provides plenty of evidence that Horace's childhood was by no means so serene as he remembers, and that his conscious memories of that childhood as stable and secure are simply evasions of certain truths, never directly articulated in the novel, that he does not want to face.

Horace's impulse toward evasion in fact is the narrative gesture that brings all of *Sanctuary*'s disparate elements together. Standing at the curtained windows of his study in Kinston, like Quentin at his Harvard dormitory window, he looks out at the "green-snared promise of unease" just outside in the ripening garden; he thinks first of the rankness of his marriage to Belle, and then, inevitably, of Little Belle. He leaves the window, goes to Little Belle's room, removes her picture from its frame and puts it in his pocket, and sets out walking to Jefferson—back, ostensibly, to the security of his childhood home, all that stability. He tells himself that he is counting on Narcissa's "imperviousness," which is, of course, like the dungeon, a kind of stability. Instead of escaping through the window, he consciously sets out to return to the dark house, to its innermost dungeon-darkness, to the very site of the repressed traumas that have created the nightmare shapes. Like Joe Christmas's his return, too, will prove disastrous.

It is precisely on the way back home to Jefferson that all his nightmares come to life. In the reflecting waters of that mysterious pond, just away from the road, kneeling, a twentieth-century Narcissus, Horace comes face to face with all the conflicting elements that compose his inner life. Irwin, deriving from Otto Rank, describes the Narcissus myth in ways that apply profoundly to Horace:

> In the myth, Narcissus sees his image reflected in the water; he recognizes the image as himself, yet sees that it is shadowed on a medium whose fluidity, whose lack of differentiation, whose anarchy continually threaten to dissolve the unity of that image at the very moment that the medium itself seems to supply the force to sustain that image. What Narcissus sees is that unified image of his conscious life buoyed up

from moment to moment by a medium whose very constitution, in relation to the ego, seems, paradoxically, to be dissolution and death. (33)

Popeye, whose face merges with Horace's in the water, and at whom
Horace stares, petrified with fascination, is much more Horace's double than has generally been allowed. He is, again following Irwin, a
"double" who represents his "rejected instincts and desires," which
are

> cast out of the self, repressed internally only to return externally per-
> sonified in the double, where they can be at once vicariously satisfied
> and punished. The double evokes the ego's love because it is a copy of
> the ego, but it evokes the ego's fear and hatred as well because it is a
> copy with a difference. (33)

John T. Matthews correctly "proposes a radical intimacy between
Horace and Popeye defined by a dynamic of projection and self-eva-
sion" ("The Elliptical Nature of *Sanctuary*" 263). Thus Popeye is
Horace's twin and alter-ego, at the same time his id and his superego:
he is at once the reductio ad absurdum of Horace's darker sexual
impulses and the punishing, vengeful father—whom he must inevitably face. Popeye is both the core, the totem, to which Horace clings
for coherence (we cling to that which robs us [CS 124]) and the
singular, looming agent of the dissolution of that coherence.

In yet another scene in the original but not in the revised *Sanctuary*,
Horace leaves the Sartoris household where his sister and Miss Jenny
live, and returns to town determined to open up his childhood home,
the house where he and Narcissa grew up, and on which he has se-
cretly paid the taxes for the past ten years. He approaches the old
house through a "fence massed with honeysuckle," another association with Quentin Compson we cannot miss; he walks over a lawn
whose "uncut grass" has gone "rankly and lustily to seed." As he
wanders about the yard he feels it as a "tight and inscrutable desola-
tion" in which he moves "in a prolonged orgasm of sentimental loneliness" (SO 61). The specific terms describing the foul vegetation
around the old house suggest a symbolic relationship, at any rate,
between the childhood home and the Old Frenchman place: the "un-

pruned cedars" at home are a "jagged mass like a black wave breaking
without foam upon the May sky" (SO 61); at the Old Frenchman
place, the cedars are "massed and matted with long abandonment"
and the house itself rises above their "jagged mass the stark shape of
the house [rising] squarely like an imperishable and battered landmark above an extinct world" (SO 26). His old home place hardly
inspires in him the serenity and stability he thinks he has always
known there. Quite the contrary: the surrogate family from the Memphis underworld he finds living at the Old Frenchman place are
merely an augury of the underworld he is to find at home—and, by
comparison, relatively harmless.

At home, he examines the windows of the house, which are exactly
"as he had nailed them up ten years ago":

> The nails were clumsily driven. . . . Rusted, mute, the warped and
> battered heads emerged from the wood or lay hammered flat into it by
> clumsy blows. From each one depended a small rusty stain, like a dried
> tear or a drop of blood; he touched them, drawing his finger across the
> abrasions. "I crucified more than me, then," he said aloud. (SO 62)

He pulls the nails with a hammer, opens the shutter to let in light
and, going from room to room, discovers his conscious past, a highly
evocative tableau, much like Quentin's and, like Quentin's, set in the
powerfully liminal moment of twilight:

> It seemed to him that he came upon himself and his sister, upon their
> father and mother, who had been an invalid so long that the one picture
> of her he retained was two frail arms rising from a soft falling of lace,
> moving delicately to an interminable manipulation of colored silk, in
> fading familiar gestures in the instant between darkness and sunlight.
> (SO 62–3)

As in Quentin's tableau, Horace's mother is provocatively at the center of his memory, though Quentin remembers a whining jailor and
Horace recalls a frailer creature, in bed or in bedclothes. The language of his memory is not specifically erotic, but the languid gestures, the "manipulation" of the colored silk across her frail body,

certainly suggest her seductiveness: every other time the word "silk" appears in *Sanctuary* it is connected to Ruby and Miss Reba and her whorehouse.

Those windows are Horace's eyes, long since nailed tightly shut upon some trauma, some pain, particular or general, associated with his childhood in this house, that he has suppressed from his conscious memory, but that has remained at the center of his unconscious. Faulkner never takes us directly to the site of Horace's trauma, as he does Joe Christmas's; but since what he sees when he opens those symbolic window/eyes is his seductive mother in bed, it seems clear that the trauma is directly connected to his mother's sexual life.

I propose, then, that Horace's trauma is what Freud called the "primal scene," or some variation of it. There are an arresting number of similarities between *Sanctuary* and Freud's essay, "From the History of an Infantile Neurosis," the subject-patient of which is popularly known as the "Wolf Man," first published in English in 1925. "The Wolf Man" case history is an analysis of a young man who had dreamed of waking in the middle of the night to see the window of his room open suddenly and inexplicably upon a tree in which five motionless white wolves sat, staring at him. Under analysis unnecessarily long and complex for our purposes here, the Wolf Man revealed to Freud that as a child he had awakened from sleep in his crib to see his father and mother engaged in intercourse, his mother on her hands and knees and his father behind her. The child's immediate response was to defecate in his bed. His long-range response was to suppress the incident entirely, both what they did and what he saw.

From the patient's recurring dream of the staring wolves, Freud reconstructs for the Wolf Man a childhood whose components are familiar to readers of Faulkner: a mother in ill health, a depressed and frequently absent father, an older, seductive, dominating sister. The analysis traces the Wolf Man's neuroses directly to his shame over his defecation, his guilt over his incestuous desire to take his father's place with his mother and the homoerotic desire to take his mother's place with his father. According to Freud, then, the Oedipus complex is central to understanding the Wolf Man's dream. It is no less central to Faulkner's work. Particularly in the period from 1927 to 1932, the Wolf Man's confrontation with his parents' sexuality, and so with his own Oedipal desire, is the crucial event to which Faulkner returns, more or less explicitly, over and over again.

Sanctuary gives us no direct replications of the Wolf Man's primal scene, as *Light in August* does, partly because that is precisely what Horace is repressing. But the scene recurs percussively, insistently, throughout *Sanctuary* in a variety of guises and reformulations. Clearly, for example, Popeye's position at the foot of the bed, watching and whinnying while Red and Temple make love, is a re-enactment of the primal scene, and Horace's agitated reaction to Ruby's offer to pay him with sex, accompanied by her apologetic admission that she will have to bring the baby with her when she pays is his automatic, even if perhaps unconscious, identification with the child's probable terror at discovering parental sex: "You mean," he says, "with him at the foot of the bed, maybe? perhaps you holding him by the leg all the time, so he wouldn't fall off?" (SO 267).

But we must understand that the primal scene is not just the actual witnessing of parental intercourse; it also includes the variety of cultural and familial evasions that treat sexuality as something shameful, something to be hidden, kept in the dark and behind closed doors. Dr. Ralph Roughton, a practicing psychoanalyst, suggests that

> *Sanctuary* grows out of, and is an expression of, a child's mixed reaction of excitement and horror at having seen, or fantasized seeing, his parents in sexual intercourse. And I'm thinking of this, not so much as one discreet experience, but as the whole murky developmental process of sexual awareness, curiosity, tension, fear, excitement, shattering of idealization and much more. The great mystery that surrounds this in little children, the fantasies that it stimulates (whether they see anything or not). When there is an actual witnessing two adults in sex, it often is interpreted by the child as a fight, or as one doing something bad to the other. Often, of course, it occurs in the dark, which makes even more mystery, misunderstanding, and distorted fantasying. And often, when a child bursts into their bedroom at such a moment, the child is harshly and hastily dealt with by parents who are angry and/or anxious

about the event. Those are some of the realities. Add to this the whole constellation of oedipal desires and fears, jealousy and guilt. Especially in older children, where it is not an accidental event, but an attempt to spy, there is disbelief that his parents would do such a thing. Often a boy will feel his mother has been unfaithful to him; he may experience a shattering disillusionment that his madonna mother would indulge in something so base. Whatever sexual desires he may have himself felt directed at her may produce enough guilt that fear of punishment by father becomes predominant. And I want to emphasize that all this can happen even without an actual "primal scene."

The primal scene, then, is everywhere in *Sanctuary*, in its unrelenting emphasis on voyeurism, the need to see, and on the ways in which adult sexual life, licit or il-, takes place in dark places, in the shadows, behind closed doors, enshrouded in mystery and shame.

Three more episodes, one deleted from, two retained in, the revised text, support these speculations about Horace's childhood trauma. The first episode, retained in revision, is the grotesquely funny scene at Miss Reba's, after Red's funeral, when Miss Reba and the two visiting madames indulge themselves in a bit of alcoholic socializing and mourning, swilling beer and gin and talking about Red, Temple, Popeye, normal sex, abnormal, voyeurism, and monkey glands. The pathetic, lonely Uncle Bud, already practically an alcoholic, whose central form of amusement is snitching drinks from the ladies, listens intently to their shop talk. He moves about "aimlessly" to the window where, like Horace and Quentin, he peers out "beneath the lifted shade" (SO 246; S 353). A few pages later, after more talk of sex and more drinking, the ladies finally pay enough attention to him to note that he has gotten drunk: exasperated, Miss Myrtle "grasp(s) the boy by the arm and snatch(es) him out from behind Miss Reba's chair and (shakes) him. . . . 'Aint you ashamed? Aint you *ashamed?*' " she screams at him: "Now, you go over there by that window and stay there, you hear?" (SO 250; S 357). Faulkner explicitly associates shame and windows and curtains and sexuality: the word "ashamed" occurs half a dozen times in this scene. The scene ends when Uncle Bud vomits, an act that connects him directly to

Horace: indeed, the next chapter begins by returning to Horace as he recovers from his own sickness. Like Horace and Gowan and Joe Christmas, Uncle Bud vomits up what he has been ingesting, but the immediate cause of the nausea is what he has been forced to *hear*.

The second episode also involves children at Miss Reba's, in the extended and equally funny narrative of Virgil's and Fonzo's descent into the Memphis underworld, where they come to go to barber college. Mistaking Miss Reba's whorehouse for a boarding house, they inadvertently discover that Temple Drake is there, and so provide their cousin Clarence the crucial bit of information that brings the novel to its climactic scene in the courtroom. The name *Virgil* invites us to read the episode as a dream-driven comic recapitulation of Dante's *Inferno*: one Roman poet, Horace, easily elides into another, Virgil, to become Benbow's educated counterpart, and Fonzo just as easily becomes his backwoods Mississippi self.

Though this countrified duo arrives full of Virgil's confidence that he can guide them through the Inferno that is Memphis because he has been there before, he quickly becomes confused and disoriented by the big city and abandons leadership to Fonzo, the untutored, the rustic, the base, whose instincts of course lead them directly to Miss Reba's, the dreamwork destination of all sexual instincts. At Miss Reba's they manage to avoid the truths about all the women who inhabit the rooms in the "boarding house," assume that they are Miss Reba's married daughters, all the while being titillated by their presence and by the sounds they hear at night from their bedrooms. Older than Uncle Bud, they are no less innocent than he, though, as yokels, they are too dumb to feel Uncle Bud's shame. But they are ashamed enough of their sexual escapades in other whorehouses to keep them outside Miss Reba's house and to fear what she might do if she found out that they were having sexual lives. Actually, in one scene, Virgil bravely announces that he is not afraid of her: "She caint eat us," he says. But neither he nor Fonzo is really so certain:

> They stood outside the lattice, whispering.
> "How you know she caint?" Fonzo said.

"She dont want to, then."
"How you know she dont want to?"
"Maybe she dont," Virgil said. (SO 192)

Clearly, Miss Reba is for them *vagina-dentata*, the consuming female, the mother who eats her children.

Such scenes at Miss Reba's involve children's discovery of sex and the combination of titillation and shame and nausea that accompanies their new knowledge. The scenes evoke some essential qualities of Horace's childhood, distorted to nightmarish qualities in the dream-work's manifest content, and so hidden from consciousness. It is therefore easy to understand that Miss Reba, Uncle Bud's and Virgil's and Fonzo's surrogate mother, is also Horace's and Temple's surrogate mother by the same dreamwork process of inversion and substitution: the frail, lifeless, shallow-breathing invalid mother becomes the robust, breathless, and dominating madam of a brothel. This substitution both hides and symbolically reveals exactly those attributes of his mother he wants to block from his memory— precisely that world, that is, upon which he nailed those windows shut, for the sake of those more pleasant memories he wants to retain of his childhood.

The early version, but not the revision, associates Miss Reba and Horace's mother more directly through the specific terms of a tree in the yard of the old Benbow house, the site of Horace's childhood. The tree is

old and thick and squat, impenetrable to sun or rain. It was circled by a crude wooden bench, onto the planks of which the bole, like breasts of that pneumatic constancy so remote from lungs as to be untroubled by breath, had croached and overbosomed until supporting trestles were no longer necessary. (SO 64)

The fat, wheezing, constantly breathless Miss Reba has huge billowing breasts, a bosom of "rich pneumasis" (SO 168; S 277): she moves with the two dogs "moiling underfoot" like playful children and talks in a "harsh, expiring, maternal voice" (SO 169; S 278). Miss Reba is the self-sufficient mother, all-powerful, all-maternal, not needing the support of husband or of anybody else, but constantly demanding it, and constantly mourning the loss of the support and love of her own consort, Mr. Binford. It is clearly a maternal tree and may suggest that Horace was mothered to death as a child under its iron, impervious bosom. Not incidentally, Narcissa seems well on her way to doing this to her son, especially in the Original Text, and Horace thinks Ruby is overmothering her child too when he accuses her of holding it too much, though to be sure the reader of the revised text only cannot understand *why* Horace thinks this.

Another scene in the original version of the novel, deleted in revision, evokes the Wolf Man more directly. Sleeping alone in the family house one night, Horace wakes suddenly:

> On the second night he dreamed that he was a boy again and waked himself crying in a paroxysm of homesickness like that of a child away from home at night, alone in a strange room. It seemed to him that not only the past two days, but the last thirty-five years had been a dream, and he waked himself calling his mother's name in a paroxysm of terror and grief. . . .
>
> After a while he could not tell whether he were awake or not. He could still sense a faint motion of curtains in the dark window and the garden smells, but he was talking to his mother too, who had been dead thirty years. She had been an invalid, but now she was well; she seemed to emanate that abounding serenity as of earth which his sister had done since her marriage and the birth of her child, and she sat on the side of the bed, talking to him. With her hands, her touch, because he realised that she had not opened her mouth. Then he saw that she wore a shapeless garment of faded calico and that Belle's rich, full mouth burned sullenly out of the halflight, and he knew that she was about to open her mouth and he tried to scream at her, to clap his hand to her mouth. But it was too late. He saw her mouth open; a thick, black liquid welled in a bursting bubble that splayed out upon her fading chin and the sun was shining on his face and he was thinking He smells black. He smells like that black stuff that ran out of Bovary's mouth when they raised her head. (SO 60)

Horace's mother, his sister, his wife, Ruby Lamar, and Emma Bovary, the adulteress, all the objects of his sexual consciousness, become fused with Popeye and condensed into one repulsive image that makes explicit how directly his childhood trauma is connected with sex and aggression and death and disgust and his mother.

Sanctuary, then, is Horace's nightmare. His nightmare is no static visual tableau like five motionless white wolves. Rather, outside the window of his secure dungeon-home in Kinston, he watches a teeming, overfructive garden turn into the foul, rank, overgrown jungle that surrounds the Old Frenchman place where, in the corn*crib*, Temple, his female self, is violated by Popeye while, in Temple's mind, blind Pap looks on. Horace's dream, then, substituting and transforming and inverting the actual childhood experience, manufactures out of whatever he saw, whatever he felt, whatever he was suppressing, a world of dark fantastic characters and shapes that correspond to something in his hidden life. It is a fantastic world indeed, full of dark places and bizarre, grotesque shapes that make the imagination of Quentin Compson seem, by comparison, a clean, well-lighted place.

5. Oedipus is le nom-du-pere, le nom-du-fils

If Miss Reba is Horace's dreamwork version of his mother, Popeye is Horace's father: the judge, the sober respectable family man becomes, by the substitution and inversion of the dreamwork, the impotent voyeur, the outlaw, the non-drinking bootlegger who thinks there ought to be a law to keep folks from making and selling whiskey, but still the punishing, vengeful father who in the dream kills the son for the Oedipal desire, as, indeed, Popeye murders both Red and Tommy, the first who actually has sex with Temple, the latter who merely wants to.

The Oedipus complex is everywhere in *Sanctuary*, everywhere mixed up in the numerous inversions and transpositions of identity that both hide and symbolically reveal precisely the characteristics of his parents that he is hell-bent to repress. Oedipus is present, first of all, in the number of fathers and father-substitutes whose actions in one way or another betray the Oedipal crisis. Temple has a variety of father-figures: her real father, like Horace's a "judge," of whom she is always conscious, and who overprotects her behind a wall of four mountainous brothers; as a family of males they are different in degree but not in kind from Ruby's father and four brothers, who overprotect her to the extent of killing her lover while she watches; Lee Goodwin, who with Ruby Lamar ("Reba" elides into "Ruby") forms a surrogate family at the Old Frenchman place—Matthews calls it a "nightmarish disfiguration of a family" ("The Elliptical Nature of *Sanctuary*" 256)—for her, constantly spies on her, violates her privacy; Temple's blind "Pap" watches as Popeye violates her; then Popeye himself, whom Temple calls "Daddy" during the scene at the Grotto, and who, as a father surrogate, actually fulfills her Oedipal fantasies—even if not in the manner she had intended. Horace marries Belle, whom he calls "Little Mother" in public; he also longs for Little Belle, his step-daughter, and for Narcissa, his sister. He even jokes, if nervously, about his Oedipus complex, in a scene toward the beginning of *Sanctuary* when Belle accuses him of being "in love with your sister. What do the books call it? What sort of complex?" she twits. He evades the issue entirely by punning: "Not complex. . . . Do you think that any relation with her could be complex?" (SO 16).

Finally, and most conspicuously, Oedipus Tyrannis is present in *Sanctuary* in the legal system of North Mississippi and Tennessee, in a capricious set of lawyers, judges, legislators, policemen, jurors, preachers, and even Jefferson society, all of whom, like fathers, make laws and break them with impunity, condemn and punish with little concern for guilt or innocence. The conniving and politically ruthless District Attorney, Eustace Graham, whose club foot clearly associates him with Oedipus, is more than willing to punish Lee Goodwin for his own political purposes. With Narcissa's assistance, he humiliates and punishes Horace in his own father's courtroom, in front of a judge-father substitute who sits where his own father would have sat, and who chides him publicly for his incompetence.

In 1979 I suggested in an essay on Faulkner and the Law that the courthouse and the jail in Jefferson "stand throughout most of William Faulkner's fiction as the central axis of his narrative and thematic concerns, and they are connected to each other by the strongest and most irresolvable ties" ("I Taken an Oath" 159). I argued that in Faulkner's work the courthouse represented humanity's need for security, the impulse to idealize justice; the jail, the opposite impulse toward aggression and destruction.

It is a mistake, however, I now believe, to accept this generalization about the jail-courthouse polarity as being true for Faulkner's entire career, for although the courthouse and the jail are indisputably important architectural components of the Jefferson landscape from the very inception of Yoknapatawpha County, they did not assume the thematic dimensions I identified until somewhat late in Faulkner's career. Indeed, my comments then grew out of my explorations of *Requiem for a Nun* (1951), a late work in which Faulkner attempts to bring some consistency to the ragtag history of Yoknapatawpha County he had developed in bits and pieces over the course of the previous quarter-century, in order to make Yoknapatawpha more conspicuously a part of the rest of the world. The symbolic relationship between the courthouse and the jail is thus retrospective, not one that existed from the beginning. Indeed, one is struck with the relative absence of the courthouse from the Yoknapatawpha of the twenties, thirties, and even forties. It of course exists as an architectural fact, but it is more often taken in its association with the four-faced clock atop it or with the Confederate monument on its Southern side or, simply, with the town square of Jefferson, of which it is the center. It is a constant factor in the geographical, but not much of one in the moral or legal, landscape though, to be sure, as we shall shortly see, reading backwards from *Requiem*, it does have considerable psychological significance.

The same is not true, however, of the jail, which looms considerably larger than the courthouse in the Jefferson consciousness of the early novels, particularly in *Sanctuary*. Perhaps it is only coincidental that Faulkner chose to explore the relationship between jail and courthouse in *Requiem for a Nun*, the play-novel that resurrects Temple Drake, puts her back on the witness stand if not actually in the courthouse, and forces her to the problematic "confession" that

Gavin Stevens demands of her. More particularly, Temple is in *Requiem* harassed by Gavin Stevens, the fictional descendant of Horace Benbow, who responds to the Temple of *Sanctuary* with Benbow's disgust and outrage, and who is psychologically strong enough to do what Horace only fantasizes about: to humiliate, to punish Temple for her part in his professional and personal humiliation:

> He would sub-poena Temple; [Horace] thought in a paroxysm of raging pleasure of flinging her into the court-room, of stripping her: This is what a man has killed another over. This, the offspring of respectable people: let them blush for shame, since he could never blush for anything again. Stripping her, background, environment, all. (SO 255)

This is precisely what Stevens does to Temple in *Requiem*.

It may or may not be significant that Temple Drake is at the center of both of these novels that are concerned with the functioning of the legal system. What is indisputably significant is the historical relationship Faulkner describes, in *Requiem*, between the jail and the courthouse. Like the earliest settlers in Hawthorne's New England of *The Scarlet Letter*, the early north Mississippians make their first civic building a jailhouse. Even though an insubstantial structure—it is a "morticed-log mud-chinked shake-down" (RN 475) building—and even though the settlers use it only for the relatively few "amateur" bad guys they have to deal with, they nevertheless recognize the practical necessity of having one, human nature being what it is. The courthouse, on the other hand, begins in Jefferson as merely a place to store some useless records. It is a "small . . . leanto room like a wood- or tool-shed . . . against one outside wall" (475) of the ramshackle jail, hardly a worthy embodiment of hope and aspiration, much less an assurance of justice or security. In the aftermath of a complicating jailbreak, the settlers decide that they must have a new, stronger jail, and decide to add to the new structure a second room, which would be a courthouse.

The idea for the courthouse is simultaneous with their desire to create a town; at the official founding of Jefferson, then, the jail and the courthouse are in a single structure, separated only by a single wall. As the settlers and then the later arrivals build a succession of courthouses worthy to embody their dreams and aspirations, they gradually begin to avoid the jail; they shun it for its symbolic potency as a place of punishment, its constant reminder of the factor in human nature that makes jails necessary. Jefferson repudiates the jail so completely that it separates the courthouse building from it; in building a new courthouse, they move not just the new building but the entire town to a new location, leaving the old jail building "not even on a side-street but on an alley" (616) where most citizens would not have to pass it and so think about it during a normal day. During the subsequent history of Jefferson the settlers constantly rebuild and expand the courthouse building; they leave the jail building alone; they merely whitewash it over. Through the years, it retains its symbolic relationship to something, whatever it is, that the Jefferson folk want, need, to forget.

The prologue to Act I of *Requiem*, "The Jail," is, on one important level at least, a fable of the founding of western civilization (Polk, *Requiem*; Crane). Faulkner saw, in 1951, the profound relationship between jail and courthouse as he perhaps had not seen it during the work of his early years, and it is significant that he saw that relationship arising out of the prior existence of the jail. Indeed, the jail does not have merely a *prior* existence: "there was no town until there was a courthouse," he writes in *Requiem*, and "no courthouse until [the courthouse was 'reft from the log flank of the jail'] (like some unsentient unweaned creature torn violently from the dug of its dam)" (616). The jail is thus mother/progenitor of the courthouse and so of civilization itself: no town without a courthouse, no courthouse without a jail. Civilization, in this image, derives from a collective and individual guilt somewhere far anterior even to consciousness.

In *Sanctuary*, then, the complex of prohibitions originating in infantile sexual relationships between parents and children is intimately, directly, and symbiotically related to the judicial system that originates in the absolute need of any society, primitive or modern, to have rules to govern human intercourse. This is no accident in *Sanctuary*, and once again we may turn to Freud. In *Totem and Taboo*, published originally in 1912, but published in English in this country in 1918, Freud addressed himself directly to these problems.

Freud's starting point in *Totem and Taboo* is what he and anthropologists such as Sir James G. Frazer and Claude Lévi-Strauss observed as the universal prohibition, in every known society, of incest. Freud argues that this prohibition can be traced to a rupture in the relationships that must have existed, in the earliest families, between fathers and sons. He posits a primal, historical family in which the only sexual restrictions were those imposed by the father; that is, the father held all power, all possessions, and claimed all sexual privileges with all women, including his own daughters, as his exclusive right. The sons counselled among themselves and determined that this was an intolerable state of affairs. In order to free themselves from their father's tyrannical rule, they murdered him. They celebrated their freedom vigorously, yet they also felt immediate remorse for their deed, for in spite of their fear and resentment of their father, they also loved him and depended on him for the order and social control his strength provided.

After the celebration, remorse conquered the sons: guilt entered the world. Their remorse led them to try to atone for their collective guilt by making of the dead father a totem and by identifying him with a totem animal. They collectively forbade any repetition of their patricide by making the totem sacred. They raised their father, now safely dead, to the status of hero; they made him repository and symbol of all of their ideals, and worshiped him through the totem that represented him. They also renounced their claim to the women for whom they had killed him in the first place:

> They revoked their deed by forbidding the killing of the totem, the substitute for their father; and they renounced its fruits by resigning their claim to the women who had now been set free. They thus created out of their filial sense of guilt the two fundamental taboos of totemism, which for that very reason inevitably corresponded to the two repressed wishes of the Oedipus complex. Whoever contravened these taboos became guilty of the only two crimes with which primitive society concerned itself.

The two taboos of totemism with which human morality has its beginning are not on a par psychologically. The first of them, the law
protecting the totem animal, is founded wholly on emotional motives:
the father had actually been eliminated, and in no real sense could the
deed be undone. But the second rule, the prohibition of incest, has a
powerful practical basis as well. Sexual desires do not unite men but
divide them. Though the brothers had banded together in order to
overcome their father, they were all one another's rivals in regard to
the women. Each of them would have wished, like his father, to have
all the women to himself. The new organization would have collapsed
in a struggle of all against all, for none of them was of such over-
mastering strength as to be able to take on the father's part with success. Thus the brothers had no alternative, if they were to live together,
but—not, perhaps, until they had passed through many dangerous crises—to institute the law against incest, by which they all alike renounced the women whom they desired and who had been their chief
motive for despatching their father. In this way they rescued the organization which had made them strong. . . .

Totemic religion arose from the filial sense of guilt, in an attempt to
allay that feeling and to appease the father by deferred obedience to
him. All later religions are seen to be attempts at solving the same
problem. They vary according to the stage of civilization at which they
arise and according to the methods which they adopt; but all have the
same end in view and are reactions to the same great event with which
civilization began and which, since it occurred, has not allowed mankind a moment's rest. (SE XIII: 143–45)

Thus the Oedipus complex is not just the "nuclear complex of the
neuroses" (SE XIII: 129); the murder of the primal father is in fact
the "great event with which civilization began," and, therefore, arguably, why, in Faulkner and Hawthorne, new societies begin not with a
courthouse but with a jail—not with freedom and aspiration, but with
prohibition and repression. As Freud argues in *Civilization and its
Discontents*, neurosis is the basis for civilization.

To repeat: Horace is unquestionably the central consciousness—or
unconsciousness—of *Sanctuary: The Original Text*: Horace the neurotic, Horace the lawyer, Horace the son of a judge, Horace the ideal-

ist, Horace the defender of all things civilization stands for—which are, ironically, the prohibitions of the very things that his unconscious, his id-instinct, is urging him most powerfully to do. He clings to civilization, to the law, to concepts of justice, as to a totem to prevent himself from yielding to those primal impulses that so dominate his unconscious life.

In Faulkner, the "Name-of-the-father" is Oedipus. Discussing Freud's analysis of a father's dream in which his son says to him, *"Father, can't you see I'm burning?"*, Jacques Lacan suggests that Freud's interest in the dream is

> to suggest a mystery that is simply the world of the beyond, and some secret or other shared by the father and the son who says to him, *Father, can't you see I'm burning?* What is he burning with, if not with that which we see emerging at other points designated by the Freudian topology, namely, the weight of the sins of the father, borne by the ghost in the myth of Hamlet, which Freud couples with the myth of Oedipus? The father, the Name-of-the-father, sustains the structure of desire with the structure of the law—but the inheritance of the father is that which Kierkegaard designates for us, namely, his sin. (Lacan 34)

In fact, then, when invoking her father the judge in moments of panic, Temple is not invoking her father but Lacan's "Name-of-the-father," the all-powerful arbiter of the law that stands beyond the father and is more powerful than her father, but for whom the father stands. The "Name-of-the-father" is "the symbolic function, which, since the dawn of historical time, has identified his person with the figure of the Law" (qtd. in Bleikasten, "Fathers in Faulkner," 120).

It may then be precisely to the point that in revising the final pages of *Sanctuary* Faulkner included a quite elaborate scene in which the good citizens of Jefferson, perhaps prompted by the travelling drummers at the hotel, lynch Lee Goodwin by setting him on fire and by threatening to do the same to Horace (S 384). He thus invokes the "Burning burning burning burning" lust of Eliot's "The Fire Sermon," but also Freud's dream, in which Horace is almost burned, as Lee *is* burned, for the transgressive desire for his mother that he has inherited from his father. The mob who lynch do so, however, in outrageous but perfectly understandable paradox: they condemn Lee beyond the law that the judge presiding over Lee's trial represents, and so act as agents of the "Name-of-the-father," as agents of civilization's repulsion at the idea of incest. At the same time, they commit the sin, or express the desire to, for which they are burning Lee: "She was some *baby*," one drummer says. "Jeez. I wouldn't have used no cob" (S 383, my emphasis). In adding this scene, Faulkner has thus written into *Sanctuary* his own adaptation of *Totem and Taboo*'s central event, the event with which civilization began, when the children killed their father to gain access to the father's women. The scene of Lee's conflagration occurs to Horace as "a voice of fury *like in a dream*, roaring silently out of a peaceful void" (S 384, my emphasis).

If Oedipus is central to *Sanctuary*, we may make some sense of Temple's rape, for which Lee is being burned: Popeye and Pap, whose names are reciprocal and analogous—"Pop" is a soubriquet for "father"—are involved equally in her violation: their eyes make them Oedipal twins—one is blind, one is a pop-eyed voyeur, eyes strained with bulging to see more and more of what she is doing. Temple's unconscious wants the Popeye part of her father to see her as a desirable woman capable of accepting his sexual love. He violates his child, significantly, in a "crib," and at Miss Reba's she wears a towel like a diaper to staunch the flow of blood from her injury; as noted earlier, the drummers in Jefferson refer to her as a "baby" that they wouldn't have used a corncob on. As *this* part of her father fulfills the Oedipal fantasy, she immediately becomes conscious of the *other* part, the part that condemns and shames. Faulkner is very specific: at the very moment of her violation, Pap becomes fused in her mind with her judge father, "sitting in his chair . . . his hands crossed on the top of the stick" (SO 140; S 250). Pap is blind Oedipus, from whom she wants to hide both her behavior and her desires; he is the *judge* part, the super-ego that condemns her and makes her feel guilt. Pap dominates her mind at the moment of her rape. Whatever of pain and violation she feels at the moment of her rape, that pain is clearly secondary to her fear of her father's impending disapproval: "Something is happening to me!" she screams at him in reproach, disclaiming her own responsibility for being here and, in effect, blaming him for not protecting her: "I told you it was!", she says (SO 140; S 250).[5]

This reading of her rape may also make it possible to understand why she "lies" on the witness stand during Lee's trial. Why does she swear away Lee Goodwin's life?[6] The question has perplexed *Sanctuary* criticism for years. Her lying is not a cold-blooded disregard for truth or human life, although it has often been interpreted that way. More likely, Temple *could not possibly* tell the truth about the events surrounding her rape because she has repressed the trauma so completely. Tommy's murder is intimately tied up with Temple's Oedipal desire: traumatized, she censors the truth, displaces it with a convenient and plausible substitute, because in fact she had desired Lee, teased him and Tommy, and he may in fact have had some form of sex with her prior to Popeye.[7] What Temple tells is not the truth, but it is not a lie in her conscious mind. Just as in her testimony Temple

5. Matthews' reading of the rape scene is worth noting, both for its similarities to and differences from my own: "The displacement leading to the fusion of the two figures signals Temple's intuition that fathers not only stonily countenance their daughters' defilement, but even participate through delegation. Again the conflation of the enforcement and endangerment of the incest prohibition flickers—this time through the image of Pap's face leaning over the thrashing Temple. Pap is at once menace and protector; his enfeeblement embodies Temple's understanding of a father's eventual refusal to defend what exists only in its loss" ("The Elliptical Nature of *Sanctuary*" 260–61).

6. See Elisabeth Muhlenfeld's interesting discussion of this issue, especially 54–55.

7. In one scene everyone at the Old Frenchman place converges in the room Lee has assigned Temple and Gowan; Van and Lee fight bloodily for "rights" to Temple; Ruby pathetically puts on a faded negligee to try to tempt Lee away from his desire for Temple. Lee finally succeeds in driving them all out of the room. All except Tommy go to the kitchen, waiting and listening—for something—while Tommy sits outside the kitchen door. The beginning of the next paragraph—"He [Tommy] was there when Goodwin came out with the raincoat" (S 232)—*may* indicate that some time has elapsed—enough perhaps for Lee to have raped or molested Temple in some way. In any case, he carries Temple's raincoat, which she had been reluctant to give up to Van, and it seems to be a prize of some sort. But see also the beginning of the next chapter for contradictory evidence.

substitutes Lee Goodwin for Popeye, so does she substitute the infamous corncob for the paternal penis of her fantasy.

We may also now understand why Horace crumbles so quickly upon seeing Temple in the courtroom. Here, in the courtroom, in the Yoknapatawpha County courthouse, right at the center of the civilized world, in the very spot in all the world on which all the world's disapproval of Oedipus' two related sins converge in a fury, *and* under the condemning eye of his own judge/father, represented by the surrogate actually presiding over the trial, Horace confronts not merely Temple Drake, his shamed and violated female self, but also his own shamed and desiring male self. He and Temple must tell their shameful stories to the "name-of-the-father" himself. It is really no wonder he crumbles.

In revisiting *Sanctuary* twenty years later, in *Requiem*, Faulkner added historical-mythical scope and density to the courthouse-site of Horace's undoing. As in Freud, the courthouse is second on the historical-mythical stage of civilization, following, perhaps not even closely, the settler's recognition of their mutual need to prohibit and punish. The courthouse becomes the repository of their aspirations as a displacement of their instinctual desires to transgress and the guilt and shame the desire no less than the act engenders. As Freud put it, there are no prohibitions against things nobody wants to do.

Again, it's worth noting that in *Requiem* the courthouse was "reft from the log flank of the jail . . . like some unsentient unweaned creature torn violently from the dug of its dam" (616). The repository of aspiration, of civilization's ideals, is a quiescent, nearly-vegetative creature-infant dependent upon its mother for what little of life it requires, until something tears it unceremoniously away from its vegetative existence both in its mother's womb and at her breast. For Faulkner, then, civilization proceeds from a violent rupture in the quiet nurture of the mother-child relationship, from which fathers are biologically excluded. Faulkner does not tell us who or what creates the rupture—who or what reives the courthouse from the jail. But the perpetrator can only be some power greater than that relationship, one that has the power in fact to call that relationship transgressive and so prohibit it. The father disrupts this relationship "violently" because he feels threatened by it or, like Gail Hightower's father, merely excluded from it. In forbidding the relationship, the father must also forbid even the desire for it; in claiming and exercising the power to prohibit, he, like Freud's primal father, claims power over the women and the children, and so creates the conditions that will cause his sons to commit, or want to commit, the two primal sins of Oedipus.

But in disrupting the relationship, the father pulls children from the very dungeon of the mother that both imprisons and nurtures, and at which they all stare, fascinated. In one sense, the father must forbid the relationship, not just to prove the arbitrariness of his power and to have the mother exclusively, but also to enforce his son's freedom from that dungeon-mother. As Bleikasten puts it,

> It is essential to remember . . . the crucial function which psychoanalysis assigns to the father in the dialectic of desire and law that, under normal circumstances, leads to the achievement of selfhood. In the Oedipal triangle the father appears as the obstacle to the fulfillment of the incestuous wish; he bars the son's access to the mother, yet by the same token he also forbids the mother exclusive possession of the son. He thus releases the latter from the constraints and tensions of the family circle, allows him to move on to other object-choices, and furthers his entry into the system of alliances which rules and regulates the wider world of human exchange. In prohibiting and preventing incest, the father indeed performs a major cultural function, especially if, as Lévi-Strauss argues, the universal incest taboo is to be understood as the very cornerstone of human society. ("Fathers in Faulkner" 119)

The father can thus legitimately embody his power in a language of aspiration, of communal ideals, that masks his power and allows him to move the jail, the sign of the prohibition, of his power to prohibit, into a back alley of town where folks don't have to speak of it or be constantly reminded of it. But he claims the center of communal life anyway, by putting the courthouse, his totem, at the center of town, where its imposing presence keeps him constantly at the center of everybody's consciousness. The four symbolical clocks in the courthouse cupola allow him to maintain surveillance over his children—or, rather, the clocks force the children to maintain surveillance over themselves. The four clocks are thus the eyes of the super-ego, the eyes of the Name-of-the-father that operate as a constant reminder to the children that even though they choose not to talk about their shame, they must nevertheless never forget it, never forget that they are being constantly watched and will be punished/will punish themselves for the slightest fault. The clocks at the top of the courthouse are signs of Jeffersonians' "delusions of being watched," which, according to Freud, is how guilt manifests itself.

In "Delta Autumn," a distraught and anguished Roth Edmonds finds himself agreeing with an unsympathetic Legate that "it's only because folks happen to be watching him that a man behaves at all. . . . Is that it?" "Yes," Edmonds replies, "A man in a blue coat, with a badge on it watching him. Maybe just the badge" (GDM 255). Watching. Being watched. Roth Edmonds thinks there ought to be a policeman standing behind everybody, looking over their shoulders and hitting them with a billy-club every time they misbehave or even think about misbehaving. In *Sanctuary* and *The Sound and the Fury* and other works, that policeman is already there, firmly enshrined, punishing and vengeful, unsleeping and vigilant. The Law in *Sanctuary* is an all-encompassing pair of eyes.

That Temple's and Horace's fathers are both judges in Mississippi's judicial system has particular significance in *Sanctuary*'s scheme. As has been suggested, they are essentially the same person; though mostly absent from the narrative (Horace's parents are dead), they wield powerful influence over their children through their constant presence in their children's neuroses. When Temple variously makes claims upon her father's power—"My father's a judge. My father's a judge"—in moments of crisis, it is as a mantra, a prayer for protection, and she obviously has no real reason to believe that her father will actually provide the protection that she is praying for.

Indeed, as Bleikasten has pointed out, biological fathers are noticeably absent or powerless in Faulkner ("Fathers in Faulkner"); when they are absent or powerless, aunts, uncles, foster-fathers, mothers

and grandmothers try to take over for them. Fathers directly present
in the narrative are almost always incapable of administering the law
that is their historical responsibility; their children seek either to force
them to live up to that responsibility or, failing that, to construct a
"Name-of-the-father" to whom they can look for order, security,
peace, even at the cost of their own punishment. Thus Quentin
Compson in *The Sound and the Fury* tells his father he and Caddy
have committed incest; failing to force his father's hand, he looks
backward beyond his father to his grandfather and Colonel Sartoris
for the capacity to exercise the power over life and death (SF 176).
Quentin's fascination with Thomas Sutpen in *Absalom, Absalom!* is at
several levels precisely a function of his need to give a name and form
to the nameless and the formless.

Likewise, in *Light in August*, Gail Hightower is madly obsessed with
the gallantry and the competence, if foolhardy, of his own grandfather; he spends sermon after sermon invoking him from the pulpit,
making of him both a deity and the "Name-of-the-father." Not surprisingly, Hightower's memories of his parents bear significant resonances with Quentin's and Horace's. Like Quentin and Horace,
Hightower also spends an abnormal amount of time looking out the
window of a study in a dark house he is virtually a prisoner in. Like
theirs, his mother was also an invalid, for twenty years before she
died. He remembers her and his father in a passage that sums up the
meaning of family, of the Oedipal triangle in Faulkner: it is a stunning
crystallization of the Faulkner of this period: he remembers her

> first and last as a thin face and tremendous eyes and a spread of dark
> hair on a pillow, with blue, still, almost skeleton hands. . . . at eight and
> nine and ten he thought of her as without legs, feet; as being only that
> thin face and the two eyes which seemed daily to grow bigger and big-
> ger, as though about to embrace all seeing, all life, with one last terrible
> glare of frustration and suffering and foreknowledge. . . . Already, be-
> fore she died, he could feel them through all walls. They were the
> house: he dwelled within them, within their dark and allembracing and
> patient aftermath of physical betrayal. He and she both lived in them
> like two small, weak beasts in a den, a cavern, into which now and

then the father entered—that man who was a stranger to them both, a foreigner, almost a threat: so quickly does the body's wellbeing alter and change the spirit. He was more than a stranger: he was an enemy. He smelled differently from them. He spoke with a different voice, almost in different words, as though he dwelled by ordinary among different surroundings and in a different world; crouching beside the bed the child could feel the man fill the room with rude health and unconscious contempt, he too as helpless and frustrated as they. (750–51)

He and his mother are prisoners in their own versions of Quentin's dungeon; like Horace's, his mother is simultaneously a seductive sexual presence but also the condemning maternal fury whose "allembracing" eyes constantly monitor his every movement, his every thought. His frustrated and alien father is the threat to their relationship. His parents are the dark house indeed.

6. Life Is Terrible for Women

Temple's fantasy of becoming a school teacher is not difficult to understand. A teacher was a formidable person in Temple's world, teaching perhaps the only position of authority, outside of motherhood itself, to which a girl of Temple's era could aspire. The other part of the fantasy, the part in which she projects herself as forty-five years old and having both "iron-gray hair and spectacles" and a huge maternal bosom—"I was all big up here, like women get"—is very interesting, for this powerful woman, whom Temple imagines herself to be, is something of an epicenter in Faulkner's work, particularly of the early period. She is one, but she is also many: male, she is often a judge or a sheriff; female, she is grandmother and mother, maiden and widowed aunt; she is often seen framed in windows looking out at the world passing by or at children playing in the yard; she is frequently bedridden, frequently invalid, and she is often seen juxtaposed against the pillow, her hair splayed out, Medusa-like, in grotesque parody of the sexuality she abhors, fears, and represses in herself and in others, eliding back and forth between the seductive mother and the condemning maternal Erynnis. She may be an active participant in a story or she may be merely part of a story's background. But if she is not in fact in *every* story, she is nevertheless, like Oedipus, *everywhere* in Yoknapatawpha, the county's resident genius of guilt and repression, the root of all problem, Oedipus's feminine self. She doesn't always have gray hair, she doesn't always wear spectacles, but in one or more combinations and permutations of these elements, she hovers close above huge areas of Yoknapatawpha: iron, imperious, fanatical, frustrated herself, and withal pathetic.

To be sure, the women of Yoknapatawpha have their own problems; they do not become what they become in a historical vacuum (Trouard, "Faulkner's Text"; Williams). Mothers, on to whose lives Faulkner's male narrators inscribe the language of domesticity and nurture, become dungeons and jailors when they do not give what males demand of them. And so, as Quentin Compson's and Gail Hightower's memories make clear, the women who symbolize the dungeon also live in it. They too have invariably grown up in dark houses, which they are now willy-nilly perpetuating, in families racked with dysfunction because of husbands and fathers who cope with their own lives through either domination or escape.

In the holograph manuscript of "Dry September," Faulkner wrote: "Life in such places is terrible for Women. Life in all places is terrible for women" (WFMS 9:264). He did not retain this bleak pronouncement when he typed the story, but it remains, in the manuscript, as a poignant and pointed summation of a central truth in Faulkner's fiction of the years 1927–1932. Life for women is not always significantly better in the fiction of the later years, but it is particularly terrifying in these crucial years, and the terror and despair are always rooted in family dysfunction caused by Oedipal tensions and sexual repression in general. That is, whatever terror these gray-haired Medusas inflict on their own children and grandchildren, they, too, like Caroline Compson, live in the dungeons, the dark houses, that they grew up in.

What follows in this section is a brief catalog of women of the years 1927–1932, a quick overview to demonstrate just how pervasive this woman is in Faulkner, and how problematic the lives of women in Faulkner are. The catalog demonstrates a dazzling variety of modulations and permutations of these women, who are all, in basic ways, avatars of the same woman.

♀ With one exception, Miss Jenny DuPre is perhaps the best-known of Faulkner's old ladies; she has prominent roles in *Flags in the Dust, Sanctuary,* and "There was a Queen." She is generally admired by readers, and it is easy to see her in these three works as merely exercising the privileges of her age in being a crotchety and sharp-tongued but finally wise and sympathetic old lady, one of Faulkner's unvanquished, one of his irreconcilables. But she is at the same time frequently and unexplainably querulous, impatient, intolerant, downright mean and racist, and she is in her own way as nihilistic as Jason Compson and Addie Bundren's father. She was married for two years, widowed in the Civil War, and never remarried. When she comes from Carolina to stay with her nephew, old Bayard, she brings with her a "narrow" window "with leaded varicolored panes" (FD 34). Along with Miss Jenny herself, the window is his mother's deathbed legacy to old Bayard. In the manuscript, but not in the published book, Miss Jenny is Bayard's sister, not his aunt (WFMS 5:1, 36): it is not clear why Faulkner changed the relationship in *Flags,* but the significance of the brother-sister relationship there so stuck in his mind that three decades later, writing *The Town,* Faulkner remembered their relationship as that of siblings (T 139).

Under Miss Jenny's soft graying exterior lurks the same sorts of frustrations that we find in other women of her type. She diverts that energy into acceptable channels: she

> enjoyed humanity in its more colorful mutations, preferring lively romance to the most impeccable of dun fact, so she took in the more lurid afternoon paper even though it was yesterday's when it reached her, and read with cold avidity accounts of arson and murder and violent dissolution and adultery; in good time and soon the American scene was to supply her with diversion in the form of bootleggers' wars. (FD 35)

In the manuscript the final sentence of this passage reads: "in good time and soon the American scene was to furnish her with soul's ease in the form of bootleggers' wars" (FDMS 5:1, 29). Clearly her sharp tongue, her avidity for the sensational, are vicarious thrills, substitutions for a kind of experience she has been denied, but for which, at some level, she longs. It is not absolutely clear why she dies at the end of "There Was a Queen," but it seems clearly related to her adamant, self-righteous, and racist disapproval of Narcissa's liaison with a Jew; how much of envy is involved is impossible to say, but one early version of "There Was a Queen," is titled "Through the Window." In "There Was A Queen," she dies while staring out the window through which she has watched Narcissa being courted.

♀ In *Flags in the Dust* Narcissa Benbow is associated many times with windows, both those she looks out of and those through which Byron Snopes not only spies on her but actually invades her bedroom. It is manifestly clear throughout *Flags* that her feelings for Horace are more maternal than sexual; in one scene that suggests her true place in Horace's psyche, Horace comes to her to talk while she is lying in bed, "beneath the shaded light, with the dark splash of her hair upon the pillow, and only her eyes moved as he crossed the room . . . watching him with sober interrogation" (FD 241). She too is both condemning judge and seductive mother.

♀ In *The Sound and the Fury* Quentin precedes the little Italian girl into a bakery where they are greeted by a woman who thoroughly disapproves of the Italian girl's presence in her store, though perhaps Quentin interprets her disapproval somewhat otherwise. The woman enters, "her neat gray face her hair tight and sparse from her neat gray skull, spectacles in neat gray rims riding approaching like something on a wire. . . . She looked like a librarian" (SF 125); a deleted line in the manuscript adds, "Or at least, a school teacher" (WFMS 6:1, 60). She glares at Quentin: "She just needed a bunch of switches, a blackboard behind her 2 x 2 e 5," he says (SF 126). She gives the little girl a loaf of bread, but does so ungenerously. She appears later in the sequence in the form of the justice of the peace who tries Quentin for his depredations with the little girl; the justice is "a man with a fierce roach of iron gray hair [peering] at us over steel spectacles" (142).

♀ In *Sanctuary* one of the prim madames who sits around with Miss Reba after Red's funeral swilling gin and beer and talking about their trade is a woman "primly erect, in gold nose-glasses on a gold chain and neat iron-gray hair. She looked like a school-teacher" (SO 246). Temple herself is described in Miss Reba's bed, "the covers to her chin and her face small and wan, framed in the rich sprawl of her hair" (SO 170; see also 175).

♀ In "The Brooch," Howard Boyd's invalid mother controls his and his wife's life from her bedroom, at the bottom of the stairs behind a closed door. When they see her, or even imagine her, she is "high-propped on the pillows, with her tallow face and dark inscrutable eyes and the hair which Amy said resembled weathered cotton" (CS 655). Howard's way out, like Quentin Compson's, is to commit suicide. Her constant observing presence is symbolized by the light from her room shining through the transom over her door.

♀ "Miss Zilphia Gant" is perhaps Faulkner's least subtle and so most revealing treatment of these themes. Faulkner wrote "Zilphia" before December of 1928, less than a month before he was to start the final push to finish *Sanctuary*. Zilphia's father is a travelling man who leaves home for another woman; Zilphia's mother hunts him down with a shotgun and kills him; she seeks him "with the capability of a man, the pertinacity of a Fate, the serene imperviousness of a vestal out of a violated temple, and then returned to her child, her face cold, satiate and chaste" (US 370). She raises Zilphia in a house that is literally a prison, even to the barred windows. The townspeople see Zilphia's "wan small face watching them, or, holding to the bars, coughing" (US 371). As she gets older, Zilphia becomes a "neat woman, with neat hair. Her skin was the color of celery and she was a little plump in a flabby sort of way. Her glasses lent a baffled, ascetic look to her face" (US 375). She becomes enamored of a housepainter who first sees her and then continues to stare at her through the window as she sits sewing, and at whom she obviously stares through the same barred window; she dreams at night of things which "the painter performed monstrously with his pot and brush." Now and then "she dreamed of the pot and brush alone. They would be alive, performing of themselves actions of monstrous and ritualled significance" (US 375). She marries the painter, but her mother, again with shotgun, denies him entrance to the house, and denies Zilphia escape from it. Though the painter begs, Mrs. Gant remains adamant, and he takes off. Mrs. Gant maintains a vigil to make sure he doesn't sneak back, "in a chair at the front window, the shotgun leaning at her hand. For three days she sat there, rigid, erect, her eyes closed, sweating slowly. . . . That night Mrs. Gant died, erect and fully dressed in the chair" (US 378).

Alone, Zilphia hires a detective to follow her husband, and lives vicariously through the reports: "Sometimes at night she would become one of the two of them [her husband and his new wife], entering their bodies in turn and crucified anew by her ubiquity, participating in ecstasies the more racking for being vicarious and transcendant of the actual flesh" (US 380); a passage deleted from the manuscript tells us that when she received word that the wife was pregnant, she "dreamed that night that she was shackled to the wall of their bedroom, her eyelids wedged [open]" (WFMS 24:174). She tries to commit suicide, but fails. She spends ten years dreaming and weeping. Then she begins to realize that "for some time now she had been dreaming of negro men. 'Something is about to happen to me,' " she thinks, like Temple Drake and Joe Christmas. When she learns that both her husband and his wife are dead, she goes to get the child, brings her to Jefferson; repeating her own life, she becomes her own mother and begins to raise her little girl as she had been raised, in a house with barred windows.

♀ "Elly" is also particularly interesting because Elly is compounded of parts of Temple Drake, Caddy, Miss Quentin, Addie Bundren, Zilphia Gant. She is an eighteen-year-old woman who lives in Jefferson, in a "dark house"—called so several times—with her parents and her deaf grandmother who, she feels, watches her all the time. Like Caddy and Quentin, she lies "almost nightly" in the shadows created by the house's "deep veranda with screening vines and no lights" (CS 208) with just about any male—though, fearing pregnancy, she always stops short of intercourse. Afterwards, she must walk up the stairs to her room, passing her grandmother's room at the top of the stairs, from the door of which "a single square of light" falls "upon the upper hallway." She passes the room and sometimes looks in, sometimes not, to where her grandmother sits in the bed, "erect, an open book in her hands, facing the hall" (CS 208). What part her parents play in her life we do not know, except that her grandmother's most potent threat, what Elly fears most, is that she will tell her father about her promiscuity.

But like Caddy, Elly's furtive amorous experimentations bring her no particular pleasure; quite the contrary, they fill her with self-loathing. She stares at herself in the mirror, sees her face "flattened . . . and weary and dulled with kissing," and she thinks with disgust:

> "My God. Why do I do it? What is the matter with me?" thinking of how tomorrow she must face the old woman again with the mark of last night upon her mouth like bruises, with a feeling of the pointlessness and emptiness of life more profound than the rage or the sense of persecution. (CS 209)

"My God," she says. "How could I. How could I. I don't want any man, anything" (CS 211).

At a crucial moment she does what so many of Faulkner's trapped characters do. She looks out a window at a fecund, burgeoning world that both attracts and repels her: from her mother's bedroom window, she watches the "infinitesimal clematis tendrils as they crept and overflowed up the screen and onto the veranda roof with the augmenting summer" (CS 214). As she looks, she meditates over her rage and frustration at her impending marriage to a very dull childhood friend, a cashier in the bank. She thinks of that marriage "with quiet despair and resignation," in language like Addie Bundren's:

"Anyway I can live quietly now. . . . At least I can live out the rest of my dead life as quietly as if I were already dead" (CS 213). It is not just her present life in that dark house that causes her grief, then, bad as it is; more than anything, she despairs over the long life to come, in which, married to her dull banker, she will continue to live in such a prison. When her grandmother interrupts her first attempt to have sexual intercourse, she is driven to rage against the old lady because she caught them *before* they had a chance to do anything: "At least, I would have had something, something" (CS 212). Her decision, then, to give her virginity not just to someone besides her husband but to a Negro, Paul de Montigny, fulfills Zilphia Gant's fantasies: it is a doubly intense sin, a doubly intense entry into the forbidden, a sin no less potent than incest. It is not just an act of rebellion against her grandmother and the mores of Jefferson, nor is it for her merely an attempt to escape from that life. Sex with the Negro, with the forbidden, is a chance to store up some excitement that she will have as a memory in the long, dull life to come. The decision, however, doesn't make her very happy; she cannot escape feelings of guilt, however strong her feelings of resentment.

She is named for her grandmother—Ailanthia—and Faulkner frequently depicts them staring into each other's eyes in ways that remind us of Popeye's and Horace's two-hour séance across the pond. Since her grandmother is deaf, Elly must communicate with her by writing on small cards. During one of their fights they have a tug of war over one of the cards: it connects them "like a queer umbilical cord" (CS 218). Her grandmother, then, is first the very model of what Elly is afraid she herself will eventually become, and Elly is terrified of that. Second, and more obviously, her grandmother is Elly's own vengeful superego, the part that disapproves of her, that forces her to hate herself, the very model of the gray-haired punitive Medusa, the controlling genius of the dark house. When she and Paul and her grandmother ride back home, her grandmother sits between them, between Elly and the object of her shame, separating even while connecting them. In trying to horrify her grandmother, by flaunting her liaison with a Negro, Elly, like Quentin Compson, begs for punishment. She schemes to kill her grandmother, but it is herself whom she wants to punish.

♀ "A Rose for Emily" is the best-known of Faulkner's female characters, and she is a classic study of this type. We know nothing of Emily's mother, but her father is cast from the same mold as Temple Drake's father, Zilphia Gant's mother, and Elly's grandmother. He drives her potential suitors away. The town thinks of Emily and her father "as a tableau": "Miss Emily a slender figure in white in the background, her father a spraddled silhouette in the foreground, his back to her and clutching a horsewhip, the two of them framed by the back-flung front door" (CS 123). Long after her father dies, she keeps her crayon portrait of him on a gilt easel before the fireplace, the relentlessly-dominating presence over that hearth—and dominant by her own design. The town sees her over the years sitting in one of the many windows of that huge dark house, "the light behind her, and her upright torso motionless as that of an idol" (CS 123). The city fathers who come to call on her about her taxes, find her

> a small, fat woman in black, with a thin gold chain descending to her waist and vanishing into her belt, leaning on an ebony cane with a tarnished gold head. . . . She just stood in the door and listened quietly. . . . Then they could hear the invisible watch ticking at the end of the gold chain. (CS 121)

We can only infer her desire from the cumulative events of the story. But her black dress and the cane suggest that she has *become* her father, her own superego.

Emily dies "in a heavy walnut bed with a curtain, her gray head propped on a pillow yellow and moldy with age and lack of sunlight" (CS 129). Those who come to the house out of curiosity to look at her body find her laid out in the parlor, "with the crayon face of her father musing profoundly above the bier" (CS 129); upstairs, on the pillow beside Homer Barron's skeleton, is the gray-hair evidence of Miss Emily's necrophilia.

It is more than necrophilia, however. Homer Barron, whose name signifies not just "barren home" but also blindness—the blind poet, perhaps blind Oedipus himself—is also a father-surrogate. Like her father, he carries a "whip in a yellow glove" when they ride through the streets during their "courtship." She thus completes with Homer's body the gesture she began when her father died, of refusing to give up the body to the authorities. After his death she "consummates" the Oedipal dream, at least to the extent of lying with him in bed. The townspeople are more correct than they know when they surmise that "with nothing left, she would have to cling to that which had robbed her, as people will" (CS 124).

If Oedipus is the courthouse-totem of the house of Yoknapatawpha, this gray-haired bespectacled matron is its resident concierge, the keeper of more than keys. Mantled in the imperious iron-gray of respectability, she is blind Oedipus's, blind justice's, unwavering eye. On the one hand she sees all and at least threatens to tell all to the punishing father; on the other hand, clothed in the colorless gray of her colorless life, she colludes with the children in their transgressions of the father's law, she too a prisoner in the dark house. In her bed, she is both seductive and judgmental, simultaneously offering and denying; thus her children often approach her in her bed-throne, in supplication, fearing her disapproval and her condemnation of what they ask.

In *Intruder in the Dust* (1948), recall, Gavin Stevens and Sheriff Hampton arrange to have the elderly Miss Habersham sit in the doorway of the jail to protect Lucas Beauchamp from the lynch mob developing just outside, while they go back out to do more digging. Who but men afraid of what she represents could really believe that this little old lady, alone, sewing, in the doorway to the jail, is iconically powerful enough to stop a lynch mob of Yoknapatawpha citizens? In all cases, this Faulknerian woman is an icon to which the fiction as a whole pays obeisance. Her brooding presence, implied or actual, monitors Yoknapatawpha as powerfully as the four eye-clocks atop the courthouse: maternal, frustrated, and pathetic in herself, but imperious and powerful in her effects on those she watches.

7. Joanna's Burden

Joe Christmas's childhood is so dreary and bleak as to make it a reductio ad absurdum, a grotesque parody, of all childhoods in Faulkner. It is so bleak that Joe represses most of it from his conscious memory, and Faulkner presents the long flashback of chapter 6 that recounts his earliest years as the content of his Joe's *unconscious*: "Memory believes before knowing remembers" (487): Memory (the unconscious) believes (retains all of the trauma) before knowing (consciousness) remembers (brings it to the surface). Embedded in his unconscious is the prison world wasteland of the orphanage, a dark house indeed. The orphanage and his unconscious are

> a corridor in a big long garbled cold echoing building of dark red brick sootbleakened by more chimneys than its own, set in a grassless cinder-strewnpacked compound surrounded by smoking factory purlieus and enclosed by a ten foot steel-and-wire fence like a penitentiary or a zoo. (487)

The building has "bleak windows where in rain soot from the yearly adjacenting chimneys streaked like black tears" (487); it is thus the dark house of Horace Benbow's childhood, too, its weeping window-eyes shut tight upon childhood trauma. Even so, it is no darker than the McEachern's house, into which Joe will move as an alien foster child. As he and McEachern approach his new home, Joe's foster father raises his "mittened fist which clutched the whip, toward a single light which shown in the dusk," and says "Home" (505)—an image as grim and punitive as the avenging Percy who will kill and castrate the adult Joe.

If the narrative indirection of *Sanctuary* makes it impossible to do more than posit a primal scene, there can be no doubt that it is the central episode in Joe Christmas's childhood, the event of which all the misery of his later life is a repercussion. Joe's experiences replicate the Wolf Man's explicitly; indeed, the Joe Christmas portions of *Light in August* are, I believe demonstrably, a virtually programmatic inscription of Freud into the novel.[8]

Joe's primal scene is the intercourse between the dietitian and the young intern Charlie, who have been carefully established as the orphan's surrogate parents—the dietitian through her constant association with Joe's food, a common factor among all of the women in Joe's life, the intern through finding him on the orphanage's steps on Christmas Eve. The Wolf Man defecates, Joe vomits. Joe after this episode associates all things sexual with filth and shame: women become cracked, dripping urns and, later, he thinks of his relationship with Joanna Burden that it is "as though he had fallen into a sewer" (588); such associations are richly resonant with the reasons Quentin wants to smear mud on himself and on Caddy when Caddy catches him with Natalie. Joe torments the dietitian by constantly putting himself in her way, to get his punishment over with; he spends the rest of his life unconsciously looking for, trying to provoke, the beating he cannot get from her. Even as a child he invites regular beatings from his foster father and accepts them not just as his due but as something he must have; Simon McEachern is more than happy to oblige him. In the well-known scene during which McEachern punishes him for refusing to learn his catechism, Joe stands masochistically erect, holding the pamphlet containing the catechism, "his face and the pamphlet lifted, his attitude one of exaltation" (509).

Mrs. McEachern, who tries to be kind to him, is physically at least a prototype of the woman/mother/judge I have been describing. Joe first sees her standing on the porch of the dark house to which McEachern has just pointed with his whip and designated "home." She is

> waiting on the porch—a patient, beaten creature without sex demarcation at all save the neat screw of graying hair and the skirt. . . . It was

8. In this discussion of *Light in August*, as well as in that of *Sanctuary*, I am moving in directions already provocatively mapped out by André Bleikasten in *The Ink of Melancholy* and in "Terror and Nausea: Bodies in *Sanctuary*." I am particularly grateful to Bleikasten for suggesting that I look into Freud's Wolf Man.

as though instead of having been subtly slain and corrupted by the ruthless and bigoted man into something beyond his intending and her knowing, she had been hammered stubbornly thinner and thinner like some passive and dully malleable metal, into an attenuation of dumb hopes and frustrated desires now faint and pale as dead ashes. (521)

She thus also makes one with Horace's and Quentin's mothers, a captive in the very house that she, not McEachern, will turn into a dungeon from which Joe must escape. Joe feels more oppressed by her long-delayed mothering than by McEachern's harsh uprightness, and he perceives her, rather than McEachern, as one of his "enemies" (551). Like Caddy and Quentin and Lena Grove, he escapes periodically from that house through the window of his bedroom, by means of a rope he maliciously allows Mrs. McEachern to help him hide. After he kills and repudiates McEachern, he returns to steal the money she has hidden and to repudiate her too.

Joe escapes the McEachern house; but he never escapes the patterns that were established in him during his childhood at the orphanage. His appearance at the equally dark house of Joanna Burden is a return to the McEachern home. Joanna combines all the most potent characteristics of his foster parents, Simon's rigid puritanism, Mrs. McEachern's frustrated and hopeless female life; her hermaphroditic first name and the historical baggage of her family name are rife with implications for an Oedipal reading of her relationship with Joe. Joe helps us along, perhaps a bit mechanically, by thinking of the McEacherns at crucial times in his relationship with Joanna, so that we won't miss the connection, when he steals the cold peas from the stove, when he climbs in and out of her windows, and when he throws her proffered food on the floor as he had thrown Mrs. McEachern's.

Joe first sees Joanna through the window of her dark house as a shadow moving across the wall of the only lighted room (567), as Jefferson frequently sees Emily Grierson. He climbs through the window to steal food from the kitchen. Curiously, Joanna has left the window open, and we surmise later that Joanna has, all of her life, fantasized about just such an occurrence: like Elly, like Miss Zilphia Gant, she fantasizes about Negro men.

Nor, in her sexual frustration and loneliness, is she alone in *Light in August*: she has many sisters. The opening chapter, for example, offers us a Mrs. Armstid with a "savage screw of gray hair at the base of her skull and a face that might have been carved in sandstone" (411); she is a "gray woman not plump and not thin, manhard, work-hard, in a serviceable gray garment worn savage and brusque, her hands on her hips, her face like those of generals who have been defeated in battle" (410). She is hospitable to Lena Grove, even gives her money; but she is not *kind* to her. While Lena is her "guest" Mrs. Armstid is virtually irrational with rage: she cooks with "an amount of attention out of all proportion to the savage finality with which she built the fire" (411). The intensity of her hospitality suggests a tumultuous ambivalence as she contemplates Lena's presence in her respectable house. At the top of her reaction is her moral outrage; just under the surface of the outrage, and bubbling furiously, is a lot of envy—perhaps unconscious, certainly never verbalized—of Lena's youth, of her freedom, and, doubtless, of Lena's untroubled sexuality. Lena's presence, then, fills her with a hatred of her own life, which she disguises as moral indignation at men.

In another scene, the townsfolk gather around Joanna's burning house, the scene of the crime. They are grateful to Joanna for supplying them with an "emotional barbecue," a "Roman holiday almost." They hope that Joanna has been raped as well as murdered, though this hope is not so cold-blooded and heartless, nor the townsfolk so pitiless, as the mere words suggest, for there is not so much hatred as envy in their hearts. The women come,

> the idle ones in bright and sometimes hurried garments, with secret and passionate and glittering looks and with secret frustrated breasts (who have ever loved death better than peace) to print with a myriad small hard heels to the constant murmur *Who did it? Who did it?* periods such as perhaps *Is he still free? Ah. Is he? Is he?* (612–13)

They are like Miss Minnie Cooper's friends in "Dry September" who take an extraordinary interest in the details of Minnie's putative rape: "Do you feel strong enough to go out?" they ask her when they come to take her to a movie. Their eyes bright, "with a dark glitter": "When you have had time to get over the shock, you must tell us what happened," they tell her. "What he said and did; everything" (CS 180). Clearly their desperate fantasies have taken routes similar to hers. Such are their own terrible lives that death, particularly a violent, sexual death, is better than the boredom of peace. They lead the life that terrifies Elly.

Unlike Zilphia, however, Joanna can with Joe actually live out her fantasies, all of them, as Joe can with her. He plays her games, eats her food, listens to her use the foul forbidden epithets that excite her as they make love. But they live in a state of constantly growing shame, and her guilt at last overpowers the relationship. Joe goes to her bedroom and finds her not in bed but at her desk. She has assumed Faulkner's costume: her hair, Joe notices, is "just beginning to gray" and it is "drawn gauntly back to a knot as savage and ugly as a wart on a diseased bough. . . . (S)he looked up at him and he saw that she wore steelrimmed spectacles which he had never seen before" (602). Trying to deal with her own guilt, she becomes their mutual repressive superego, and tries to make Joe pray too, as McEachern had. Thus Joanna, with her hermaphroditic name, is for Joe Mother, who feeds him and creates a dungeon for him in her dark house; she is also the hard, puritanical father. When they make love, Joe fulfills all his own Oedipal fantasies, whereby he, like the Wolf Man's desire, has sex with both mother and father: "My God . . . it was like I was the woman and she was the man" (572), he thinks. Their names, Joe and Joanna, imply a close relationship, like that of twins, perhaps, so that Joe is also fulfilling the incestuous fantasies of Quentin, Horace, and Darl. From this point of view, Joanna's name much less signifies the historical *racial* "burden" of Southern history than their mutual psychic burden, which he has, completing the circle, come back to the dark house to face, and with which she has lived all these years.

Their final confrontation takes place with Joanna "sitting up in the bed, her back against the headboard" (607). In killing her, Joe kills both his father, who will not stay dead, but also his mother, the complicating source of much of Yoknapatawpha's grief, the original dungeon.

But Joe cannot escape himself or his Oedipal guilt. He has actually committed Oedipus's two primal crimes. All of his running after the murder, like his efforts to get the dietitian to beat him, is mostly an effort to get caught, to get his punishment over with; he walks up and down the streets of Mottstown, waiting for somebody to recognize him (657–58). Nor can he escape the maternal Erynnis, who also will not stay dead. In jail he awaits his trial and execution (like another black man, in *Sanctuary*, in the same jail, also awaiting execution for the same crime of cutting his wife's throat). He thinks he is safe until Byron Bunch brings into his dungeon-sanctuary yet another mother intent on helping him. Mrs. Hines, a woman claiming to be his actual grandmother, has the audacity to tell him that she is going to inter-fere, to help him by getting Hightower to lie for him. It is the same sort of slimy collusion that he so detested in Mrs. McEachern. He runs from the police guard on his final day, then, not because of any conflict between his black and white blood, as Gavin Stevens pontificates. He runs in a desperate ultimate repudiation of the dun-geon who is mother herself, trying in one last furious effort both to escape his desire for her and to provoke the punishment he deserves for that desire. What more appropriate punishment than castration and death for one who has sinned as he has?

8. Fort-Da

It is worth a final word to suggest the ways in which this complex of images remain an active part of Faulkner's fictional language for the remainder of his career. Though houses, Oedipal dysfunction, and gray-haired old ladies appear with less intensity and frequency in the fiction following 1932, they occur frequently enough to establish their own significance and they are no less meaningful images to the later Faulkner, no less powerful referents in the later works.

Indeed, for example, *Absalom, Absalom!* begins with a scene in which Quentin visits with Rosa Coldfield, who sits "like a crucified child" (6) in a chair too large for her, in a "dim hot airless room" "called the office because her father had called it that" and closed to the outside light because "when she was a girl someone had believed that light and moving air carried heat and that dark was always cooler" (5). If Joe Christmas's orphanage is a grotesque parody of all childhood homes in Faulkner, Rosa's life is equally a parody of the lives of others of Faulkner's old women. She is a victim, too, like them, of an outrageous childhood: raised by a maiden aunt who escapes through a window to elope; then by a McEachern-esque puritanical father who sublimates himself above his own fatherhood by removing himself to the attic of the house, to become the insane spirit of the house, no longer a father but the name-of-the-father personified in and by his absence, who demands Rosa's total self-denial in his name and for his sake. She lives in this prison-room of an office, the shutters indeed closed to the outside world so that she could not look out them if she would. She sits "bolt upright in the straight hard chair that was so tall for her that her legs hung straight and rigid as if she had iron shinbones and ankles, clear of the floor with that air of impotent and static rage like children's feet" (5). As he listens, Quentin envisions her as

> a little girl, in the prim skirts and pantalettes, the smooth prim decorous braids, of the dead time. She seemed to stand, to lurk, behind the neat picket fence of a small, grimly middleclass yard or lawn, looking out upon the whatever ogreworld of that quiet village street with that air of children born too late into their parents' lives and doomed to contemplate all human behavior through the complex and needless follies of adults—an air Cassandralike and humorless and profoundly and sternly prophetic out of all proportion to the actual years even of a child who had never been young. (17)

Likewise, Thomas Sutpen's central enterprise is to build a house through whose doors he can move with absolute impunity, as he had been denied entry as a child: he installs doors, but he refuses to install windows in the frames until Ellen marries him and moves in. Like Rosa's, Sutpen's childhood is also a horror story equal to any in

Faulkner, and his story ends, like Joe Christmas's, in an Oedipal confrontation when Wash Jones, his father-surrogate, kills him with a
castrating scythe for his incestuous union with his surrogate sister
Milly ("The Artist as Cuckold"), and then burns down his own shack,
the dark house in which he and his granddaughter had lived under
the terms of Sutpen's abuse.

Faulkner never completely escaped these intensely private, often
solipsistic concerns in his fiction. Oedipus is never completely absent,
and in *The Hamlet* and especially in *A Fable* ("Ratliff's Buggies" and
"Woman and the Feminine in *A Fable*") he is again the root cause of
problem. When Faulkner does not address him directly, he nevertheless returns, again and again, to those powerfully iconic images — of
gray-haired women wearing steelrimmed spectacles; of whip-bearing
men dressed in black; of windows stealthily breached or closed upon
the promise of the burgeoning world; of houses fearfully dark; of
women framed in bedroom windows, sitting like idols looking out
over a world they can have no part of.

We now know these images to be tied to the Oedipus complex, and
they recur deliberately, even if perhaps unconsciously, throughout
Faulkner's fiction, very much as Freud's grandchild played the *fort-
da* game that so fascinated Freud. "The Patient," Freud argues in
Beyond the Pleasure Principle,

> cannot remember the whole of what is repressed in him, and what he
> cannot remember may be precisely the essential part of it. Thus he
> acquires no sense of conviction of the correctness of the construction
> that has been communicated to him [by the psychoanalyst]. He is
> obliged to *repeat* the repressed material as a contemporary experience
> instead of, as the physician would prefer to see, *remembering* it as some-
> thing belonging to the past. These reproductions, which emerge with
> such unwished-for exactitude, always have as their subject some por-
> tion of infantile sexual life — of the Oedipus complex, that is, and its
> derivatives; and they are invariably acted out in the sphere of the trans-
> ference, of the patient's relation to the physician. (12)

Patients "repeat all of these unwanted situations and painful emotions
in the transference and revive them with the greatest ingenuity" (14).

In Faulkner's case, the "patient" transfers the repressed material to his fiction.

Perhaps Freud's construction here at least partly explains Faulkner's compulsion, in his later works, to revisit certain crucial sites of his early career—the Old Frenchman place, the Jefferson jail, Miss Reba's whorehouse. In these revisitations he reinscribes on them his older, somewhat wiser, self who had, by the fifties, watched his own daughter grow up and doubtless became aware of what kind of dark house Rowan Oak had been for Jill because of his and Estelle's alcoholism and constant marital dysfunction. By the fifties the man who all his life had resisted bourgeois respectability was giving speeches about the meaning of home for an audience of which Jill was a part ("Pine Manor"), waxing even a bit sentimental about the value of normalcy at home.

Indeed, just as in the fiction he wrote between the two *Sanctuarys* he seems to have worked through many of the problems that he had faced in the first version, he also seems, by the time of his late-career return to those Memphis scenes, in *The Mansion* and *The Reivers*, to have worked through more at least of the specifically gender issues that so troubled *Sanctuary*, and many of the family issues as well, so that gender and family problematics are not so intense, so personal, perhaps, as in the early works. Irwin, arguing out of Freud, suggests that the act of writing puts the writer in an active, rather than the formerly passive, relationship to such repressed material, so that "one actively repeats an unpleasant occurrence as a source of pleasure" in order to make it pleasurable or, simply, to master the repressed material (115 and *passim*).

In his later works, Faulkner addresses the issues more as cultural than as psychological problems. But he never forsakes that cluster of images that were so evocative for him, and their various reoccurrences throughout his fiction tie the current work directly to all those old Oedipal issues, so that, again, it is clear that the Oedipus complex is one of the constants of Faulkner's fiction from beginning to end; even if he does not always foreground it, as he does in the 1927–1932 period, it is always there, always operative, a base to which so many of his characters, and perhaps he himself, must return periodically, clinging, as people will, to that which robs them (CS 124).

From this point of view, one of the most poignant moments in *The Hamlet* is the scene following the horse auction, in which Mrs. Flem Snopes, née Eula Varner, uncontained and uncontainable, stands framed and contained indeed, inside the upstairs bedroom window of the dark house into which she has just been sold, looking out at a "tremulous April night murmurous with the moving of sap and the wet bursting of burgeoning leaf and bud" (H 1016). Ratliff and his cronies stop in front of Varner's house, which is "dark, blank and without depth in the moonlight":

> They stood, clumped darkly in the silver yard and called up at the blank windows until suddenly someone was standing in one of them. It was Flem Snopes' wife. She was in a white garment; the heavy braided club of her hair looked almost black against it. She did not lean out, she merely stood there, full in the moon, apparently blank-eyed or certainly not looking downward at them—the heavy gold hair, the mask not tragic and perhaps not even doomed: just damned, the strong faint lift of breasts beneath the marblelike fall of the garment; to those below what Brunhilde, what Rhinemaiden on what spurious river-rock of papier-mache, what Helen returned to what topless and shoddy Argos, waiting for no one. (H 1016–17)

Waiting for no one, waiting for anyone, it is all the same to those, in the early works, no less enshrined in the window-niches of their homes than prisoners are enshrined—their hands at any rate—in the windows of the Jefferson jail.

In the elegiac prologue to Act III of *Requiem for a Nun*, "The Jail," Faulkner builds a veritable domestic and historic epic around Cecilia Farmer's diamond-scratched signature in the window of the Jefferson jail, while combining jail and house and family into one metaphorical structure. The jail looks like a house and indeed it is a family affair; the jailor lives there with his daughter Cecilia and his wife, who as part of the jailor's duties feeds the prisoners. Cecilia thus lives literally in a jailhouse, with a literal jailor for a father, and like other women in such circumstances, she spends a good deal of her time looking out that window.

But she does more than look: she writes, on the very symbol of her entrapment, a simple name and date on a fragile piece of glass that locate her in time and space. Her writing evokes for generations of Jeffersonians and visitors her face in the window, which becomes a magical summons to viewers to recreate her life in terms of the romance of her departure from Jefferson, as the wife of a Confederate soldier from Alabama, who saw her in one fleeting moment as he rode through town fleeing the Yankee army and returned at war's end to claim her, to take her away to Alabama to start a new life. So far as we are told she shares none of her Faulknerian sisters' sexual frustrations, has no particular desire to escape, or to do anything else; though she has a literal jailor for a father, and a mother who feeds her prisoner-siblings, they do nothing to stop her from marrying a stranger and moving to a land where they will probably never see her again.

In Cecilia Farmer's fragile, delicate signature, the communal memory of her face enshrined in the window, and the legend of her courtship and marriage, Faulkner allows the prisoner-woman of his earlier fiction to relax her grip on his imagination and to push it in new directions. Cecilia is no icon of feminine limitation: "no symbol there of connubial matriarchy, but fatal instead with all insatiate and deathless sterility; spouseless, barren, and undescended; not even demanding more than that: simply requiring it, requiring all" (647). She is, quite to the contrary, the very icon of limitless possibility: looking at the window, you, the outland visitor, stand

> among the roster and chronicle, the deathless murmur of the sublime and deathless names and the deathless faces, the faces omnivorous and insatiable and forever incontent: demon-nun and angel-witch; empress, siren, Erinys: Mistinguette too, invincibly possessed of a half-century more of years than the mere three score or so she bragged and boasted, for you to choose among, which one she was,—not *might* have been, nor even *could* have been, but *was*: so vast, so limitless in capacity

is man's imagination to disperse and burn away the rubble-dross of fact and probability, leaving only truth and dream. . . . (648)

Charles—Chick—Mallison is one of Faulkner's later children, the only male child in the fiction whom we see grow from childhood to adulthood over the course of Yoknapatawpha's history; Linda Snopes Kohl is the only female child. Chick enters the fiction only in 1948, with the publication of *Intruder in the Dust*, as Gavin Stevens's nephew, the son of Stevens's twin sister Maggie. Maggie may be Faulkner's sanest, least neurotic woman, and her marriage with Chick's father is the most normal, the healthiest, marriage in Faulkner's fiction. There is a good deal of mildly sexual but goodnatured humor buzzing around in their adult conversation, most of it centered around Charles's father's humorous denials that he finds Eula Varner Snopes attractive; but clearly Chick does not grow up in a dark house of the sort we have been describing.

Even so, in *The Town*, an older Charles Mallison, trying to explain why his mother could not talk to him about sexual passion, especially that between Eula and Manfred, articulates the older Faulkner's version of the primal scene and the Oedipus complex. Doubtless because his own childhood was not traumatic he has enough distance to understand what the earlier children could not:

> She wanted to tell me. Maybe she even tried. But she couldn't. It wasn't because I was only twelve. It was because I was her child, created by her and Father because they wanted to be in bed together and nothing else would do, nobody else would do. You see? If Mrs Snopes and Mr de Spain had been anything else but people, she could have told me. But they were people too, exactly like her and Father; and it's not that the child mustn't know that the same magic which made him was the same thing that sent an old man like Mr Will Varner into town at four oclock in the morning just to take something as sorry and shabby as a bank full of money away from another man named Manfred de Spain: it's because the child couldn't believe that. Because to the child, he was not created by his mother's and his father's passion or capacity for it. He couldn't have been because he was there first, he came first, before the passion; he created the passion, not only it but the man and

the woman who served it; his father is not his father but his son-in-law, his mother not his mother but his daughter-in-law if he is a girl.

So she couldn't tell me because she could not. And Uncle Gavin couldn't tell me because he wasn't able to, he couldn't have stopped talking in time. That is, that's what I thought then. I mean, that's what I thought then was the reason why they—Mother—didn't tell me: that the reason was just my innocence and not Uncle Gavin's too and she had to guard both, since maybe she was my mother but she was Uncle Gavin's twin and if a boy or a girl really is his father's and her mother's father-in-law or mother-in-law, which would make the girl her brother's mother no matter how much younger she was, then a girl with just one brother and him a twin at that, would maybe be his wife and mother too.

So maybe that was why: not that I wasn't old enough to accept biology, but that everyone should be, deserves to be, must be, defended and protected from the spectators of his own passion save in the most general and unspecific and impersonal terms of the literary and dramatic lay-figures of the protagonists of passion in their bloodless and griefless posturings of triumph or anguish; that no man deserves love since nature did not equip us to bear it but merely to endure and survive it, and so Uncle Gavin's must not be watched where she could help and fend him, while it anguished on his own unarmored bones. (T 304–05)

Wry, witty, perhaps even a bit melancholy: sexual passion is not frightening nor exploitative nor dangerous, but "magical" enough to be protected from voyeuristic eyes. It is not a matter of shame, but simply of privacy.

One important difference between Sutpen's mansion and Flem Snopes's is that the first constructs his out of deep psychic anxieties rooted in his childhood, while the latter *buys* his mansion, and at the same time buys into a social contract not of power so much as of respectability. Flem knows, as Sutpen and others in Yoknapatawpha do not, that sexual desire and shame need not be neuroses to be feared and repressed, and he easily converts them into commodities to be traded and bartered. Flem simply buys the dark house that

Sutpen tries to create, conquering with possession what Sutpen believes he must create anew. Ratliff believes that the house Flem
Snopes has "would have to be the physical symbol of all them generations of respectability and aristocracy"; and indeed, to that end, when
Flem moves in to Major de Spain's house, he hires his cousin Wat-
kins Products Snopes, a carpenter, to tear off de Spain's front gallery
and replace it with "colyums [that] reach all the way from the ground
up to the second-storey roof" (M 153–54). His mansion, then, is a
"product" of his desire and of his purchasing power. He knows, as
Sutpen does not, that you cannot start over, cannot create the world
again out of the primal edenic north Mississippi ooze, you cannot
make of yourself the original father/Father maker of laws: you cannot
be progenitorless. He knows that you cannot abrogate history, but
that you can buy it and make it serve your own public purposes if you
know how history works on other people: that is, if you know how
their private histories make them vulnerable to their own desires.

The Snopes Trilogy originally began, in "Barn Burning," with
Sarty Snopes's equation of Major de Spain's mansion with a courthouse and his assumption that wealth was therefore to be equated
with justice, and he learns that mansions do not mean justice but
merely order, two different things. In *The Hamlet* Flem appropriates
the Old Frenchman place, the place where Horace Benbow's nightmares come to life and bring about his undoing; he essentially trades
in his own passions for possession of this symbolic relic of another
time, and trades the historical relic for a newer, brighter, emptier
mansion in town, one free of the historical baggage the Old Frenchman place represents—but also, one is compelled to say, empty of
history, and so perhaps of meaning, too.

In *The Mansion*, Mink Snopes kills Flem and disappears. Stevens
and Ratliff instinctively know to look for him in Frenchman's Bend:
home. Though Faulkner doesn't name it, they find him in the cellar
of the now completely gutted Old Frenchman place. It *must* be the
Old Frenchman place, because that would be the only house in
Frenchman's Bend to have a cellar; certainly Mink's old sharecropper
cabin of nearly a half-century earlier would have long since disap-

peared, and in any case its walls would not have had a "foundation" (432), as does the collapsed building where Ratliff and Stevens find Mink. Ratliff recognizes it, even at night, by the same cedar-framed skyline of its roof that Horace Benbow sees, though by now of course time has taken its toll on it too. Ratliff recognizes "a canted roof line where óne end of the gable had collapsed completely (Stevens did not recognise, he simply agreed it could once have been a house) above which stood one worn gnarled cedar." As they approach, Ratliff, who apparently still owns it, wryly advises Stevens to "Walk behind me. . . . They's a old cistern. I think I know where it is" (432).

Although he does not use the term "Mother Earth," Mink's reverie leads him to connect womb and earth, womb and return, directly, as part of Old Moster's general plan that men should desire and resist until they had accomplished, and then yield:

> So he would walk west now, since that was the direction people always went: west. . . . it was always west, like Old Moster Himself had put it into a man's very blood and nature his paw had give him at the very moment he squirted him into his maw's belly.
>
> Because he was free now. A little further along toward dawn, any time the notion struck him to, he could lay down. So when the notion struck him he did so, arranging himself, arms and legs and back, already feeling the first faint gentle tug like the durned old ground itself was trying to make you believe it wasn't really noticing itself doing it. (434–35)

Mink Snopes, having gotten out of one dungeon in order to perform his revenge, has no more need of the freedom that he can now claim. He has killed his own clan's totem father and feels none of the remorse or guilt of Faulkner's early characters; he feels only the peace that allows him now to lie down safely on mother earth, which until now has been his antagonist, requiring his constant vigilance to keep from being absorbed and annihilated by her. He now can relax; he can relish that very absorption, "down into the ground already full of the folks that had the trouble but were free now" (435), and envision himself, very like the dreamer of "Carcassonne," as soaring into the heavens, making one among "the beautiful, the splendid, the proud and the brave, right on up to the very top itself among the shining phantoms and dreams" (435–36).

Ratliff and Stevens find Mink in a "cellar—the cave, the den" (432). Faulkner thus linguistically connects his return to the Old Frenchman place to Quentin's return to his mother-dungeon, his peaceful grotto at the bottom of the Charles River, to Horace's return home, to Joe Christmas's return to Joanna Burden's: each returns to "the old fetid caves where knowing began" (LA 611). Their return is also Faulkner's own return to the site of the original Faulknerian trauma, a return to the deepest parts of the darkest of houses that fretted and troubled him so during the early years of his career. He would return once more, in *The Reivers'* comic remake of *Sanctuary's* terror. But *The Mansion* works toward some form of closure with the terrors of childhood violation, of Oedipal desire, that define the life contained—proscribed—within Faulknerian walls. Indeed, in *The Mansion*, while waiting for Linda Snopes Kohl to work her vengeance on Flem Snopes, we discover that Benjy Compson, after a time in the state asylum, had returned home and "set himself and the house both on fire and burned up in it" (322). The House of Compson and the House of Snopes fall almost simultaneously, and the Compson mansion becomes one with Thomas Sutpen's and Joanna Burden's dark houses, burned to the ground by their own children. Thus *The Mansion*, though dark enough, is also a *Götterdammerung*, a twilight in which the father-gods and the mother-gods of the old familial order fall at last to the hands of their own devastated children.

Trying Not to Say

A Primer on the Language of *The Sound and the Fury*

Flower spaces that curl, a fence, a search, a table, a movable flag, and a pasture in which people are "hitting," all without any apparent relationship to one another, dot the visual landscape of the opening lines of *The Sound and the Fury*. And, as if the first paragraph didn't throw enough problems at the reader, the opening words of the second paragraph, the novel's first spoken words — "Here, caddie." — are relayed to us by the same narrator who has thrown us asea in the first paragraph, who transmits them without identifying their source, and who misunderstands them. They contain an aural pun, a homophone, and are related, though we don't yet know how, to the narrator's inexplicable reaction to them; indeed, we do not yet know what the narrator is reacting to. Careful readers will pretty quickly figure out that the narrator is looking through the fence at a golf course, and a really alert reader might, even this early, suspect that the course was once a pasture, and so be able to negotiate an uneasy narrative collaboration with the opening paragraph; but these two "spoken" words, which both are and are not what they seem to be, throw us back into uncertainty.

For the speaker, the word "caddie" has a specific, unproblematic referent, and he or she assumes that the person holding the golf clubs will know what he or she means; readers, who see the words' written representations rather than hear their sounds, perforce share this assumption and adduce from it that the speaker is probably a golfer (the speaker could be a supervisor or even somebody on the narrator's side of the fence who needs the caddie's attention). Our narrator, to the contrary, does not read the words but rather hears the sounds that stand for the words, and what he (or she: we don't yet know gender either) hears is "Caddy" or, more precisely, some form of the sounds a phoneticist would transcribe as *[kædi]* (or, probably closer to Faulkner's pronunciation, *[kædI]*), which sounds also have a single referent for the narrator, a referent quite different from the golfer's and, at this point in the novel, quite different from the reader's.

The narrator's response to this lingual, aural, and visual crux—"Here, caddie."—is curious indeed. He does not, really, describe his response or even identify it as a response. We understand that he is thinking or doing *something* only because he quotes a character named Luster, so that we have access to the narrator's response, whatever it is, only through a triangulation off of the secondary reaction of Luster, who also does not in fact describe it but merely comments about it in a way that indicates it is some kind of sound, vocal but not necessarily verbal: "Listen at you now. . . . going on that way" (3). The narrator's vocal "response," then, which we later learn can range from simple whimpering and slobbering to horrific bellowing, is at very least an unsettling narrative non sequitur; at most it is a monstrous violation of the fictional tradition that identifies a "narrator," especially a first person narrator, with a point of view and demands that narrators be self-conscious enough to describe what is happening to others and to themselves: to let us know that something is happening, to give us reason to believe that they have some communicable sense of the possible relationships among events and of the events' significance, even if that sense is only fragmentary and speculative, and even if they don't, won't, or can't tell us all they know. The tradition assumes a direct, complex, relationship between the language narrators use and the events they narrate or objects they describe; it has thus allowed us to assume that narrators *have* a point of view and a reason for narrating, and that they are necessarily engaged in some conscious control of the materials they narrate.

Readers looking for such narratorial control in the opening paragraphs of *The Sound and the Fury* will not find it. Nothing that happens, nothing seen, heard, or felt is causally related to anything else:

golfers do not hit balls, they just "hit"; Luster doesn't throw a rock at the bird on the flag, he just "throws"; the narrator doesn't even register his own reaction to stimuli as a reaction. Since he sees no relationship between one thing and another, he can't even grasp his own relationship to the world. He assumes himself to be the unmoved and unmoving center of the world: falling, he feels the ground come up to hit him; whirling, he sees stationary cows run up hill (20–21). Thus he experiences the world as a jumbled and unstable convergence of unconnected phenomena, and so to the extent that we share his disorientation and confusion, Benjy may be taken as a sort of surrogate "reader" in these opening pages, though our disorientation and confusion become more acute than his as Faulkner broadens the range of unattached signifiers in the next few pages. Benjy doesn't have any trouble understanding which of the two "Quentins" or "Jasons" is meant, but we do, until we have enough information from other parts of the novel to allow us to figure it out.

Benjy can register simultaneity, but not temporal or spatial relationships, except of the most primitive kind: when the golfers "go away" from him, for example, he sees them "hitting little" (3). John T. Matthews observes that "little" in this phrase is an adjective that has "usurped" an adverb's place and in doing so has "drain(ed) the verb of its energy and slow(ed) it into a picture" (*Play* 75). It is even more to the point to think of "little" as the predicate adjective in a version of Benjy's sentence that we might reconstruct, translate, as "Then they were little, hitting" or, more completely, "Then they seemed small, all the way across the golf course, and were hitting the ball." The golfers are not necessarily putting, which many readers have taken the phrase to mean; rather, Benjy is gauging the golfers' size at their distance across the pasture relative to their size when they were closer to his fence. The words thus represent the perspective of a primitive painting, in which all images appear on a flat vertical plane that has no calculus for spatial relativity, which plane Faulkner will specifically evoke in the fourth part of the novel when he describes Dilsey's church as belonging to a scene "as flat and without perspective as a painted cardboard set upon the ultimate edge of the flat earth" (292).

Benjy, then, exists as much outside of space as outside of time. He has no language, since language can exist only at the juncture of time and space: signifiers and signifieds find each other and create meaning only at pinpointed cruxes where word-sound and referent become one by mutual agreement between sender and receiver. The opening section of *The Sound and the Fury* is awash in signifiers that are attached to no particular signifieds—or seem that way, until readers get enough information from other sources to be able to attach them meaningfully. Nearly everything we presume to know from Benjy's "narration" we must reconstruct from various triangulations between what Benjy hears and sees and feels and what he reports somebody else saying or doing.

The author's place in this triangular structure is deliberately complex and problematic; he is concerned not so much to narrate as to represent narration or, more specifically in the Benjy section, to represent the world in ways that bypass the filters of language that modify our relationship to experience. But Faulkner first had to force his readers to reconsider the relationship between words and the things they pretend to name. The opening pages of *The Sound and the Fury* rip signifiers from signifieds radically and dramatically, and those first "spoken words"—written representations of vocal sounds which we encounter as silent marks on a sheet of paper—are an important clue to what Faulkner is about in this most linguistically radical of all his novels: to explore the relationship between language and experience, between language and reality, and between language and its oral and written representation. This essay is primarily concerned with the last of these.

Benjy's response to the golfer's command is not a matter of misunderstanding the sounds the golfer makes; he does not misunderstand what he hears, though he does misunderstand what the golfer says. Inscribing the scene on paper, Faulkner had to decide how to represent that sound, *[kædI]*, visually—whether to use some form of standard or dialectical written English, which is both more and less referentially precise than the sound itself. He chose a deliberate misdirection, a miscommunication, or perhaps *dys*communication, with his reader *and* with his narrator. If he had written that the golfer says "Here, Caddy." he would have misrepresented the unambiguous intent of the golfer's oral communication, though of course he would have more accurately represented the meaning that Benjy ascribes to those phonemes. He chose to misrepresent what Benjy hears rather than what the golfer says.

One of the great achievements of *The Sound and the Fury* is that in a novel which most critics now agree is centrally concerned with language, in a novel three of whose sections are "monologues" that gesture toward orality, Faulkner turns the clumsy mechanics of the representation of that language on paper, what Stephen Ross calls "the visual discourse of our reading" (44), into a highly expressive part of the language itself. At one very simple level, reading, especially the reading of dialogue, involves translating one sense impression into another: the author translates the aural into the visual, readers translate the visual back into the aural—or should, if they want to understand *The Sound and the Fury*. For just as he plays with Benjy's hearing of the phonemes *[kædI]*, so does Faulkner play with the way we read, with the mechanical signs of punctuation and spelling that harness and control, that give rhythm and shape and weight and expressive meaning to, the silent words that appear on the paper. Throughout the novel he uses an inventive array of visual devices in punctuation—or the lack of it—and spelling and grammar to help us focus on the way we comprehend language, written and oral.

Each brother, Judith Lockyer argues, "reveals an aspect of the power in language. That power is born out of the relation of language to consciousness" (53). I'd suggest more: Faulkner uses the mechanics of the English language—grammar, syntax, punctuation, spelling—as a direct objective correlative to the states of each of the narrators' minds. The mechanical conventions of the writing, then, sometimes work *against the words themselves*, so that they reveal things other than what the characters are saying; they work, in fact, to reveal things that the narrators are incapable of saying or are specifically trying to keep from saying, things that have caused them pain and shame. Words are, for Quentin and Jason, lids they use to seal that pain in the unconscious, though it constantly insists upon verbalizing itself. We have access to their pain largely through what they *don't* say, and also through the visual forms of the language in which Faulkner has inscribed their thoughts and feelings on paper. Benjy's section prepares us powerfully for the much more complex linguistic situations in the next three sections.

Benjy

Faulkner captures the disrelatedness of Benjy's various perceptions by drastically simplifying the referentiality, and the mechanics, of his language. Irena Kałuża describes Faulkner's prose in this section very usefully:

> Benjy's nouns do not admit synonyms, are never modified and are rarely replaced by pronouns. Thus Benjy's beloved sister is always "Caddy", whether she is seven or nineteen years old; she is rarely referred to as *she*, and never as *sister, girl*, etc. The same happens with the names of the other members of the Compson "family", white and black, each of them being usually designated by only one name, such as Quentin, Luster, Father, Mother. Only twice in Section One does Benjy meet strange people: a group of Negro washerwomen . . . and two girls in the street. . . . Their conversations are recorded as heard by him, but are not accompanied by the routine formula "he/she said" or "(a name) said." Benjy does not know their names and to give them identity in terms of description is beyond him. The same is in a way true about names of things. For instance in
>
> > She broke the top of the water and held a piece of it against my face
>
> more is involved than lexical poverty or ornamental metaphor. . . . By attaching to what really is a piece of ice the name of "a piece of water" the rigid inflexibility of Benjy's world asserts itself: he used to know this thing as "water" so "water" it remains for him. (49–50)

Many have noted that Benjy is "pre-lingual," that he "could never really narrate his section" (Lockyer 53) because he has no language.

I'd argue that he is rather *non*lingual: the language of the Benjy section is *Faulkner's* language. Properly speaking, Benjy is not a narrator at all, but the "very negation of narrative," as André Bleikasten has suggested (*Most Splendid Failure* 86); he is merely a filter, and not necessarily an ordering one (but see Godden 102f), for the thousands of sense impressions he processes every day, which may remain just as confusing for him as they do for readers. Benjy exists in a direct relationship to things: his world contains a multitude of signifieds, but only a severely limited number of signifiers. Even the signifiers that Benjy does attach to certain referents—Caddy, Mother, Luster—are for the most part vocal equivalents that he associates with those signifieds, although, to be sure, that is what spoken words are. Nevertheless, there are few verbal filters between him and the world he experiences, and it is useful to keep in mind that Benjy does not use words; he does not *tell* us things, but experiences them directly.

Benjy's "narration," then, is almost completely visual, cinematic, and what rolls through his mind is not "memory," although it is convenient to call it that in this essay, but rather more nearly different reels, perhaps, from a movie of his life. We can best "read" Benjy if we do not take it that he actually says, or thinks, "Between the curling flower spaces, I could see them hitting" (3), but rather that the words are Faulkner's verbal representation of what Benjy sees, at the precise moment of seeing; Benjy does not actually verbalize that the golfers are "going away," he just registers visually that they are doing so. Moreover, since Benjy is not capable of describing and so of differentiating one sensation from any other, we can account for the profusion of synaesthesia in his section; he does not actually *say* that "The sun was cold and bright" or that he could "smell the bright cold" (6), but rather reflects the physical sensations of what we would call "cold" and "bright" and the visual sensation of "sun" as registering on him simultaneously.

The written language of the Benjy section stands as a direct objective correlative to Benjy's physical and visual sensations and may best be taken as the direct linguistic counterpart to a primitive painter's technique. As many others have pointed out, for example, the section

consists almost entirely of simple sentences, sometimes strung together with coordinate conjunctions. Just as his mind allows no distinctions among his sensations that would put them in some kind of
ordered relationship, so does his language refuse what Kałuża calls a
"syntactical hierarchy" (52): there are almost no subordinate clauses
in Benjy's section, and so almost no subordination, no adjectival or
adverbial modifications, that would demonstrate hierarchical or
causal or value relationships among the sensations Benjy registers.
Mechanically, there are not even variations in end-punctuation that
would register differences in the way he processes sensation, much
less how they affect him or even whether they affect him at all. Faulkner uses only periods for sentence endings, even in quoted matter,
not question marks, exclamation marks, dashes, colons, or commas
(Polk, *Handbook* 8–12): a device that flattens all emotion out of Benjy's "quotations," forces grammatical equality on them, and even de-
taches them from their sources. Just as all his statements, then, are
grammatically equal, so are the ideas, the sensations they convey.
That Benjy's bellowing is grammatically the equal of the bright
shapes which accompany him to sleep may suggest that if there is an
emotional hierarchy at whose top is loss—of Caddy particularly, but
also of everything else—it nevertheless remains true that all sensations seem to register equally, and unrelatedly, on him.

We can gauge the relative strength or complexity of his reactions—
indeed, determine whether he is having a reaction—only by listening
to how other characters react to, verbalize, his vocalizations as bellowing or whimpering: of his own vocalizations, whether bellowing or
whimpering, Benjy can only note that he "stopped" or "started," not,
usually, what he is doing; later in the section he does several times
note it when he is crying, but readers cannot tell whether he means
to indicate simple weeping, or something more aggressive, like bellowing. The loss of Caddy and reminders of that loss register more
strongly on him than other sensations do; but he registers them at an
emotional level to which he does not have verbal access. Obviously he
has strong *feelings*, but because he has no access to normal language
conventions, he may be as estranged from them as he is from his

testicles. Benjy's brothers, as we shall see, also relate language and feelings to their own problematic sexual urges.

April 7, 1928, begins with Benjy and Luster at the fence which separates Benjy from the pasture, and follows them as they work their way back to the house toward the end of the day. From the site of one of the important things he has lost—his pasture, but we cannot help noting (Faulkner's little joke) that Luster, too, is looking for "balls"—they move steadily back to the dark and forbidding Compson house, the locus of all loss in the novel. On their way they pass various places on the Compson grounds that trigger Benjy's "memory" of events that have taken place there. He does not experience these excursions into the past as memory, because he cannot distinguish past from present. He is rather transported in his mind to these scenes of his childhood, most centering on trauma and transition, loss; all of them together give us a partial history of the Compson family. His transportation is triggered, as in Proust, by the repetition of something familiar and significant. Thus when he gets caught, yet again, on the fence that he and Luster crawl through, he remembers a similar incident when Caddy "uncaught" him (4) from the same fence when they were delivering Uncle Maury's note to Mrs. Patterson.

Faulkner signals these movements through time by using italics, but as he uses them, the italic passages are more than just visual signals of time shifts. They represent images buried in Benjy's unconscious which then work their way into the front of his conscious life, his own narrative present, elbowing April 7 out of the way, until it, too, pushes its way back into what registers, also in italics. Thus *"Caddy uncaught me"* (4) opens a passage of two italicized paragraphs that recount the episode in which they deliver Uncle Maury's letter to Mrs. Patterson. The episode begins as a dim and fuzzy italic shape in his memory as he gets caught on the fence, then emerges completely in focus as a full-blown scenario in the next paragraphs, in roman type, which throughout his section represents what is currently at the front of his mind. The roman passage does not continue the narrative begun in italics, however, but reverts to the time a few minutes earlier that day, two days before Christmas of an unspecified year, when Uncle Maury and Mother permit Versh to dress Benjy warmly and take him out to the gate to meet Caddy as she comes home from school. When Caddy brings him inside, Uncle Maury calls her aside, obviously to give her the letter to Mrs. Patterson, although Benjy does not know that (5–9) and readers, again, must figure this out eventually from other evidence. The narrative seems to be working its way directly forward to his getting caught on that treacherous fence which triggered the whole memory. But remembering Caddy's warmth, how she smelled like trees (6), makes Benjy moan on April 7, and he reports Luster's response—"*What are you moaning about.*"—(6) in italics. Faulkner uses the italics in this instance, then, to remind us of Benjy's narrative present. They represent the intrusion of the present into Benjy's past, and suggest just how freely dissociated from time and space Benjy is.

After the brief italicized interruption, Benjy continues the narrative of Caddy's arrangements with Mother to take him with her on her errand. Two italic interruptions—"*Hold still now*" and "*Now stomp*" (8)—float freely in Benjy's head as he is mindful of numerous other times Versh has helped him dress, but the narrative of that December 23rd continues to move forward until Benjy registers Caddy's assurances: "Haven't you got your Caddy." Again confronted with the fact of her absence, he begins to howl. Luster again responds: "*Cant you shut up that moaning and slobbering, Luster said. Aint you shamed of yourself, making all this racket. We passed the carriage house, where the carriage was. It had a new wheel*" (9). By this time on April 7, Luster lets us know, they have come to the carriage house and the sight of the "new wheel" trips Benjy's recollection of the time when T.P. drove him and his mother to the cemetery, and he follows that memory until they meet Jason and try, unsuccessfully, to get him to go to the cemetery with them (9–12). The bright shapes of the town remind him of the bright fast smooth shapes of his sleeping, which he associates with Caddy, which in turn causes him to cry yet again, and Luster to respond yet again, and he reverts to his original memory. He finally completes the December 23rd narrative (12–14), which ends, not with his and Caddy's successful delivery of Uncle Maury's note, but, traumatically, with a related occasion, layered into the December 23rd foray, when he delivered the note by himself, causing Mrs. Patterson to be angry at him and Mr. Patterson to chase him with a hoe (13–14)—a metaphorical scythe prefiguring his castration.

Faulkner thus achieves the effect of cinematic montage and he is able to juxtapose significant episodes in the Compson family history by simply alternating between episodes—his encounter with Caddy and Charlie in the swing, for example, is intertwined associatively with a similar, later, encounter with Miss Quentin and her boyfriend in the same swing; Caddy's wedding and Damuddy's funeral are intimately intertwined in this same way. Through these juxtapositions, these comparisons and contrasts of scenes, Faulkner creates meanings, hierarchies of emotions and significances, that Benjy can not. At the top of the hierarchy is, of course, his loss of Caddy, which registers most powerfully and most constantly—on himself and on everybody else.

Quentin

Benjy tries to say and can't; his brothers try *not* to say, and can't keep from it. Benjy's "memory" works in large discrete units, scenes that spring to life by triggers, a sound or an object, that can usually be located in the sentence or two immediately preceding the time shift. These scenes become interchangeable with each other as they suit Faulkner's needs, for example, to juxtapose Caddy's wedding with Damuddy's funeral and so to suggest ways in which these events are related in Benjy's mind, in Compson family history, and in the novel's movement toward significance. But Benjy is a passive receptor of these cinematic reels; he seems to have little control over what passes through his mind, and it may not be unreasonable to think that the linear separation of the scenes on the page is a function of the limitations of writing, and that Benjy experiences all of them as a simultaneous and inextricable welter of images, just as he does the "bright cold," not as separate phenomena. For Benjy all these scenes are undifferentiated, equivalent. As on a primitive painter's canvas, they appear in size and proportion as he originally experienced them, neither increased nor diminished nor distorted by perspectives of time or position.

Quentin's relationship with his past is quite different. Episodes, telling moments from that past do indeed exist in degrees of intensity, of psychic pain, which his consciousness has dwelled upon, worked through and over, in ways that continue to torture him. Like Benjy's, all of Quentin's past tries to crowd in on him at once, every painful episode tries to elbow its way past all the others into consciousness simultaneously. But whereas Benjy's memory is flat and two-dimensional, like his prose, Quentin's is like a large fluid-filled balloon that he is trying to flatten out, to control; but every time he steps on one spot, on one painful memory, the balloon erupts upward and outward at another point, constantly reshaping itself to its own pernicious energy.

Quentin cannot control the chaos of his amoeba-like memory and he finally succumbs to it. The protective walls he builds with his formal eloquence are constantly breached by visual intrusions from his past, italicized fragments of phrases and images that emerge briefly, even flickeringly, in no apparent order or relation, through the barriers of his language before he is able to stamp them down again, in his futile effort to keep them from full verbalization. His memories evolve out of scenes of trauma, all centered in his loss of Caddy: her wedding, his conversation with Herbert Head, the husband his parents trapped for Caddy; her love affair with Dalton Ames and his humiliating inability to defend her honor; and his long conversation with his father, whether real or imagined, whether a single conversation or an amalgam of several similar ones, about the meaning—or the meaninglessness—of life. The substance of his monologue is his effort to sort out, analyze, and come to terms with those scenes of pain that he *can* handle, and to evade, to repress, those that he cannot. Quentin is, in effect, trying to shape his memory into an acceptable version of his life that will both explain his present misery and justify his decision to commit suicide. Language is the only tool he has to effect the shape he wants.

Faulkner records Quentin's efforts to control his thoughts in several ways; as with Benjy, none is more striking than the mechanical representation of his syntax, grammar, and punctuation, which, also like Benjy's, are the objective correlative to the state of Quentin's mind. The more in control he is, the more intricate and sophisticated the structure of his sentences, the cohesion of his paragraphs; the less lucid his mind, the less formal or "normal" the representation of his language on paper becomes. One can trace Quentin's psychic disintegration, his movements into and out of lucidity, in the degree of normality of his language's representation, from the intricately structured sentences of some passages, to the almost complete disintegration of traditional language representation in others, and especially in two scenes close to the end of his section that abandon punctuation and paragraph indentation, and in the penultimate paragraph of his section in which he finally yields up the capital "I," the orthographical symbol of the fragile ego he has managed to cling to, to the lower case "i," which represents graphemically his disintegrated self. Each of these three scenes springs into consciousness at moments when his psychic censors are completely relaxed; the crucial one, that recounting Caddy's love affair with Dalton Ames and his ineffectual efforts to stop it, occurs when Quentin is literally unconscious, or at least floating in some twilight zone between consciousness and unconsciousness, having been knocked out by Gerald Bland. Language's grammatical formality, then, is for Quentin a conscious way to keep away from those things he does not want to think, those things he does not want to say. The mechanics of the written representation of language become Faulkner's device to let readers know how successful Quentin is: the most painful scenes are the farthest removed from representational normalcy (Ross 173–74).

Throughout the section there are passages in which he is, or seems to be, in complete control. In such passages Quentin is very much like Hemingway's Nick Adams as he minutely and preciously puts into words every possible sensation, every possible observation of the present moment, to try to control the various signs that would remind him of something painful back home. At his best Quentin can be ironic and self-reflexive, witty and inventive in his wordplay, as in this tortuously involuted mélange of negations and tenses, in which he mordantly contemplates his own demise:

> Hats not unbleached and not hats. In three years I can not wear a hat. I could not. Was. Will there be hats then since I was not and not Harvard then. Where the best of thought Father said clings like dead ivy vines upon old dead brick. Not Harvard then. Not to me, anyway. Again. Sadder than was. Again. Saddest of all. Again. (95)

Thanks to his sister's new husband, Quentin is preternaturally conscious of heads, and so of the hats which Harvard underclassmen must wear. He is keenly aware of the different states of the heads and hats he sees from his high vantage in the train window: some heads are topped by brand new, "not unbleached," hats—that will "unbleach" as they are worn for three years—and other heads, usually those of seniors, not wearing hats at all. This observation leads him to think of his own senior year, three years from now, when he won't have to wear a hat if he chooses not to: "I can *not*." But his senior year is of course highly problematic for him, knowing what he knows, so he immediately jumps to the subjunctive: "or, rather, I *could* choose not to wear a hat if I were going to be here. But I won't be here; in three years I will have been *was* for three years and hats won't matter to me, nor will Harvard. Will hats or, indeed, even Harvard itself exist if I am not here to affirm that they do? They won't exist at all as far as I'm concerned, at any rate." The final sentences, fragments, of the paragraph revert to his continual dialogue with his father over whether death—being *was*—is a sadder condition than continuing to live in eternal recurrence—*again* (178)—and having to experience pain and loss over and over.

Quentin is capable of poetic analogies, similes, and metaphors, of complicated but perfectly balanced parallel structures and modifications:

> I quit moving around and went to the window and drew the curtains aside and watched them running for chapel, the same ones fighting the

same heaving coat-sleeves, the same books and flapping collars flushing past like debris on a flood, and Spoade. (78)

Quentin's sentence works to contain, to control, all the moiling activity of the Harvard yard below his window, the running and fighting
and heaving and flapping and flushing, within its intricately parallel
compound-complex structures. Spoade intrudes upon his ordering
vision and so upon the sentence's structure. Strictly speaking
"Spoade" is the second element of a compound direct object of the
verb "watched"—I watched them and Spoade—but its placement at
the end of the sentence, following the comma, has the effect of alien-
ating Spoade from the neatly controlled rhythms of the rest of the
sentence. Spoade disrupts the order of Quentin's mind and of his
syntax because he reminds Quentin of discomfiting conversations
about homoeroticism and about virginity, a train of thought he passively follows back home to Jefferson to yet another version of his all-
consuming conversation with his father. As he moves backward
toward that conversation he loses control of syntax and of cohesion:

> Calling Shreve my husband. Ah let him alone, Shreve said, if he's got
> better sense than to chase after the little dirty sluts, whose business. In
> the South you are ashamed of being a virgin. Boys. Men. They lie
> about it. Because it means less to women, Father said. He said it was
> men invented virginity not women. Father said it's like death: only a
> state in which the others are left and I said, But to believe it doesn't
> matter and he said, That's what's so sad about anything: not only vir-
> ginity and I said, Why couldn't it have been me and not her who is
> unvirgin and he said, That's why that's sad too; nothing is even worth
> the changing of it, and Shreve said if he's got better sense than to chase
> after the little dirty sluts and I said Did you ever have a sister? Did you?
> Did you? (78)

Fragments of conversations at Jefferson and at Cambridge crowd
confusingly together in a near complete breakdown of cohesion in
the desperation of the paragraph's final sentences, which breakdown
signals the loss of the carefully controlled observation of the world
outside his window that began the passage. Reaching the juxtaposi-

tion of "little dirty sluts" and "sister," however, Quentin realizes he is on dangerous ground and quickly jerks himself back, away from this direction, and into a new paragraph, an ordered and detailed description of Spoade that forces him into the midst of the crowd, contains and controls him both poetically and syntactically by making him over into a turtle, the very model of static non-aggression: "Spoade was in the middle of them like a terrapin in a street full of scuttering dead leaves" (78).

Like Hamlet, all things inform against Quentin, linguistically and visually. In spite of all he can do to keep Cambridge and environs on his tongue and in his mind, they nevertheless become a verbal and visual replication of Jefferson; nearly everything that takes place on June 2, 1910, brings him insistently back to scenes of pain at home. Many commentators have noted how the language and imagery of numerous scenes in Cambridge, especially the episode involving the little Italian girl, run parallel to Quentin's world at home. Even the veil-wearing women recruited by Gerald and Mrs. Bland for their picnic, Miss Holmes and Miss Daingerfield, remind him—and readers—homophonically how fraught with danger and pain his home has been for him.

But even in the most lucid passages, Quentin's thoughts are constantly under siege, constantly on the verge of ravelling out into disorder, so that a typical paragraph is likely to start a different thought, a new direction for him, like the new paragraph about Spoade, and then fall apart, as the chaos of things on his mind constantly presses for his attention, gets it, and leads him down dangerous paths of association. The section's second paragraph is a striking example:

> It [father's watch] was propped against the collar box and I lay listening to it. Hearing it, that is. I dont suppose anybody ever deliberately listens to a watch or a clock. You dont have to. You can be oblivious to the sound for a long while, then in a second of ticking it can create in the mind unbroken the long diminishing parade of time you didn't hear. Like Father said down the long and lonely light-rays you might see Jesus walking, like. And the good Saint Francis that said Little Sister Death, that never had a sister. (76)

This paragraph and the following one begin by focusing on something in the present moment and end, through loose but definite associations, at the same point in his past: the fact that Quentin *had* a sister. As nearly every commentator has noted, Quentin's memory hovers, beggar-like, around his memories of what he thinks of as Caddy's abandonment of him in his need. The fifth paragraph is also particularly illustrative of the way his mind works:

> If it had been cloudy I could have looked at the window, thinking what he said about idle habits. Thinking it would be nice for them down at New London if the weather held up like this. Why shouldn't it? The month of brides, the voice that breathed *She ran right out of the mirror, out of the banked scent. Roses. Roses. Mr and Mrs Jason Richmond Compson announce the marriage of.* Roses. Not virgins like dogwood, milkweed. I said I have committed incest, Father I said. Roses. Cunning and serene. If you attend Harvard one year, but dont see the boat-race, there should be a refund. Let Jason have it. Give Jason a year at Harvard. (77)

This paragraph is almost a palindrome, which moves into and then out of the abyss of Caddy's wedding by the same route. Quentin begins by noting that he cannot look out the window because the sun is creating shadows that make him conscious of time. He thinks therefore of the boat-races that his father has advised him to see, then realizes that the weather is pretty because it is June, which, he cannot help remembering, is traditionally the "month of brides." This realization, in its turn, carries him right back into another mélange of fragments, a breakdown of syntactical control, an italicized reversion to Caddy's wedding and announcement, and a forced re-entry back into roman type. He confronts his memory of Caddy's wedding with a memory of his verbal efforts to stop that wedding (his confession of their incest)—that is, with an effort to control Caddy linguistically, as he had been able to contain Spoade—and gradually builds back to where he started, his father's advice about the boat-race, something in the present moment.

Italics here, as throughout Quentin's section, do not function as they do in Benjy's section; in most instances, they rather represent Quentin's farthest remove from language, although as for Benjy they are visual images, rather than verbal ones, pictures welling up in his mind rather than articulated, or articulatable, descriptions of his feelings: note, for example, how the italicized image of the street lamps in Jefferson blurble so regularly up throughout Quention's section, accreting toward the scene, fully recounted toward the end of the section, in which he and his father walk toward town, holding one of the conversations that Quentin is so desperate to repress. In this paragraph the visual, even sensual, markers of Caddy's wedding intrude upon his verbalization of things, and the italics represent a quick, perhaps instantaneous, scansion of what he saw and felt then, not what he is saying about it; those are things that he really doesn't want to put into words.

Jason

Jason abrupts on to the page and very nearly in to the reader's ear with a very wet sense of humor so rich in the vernacular you can almost hear him speak. He may be, as Faulkner wrote sixteen years later, and as most commentators have taken too easily for granted, "the first sane Compson since Culloden" (342; Kartiganer 87–88), but his monologue is very much of a piece with his brothers'. For all the apparent "logic" of his outpourings, he too is driven by irrational forces buried deep in his unconscious that are battering at the boundaries of articulation. His monologue is a long loud agonizing cry—Benjy's howling rage made verbal—which he sustains at such a frenetic pace precisely in order to drown out the other, to silence its insistent pounding at the edges of consciousness with the ear-splitting volume of the sound of his own voice. As Irena Kałuża has pointed out, it is

> devastatingly characteristic of Jason that he never allows his mental experience to operate beyond the conscious speech level, and always tries, by indefatigably inserting words like *because, when, where* and *if*, to organize his experience logically. But the result is far from logical,

and his efforts are futile. Thus he always aspires to rationality without ever achieving it in fact. (100)

If Benjy is non-verbal and trying to say, and if Quentin is extremely verbal and trying *not* to say, trying to maintain order by keeping his words inside his head, Jason is intensely, loudly, desperately, gloriously oral. He keeps himself talking loudly so that he won't have to listen to the voices that threaten him: he drowns out one horrendous noise with an even more horrendous one.

One of the reasons Jason has been taken as "saner" than his brothers is the relative normality of Faulkner's representation of his speech. His monologue almost completely lacks the visual markers, italics the most noticeable, of his brothers' incoherencies and psychic instabilities. It moves as much by associative logic as his brothers' do, but because his psychic censor is much stronger than Quentin's, he is always able to stop himself just short of speaking that which he most fears, and so he does manage to maintain a kind of control over his syntax—and so over his psyche—that his brothers utterly fail at. But Jason cannot hide his diversionary tactics, and although Faulkner uses no italics in Jason's section, he still plays with the conventions of punctuation and representation in ways that reveal Jason's unconscious to us.

Jason's monologue can be characterized first by its defensive posture. His rhetoric is the most verbally aggressive in all of Faulkner. As Ross has noted (170), he constantly uses his language to beat others into submission. He hardly ever engages in conversation, but in verbal combat, from which he can emerge a "winner," because he is cleverer and quicker than most of his opponents (there are exceptions), who range from the members of his family to the functionary at the telegraph office. Although his rhetoric is aggressive, however, it emerges from a defensive mentality, perilously close to paranoia, that constantly screams self-justification. Jason is as obsessively aware of the constantly observing "eye" of his own conscience as his brothers are of the lighted window from their mother's room, and he engages a good deal of his psychic and verbal energy defending himself from the accusations of idiocy and other forms of familial and genetic insufficiency that he imagines the people of Jefferson are constantly hurling at him (e.g. 232–33); his aggressive rhetoric is, in effect, a preemptory strike. And since he knows better than anybody else those points of character and blood where he is most vulnerable to accusation, he knows how to defend himself. We can thus discover his animating fears by paying close attention to the things he tries to defend himself against.

The second rhetorical characteristic of Jason's monologue is its almost complete dependence upon cliché (Bleikasten, *Most Splendid Failure* 164–65). Quentin's highly sensitive and poetic articulations of the world about him demonstrate considerable intellectual effort to keep his mind constantly, safely, and originally engaged with the externals of his final day in Cambridge. Jason's language, though equally engaged with externals, is quite to the contrary filled with clichés, aphorisms pious and secular, social and personal, mindless oral formulae that he can keep firing so rapidly precisely because they come so easily to the tongue. They never ask the speaker to question whether they actually *mean* anything, and in fact assume that he will not: they are merely noise to fill the lacks in his gaps, as Addie Bundren might put it. Though they carry a good deal of the weight of a culture's traditions, its language anyway, and profess to embody a sort of folk wisdom, they nevertheless give only the illusion of meaning. Jason is so mired in these illusions that he is not even aware when they betray him, as in this passage—

> After all, like I say money has no value; it's just the way you spend it. It dont belong to anybody, so why try to hoard it. It just belongs to the man that can get it and keep it. (194)

—in which flatly contradictory nostrums run amok, career carelessly into each other and demonstrate both his hypocrisy and the mindlessness of his ravings. Jason clearly does not listen to what he says, and so his "sanity" cannot be demonstrated by his language. But for his purposes the words don't have to make sense as long as they make noise: what he can not bear is the silence in which his real topic might articulate itself.

The quality of cliché is what gives his monologue its colloquial power, its roots in the spoken dialect and its convincing orality. But the number of clichés also suggests the degree to which, for Jason, sound and sense are separated from each other. His mouth is equally estranged from his mind. He works very hard to force the disengagement, as we shall see, but in spite of all his efforts, he gets so caught up in the sound of his words that he has no idea what he is saying; he loses control of his words and, no less than Quentin, of his syntax. At such times, his guard down, his mind and his mouth lead him directly back toward certain crucial moments in his psychic life. In fact, like Quentin's, Jason's monologue hovers around these cruxes as moths do a flame, approaching disaster and then retreating, as the conscious and the unconscious do mortal battle with each other. Like Quentin's, Jason's guard occasionally does relax and, with his mind out of gear but his mouth constantly revving up one cliché after another, his unconscious rolls inevitably toward the precipitous edge; but he finally does resist and snatches himself safely away from it. Precisely at those moments of retreat from articulation Jason leaves huge narrative gaps that reveal his psychological preoccupations. As in the other two monologues, Faulkner helps identify these preoccupations syntactically.

In certain ways Faulkner plays with the artifices of syntactical representation more daringly here than in the first two monologues. Some of them can be demonstrated by noting a couple of differences between the 1929 Cape & Smith first edition text and the 1984 Random House New Corrected Text, which relies heavily on Faulkner's carbon typescript of the novel. Two passages are especially revelatory. The first occurs in a long funny diatribe that begins "Well, Jason likes work," and moves immediately to a predictable litany into which Jason compresses all of the objects of his anxieties by the same sort of fluid association characteristic of Quentin's and Benjy's monologues; the association, though, is very revealing. From this savagely ironic acceptance of his need to work, he jumps immediately to the reasons he has to work and like it, all of which revolve around the complex of circumstances that he consciously sees as a betrayal of his chances to "get ahead" in life: Quentin's suicide, his father's death, Caddy's defalcation, Benjy's castration, and his mother's whining domination, all of which he jokes about in order to keep them at a distance:

> I says no I never had university advantages because at Harvard they teach you how to go for a swim at night without knowing how to swim and at Sewanee they dont even teach you what water is. I says you might send me to the state University; maybe I'll learn how to stop my clock with a nose spray and then you can send Ben to the Navy I says or to the cavalry anyway, they use geldings in the cavalry. Then when she sent Quentin home for me to feed too I says I guess that's right too, instead of me having to go way up north for a job they sent the job down here to me and then Mother begun to cry and I says it's not that I have any objection to having it here; if it's any satisfaction to you I'll quit work and nurse it myself and let you and Dilsey keep the flour barrel full, or Ben. Rent him out to a sideshow; there must be folks somewhere that would pay a dime to see him, then she cried more and kept saying my poor afflicted baby. . . . (196)

Clearly Jason is in pain. Though he here mostly maintains control over his syntax, the energy of the passage suggests that that pain is about to spill over into associations that he cannot control. He doesn't, for example, *name* Caddy, Quentin, or Father, although he does name his niece and Ben, who are the tangible, daily, reminders of his abandonment by the others. But the passage continues, a few lines later:

> It's your grandchild, which is more than any other grandparents it's got can say for certain. Only I says it's only a question of time. If you believe she'll do what she says and not try to see it, you fool yourself because the first time that was the Mother kept on saying thank God you are not a Compson except in name, because you are all I have left now, you and Maury and I says well I could spare Uncle Maury myself and then they came and said they were ready to start. Mother stopped crying then. She pulled her veil down and we went down stairs. (196)

Jason's narrative here runs directly into, and then backs away from, a syntactical breakdown, as he realizes that he is approaching dangerously near one of his scenes of pain, his father's funeral. He still will not name Caddy, though clearly he is about to try to convince his mother that his sister will not keep her word not to see Miss Quentin. He starts to tell her how he knows Caddy won't keep her word by recalling her return to Jefferson to their father's funeral, but as he approaches the words "father's funeral," he realizes that he has entered dangerous territory:

> because the first time that was the Mother kept on saying.

The Cape & Smith editors of the first edition, sensing that *something* was amiss, rendered this passage:

> because the first time that was that Mother kept on saying (SF [1929] 244)

which neither corrects nor clarifies what is happening in these few words (Polk, *Handbook* 63).

Jason catches himself back, just in time, from stumbling rhetorically into his father's grave. He starts to tell his mother that she can't trust Caddy because Caddy lied "the first time" she promised never to try to see her daughter again; Jason is on the verge of putting into words the scene of their confrontation over his father's grave, which scene has been triggered in his memory by his conversation with his mother about why he has to work, why he "likes" work. But he stalls. Faulkner's carbon typescript and his holograph manuscript render this passage as it appears in the 1984 New Corrected Text, and the passage is perfectly understandable as Faulkner wrote it if we try to hear Jason stumbling over his words. A more traditional novelist, using more traditional syntactical signs, might have rendered the passage as

> because the first time — that was — the — Mother kept on saying

which formulation would have visually approximated the rhythms of Jason's stumbling uncertainty at how to avoid what he is afraid he is about to say. Faulkner denies us the written punctuation that tells us how to *hear* Jason as he speaks, as he rushes blindly into a danger zone, halts, backs up, tries a couple of times to start over, and then finds a safer direction to pursue, in which he talks not *to* but rather *about* his mother.

He leaves Caddy's perfidy as a subject, but has in fact elided his narrative directly back to the funeral of his father—Jason III, for whom he is named—in as fluid an associative movement as either of his brothers manages, except that his is more evasive, and he finds a way to deal with his father's funeral on that rainy day, not by talking about Caddy but by focusing humorously, if savagely, on Uncle Maury's drinking and on his feeble attempts to share in the burial in the rain. Father's funeral is the narrative locus for the next several pages, which build toward that meeting with Caddy (196–207) at the cemetery, and which he can now confront because he has constructed a self-justifying narrative framework that permits it. But his reconstruction has its own psychic rules. A telling moment occurs when he discovers that his uncle smells like clove stems, and that Maury is trying at least for the duration of the funeral to pretend that he is not drinking, though of course he is:

> I reckon he thought that the least he could do at Father's or maybe the sideboard thought it was still Father and tripped him up when he passed. (197)

This is the passage as it appears in manuscript, typescript, and the New, Corrected Text; the first edition reads "at Father's funeral," which I believe indicates a misunderstanding of Faulkner's intent (Polk, *Handbook* 63): Jason simply will not put the words "Father's funeral" or "Father's grave" together, and again Faulkner refuses his readers the punctuation, the visual signs of reading—perhaps a dash following "Father's"—that would indicate how we are to *hear*, and so understand, what Jason is saying.

Throughout these pages, which also recount Jason's and Maury's participation in the actual digging of the grave, he refers to the grave only as "it." We cannot help but remember that Jason's first appearance in the novel is in the opening pages of the Benjy section, when Mrs. Compson, Benjy, and T.P. ride the buggy through town on the way to the cemetery; they stop at the store and ask him to accompany them, and he refuses. He is, after all, Jason *fils*, and the pain of his father's, and his own, mortality, looms large and threatening in his imagination. The rest of the passage about Maury is particularly illustrative of the way Jason's mind, and his language, work:

> After a while he kind of sneaked his hand to his mouth and dropped them out the window. Then I knew what I had been smelling. Clove stems. I reckon he thought that the least he could do at Father's or maybe the sideboard thought it was still Father and tripped him up when he passed. Like I say, if he had to sell something to send Quentin to Harvard we'd all been a dam sight better off if he'd sold that sideboard and bought himself a one-armed strait jacket with part of the money. I reckon the reason all the Compson gave out before it got to me like Mother says, is that he drank it up. At least I never heard of him offering to sell anything to send me to Harvard.
>
> So he kept on patting her hand and saying "Poor little sister", patting her hand with one of the black gloves that we got the bill for four days later because it was the twenty-sixth because it was the same day one month that Father went up there and got it and brought it home and wouldn't tell anything about where she was or anything and Mother crying and saying "And you didn't even see him? You didn't even try to get him to make any provision for it?" and Father says "No she shall not touch his money not one cent of it" and Mother says "He can be forced to by law. He can prove nothing, unless—Jason Compson," she says. "Were you fool enough to tell—" (197–98)

Even though Jason forces a kind of logic on these associations, the passage really is a series of non-sequiturs: the *becauses* are mechanical contrivances to connect them grammatically, but in fact the associations are emotional, and they nearly always lead him back to the same scenes of pain and conflict, whatever they happen to be. He and his mother refer to Caddy's daughter as "it," the same term he uses to refer to his father's grave, and doubtless they mean the same thing to Jason: his betrayal and abandonment by his father, his loss, like Quentin's, of an ordering center for his life. He would like to say "Father. Father."

But there are similar passages in which his mother figures as the locus of a series of associated images. In the passage just cited, for example, Jason says "dam sight" rather than "damn sight," which as a visual, not an aural, distinction—eye dialect—is somewhat at odds with the intense orality of his narrative. One of the really curious orthographical features of Jason's rendered "speech" is that throughout this section Faulkner invariably employs "dam" rather than "damn" when Jason speaks on the page; that it was a deliberate part of Faulkner's intention is indicated by the fact that when Jason quotes somebody else (Miss Quentin, twice on 184, for example), Faulkner uses the normative "damn." The Cape & Smith first edition editors "corrected" "dam" to "damn" throughout his section; when arguing for restoring Faulkner's carbon typescript reading in the New Corrected Text, I admitted that it was not clear why Faulkner did this, only that it was a demonstrable pattern, and I offered, rather feebly, the possibility that Faulkner was trying to make Jason's usage "less profane" than the others' (Polk, *Handbook* 15–16), but that seems hardly likely. I would now suggest that Faulkner is creating a visual pun of the sort that confuses Benjy in the novel's second paragraph, and agree with Tom Bowden that the pun relies on a variety of maternal and animal-breeding meanings associated with the word "dam." Faulkner uses "dam" to indicate how insistently "mother" and "sexuality" and even bestiality impinge on Jason's profanity and his attitudes, how profoundly they are related to his psychic problems; as a speaker Jason is no more aware of the difference in spelling than Benjy is of the differences between "Caddy" and "caddie," but the reader cannot escape it.

We can see how this works in another long paragraph, which occurs as Jason describes the beginnings of his futile search for his niece and the hated man in the red tie:

> I went on to the street, but they were out of sight. And there I was, without any hat, looking like I was crazy too. Like a man would naturally think, one of them is crazy and another one drowned himself and the other one was turned out into the street by her husband, what's the

reason the rest of them are not crazy too. All the time I could see them watching me like a hawk, waiting for a chance to say Well I'm not surprised I expected it all the time the whole family's crazy. Selling land to send him to Harvard and paying taxes to support a state University all the time that I never saw except twice at a baseball game and not letting her daughter's name be spoken on the place until after a while Father wouldn't even come down town anymore but just sat there all day with the decanter I could see the bottom of his nightshirt and his bare legs and hear the decanter clinking until finally T. P. had to pour it for him and she says You have no respect for your Father's memory and I says I dont know why not it sure is preserved well enough to last only if I'm crazy too God knows what I'll do about it just to look at water makes me sick and I'd just as soon swallow gasoline as a glass of whiskey and Lorraine telling them he may not drink but if you dont believe he's a man I can tell you how to find out she says If I catch you fooling with any of these whores you know what I'll do she says I'll whip her grabbing at her I'll whip her as long as I can find her she says and I says if I dont drink that's my business but have you ever found me short I says I'll buy you enough beer to take a bath in if you want it because I've got every respect for a good honest whore because with Mother's health and the position I try to uphold to have her with no more respect for what I try to do for her than to make her name and my name and my Mother's name a byword in the town. (232–33)

This remarkable paragraph is as close to stream-of-consciousness as any in Quentin's monologue in its abandonment of all punctuation after Jason gets launched into the third sentence. As in other passages, Jason here compresses all of his most threatening concerns: his father's drinking death, one brother's suicide, another's idiocy, his niece's sexual misconduct, his dalliance with his Memphis whore/girlfriend Lorraine, and his need to assert his own sexual potency, his physical mastery over women (his need to assure himself and others that he, unlike Benjy, does indeed have testicles), and, crucially, his paralyzing fear of the town's watchful eye. It is a mixture of important things, especially in the final lines where the syntax, on the verge throughout, breaks completely down: there is no object to the preposition "with," following the second "because," and no predicate to complete the clause "because" begins. We notice this "because" because two of them, the only two in the paragraph, are jammed into this one sentence, whereas usually, as Kałuża has pointed out, Jason constantly uses such conjunctions to try to organize his speech, to force relationships, causes and effects, that may or may not exist; thus they signal a psychic association, if not a strictly logical or rational one. In this paragraph, "because" abrupts at us precisely because it becomes a psychic bridge between Lorraine and Mother: Mother = whore.

Jason rumbles into this connection again, later, in a typically churning meditation:

> I'm a man, I can stand it, it's my own flesh and blood and I'd like to see the color of the man's eyes that would speak disrespectful of any woman that was my friend it's these dam good women that do it I'd like to see the good, church-going woman that's half as square as Lorraine, whore or no whore. Like I say if I was to get married you'd go up like a balloon and you know it and she says I want you to be happy to have a family of your own not to slave your life away for us. But I'll be gone soon and then you can take a wife but you'll never find a woman who is worthy of you and I says yes I could. You'd get right up out of your grave you know you would. I says no thank you I have all the women I can take care of now if I married a wife she'd probably turn out to be a hophead or something. That's all we lack in this family. (246–47)

The paragraph moves from his resentment of his niece's embarrassing public sexual misconduct and his irritation at having to support her, to her mother's perfidy, which in turn is the reason, he thinks, that he has to work for a living. The meditation runs from yet another assertion of his masculinity to a cliché-ridden and phony defense of his women friends to a cliché-ridden and phony attack on social morality, to a defense of his secret sexual liaison with Lorraine (secret from his mother, at any rate, and from the prying eyes of the town). Then his uncontested thoughts stampede him into a defense of his bachelorhood, for which he claims to have told his mother that he blames her: "If I was to get married you'd go up like a balloon." His reported exchanges with his mother throughout may, of course, be as imaginary as the ones Quentin claims with their father (Matthews, *Play* 103; Pitavy, "Through the Poet's Eye," 93). But what is significant about Jason's "conversations" are the contorted connections he makes, willy-nilly, between his bachelorhood, Lorraine, and his mother: again and again Lorraine and Mother collide, in the deepest, least conscious, parts of Jason's mind.

Benjy's attempts to "say" get him castrated. Quentin also associates sexuality, sexual shame, with language directly when he fantasizes castrating himself, so he can treat sexuality as he would Chinese, as a language he doesn't know (116). Like Quentin, what Jason cannot "say," what he cannot confront in language, is also precisely how much he both fears and desires his own castration and death: "That's a hog for punishment for you," he says of Benjy:

> If what had happened to him for fooling with open gates had happened to me, I never would want to see another one. I often wondered what he'd be thinking about, down there at the gate, watching the girls going home from school, trying to want something he couldn't even remember he didn't and couldn't want any longer. And what he'd think when they'd be undressing him and he'd happen to take a look at himself and begin to cry like he'd do. But like I say they never did enough of that. I says I know what you need you need what they did to Ben then you'd behave. And if you dont know what that was I says, ask Dilsey to tell you. (253)

> And if they'd just sent him on to Jackson while he was under the ether, he'd never have known the difference. But that would have been too simple for a Compson to think of. Not half complex enough. Having to wait to do it at all until he broke out and tried to run a little girl down on the street with her own father looking at him. Well, like I say they never started soon enough with their cutting, and they quit too quick. I know at least two more that needed something like that, and one of them not over a mile away, either. But then I dont reckon even that would do any good. Like I say once a bitch always a bitch. (263)

These two startling passages—the latter close to the end of Jason's section and so part of his peroration—suggest the degree to which

Jason's interlocutor throughout has been mostly himself, and he the object of his own scorn. The first passage suggests his attempt to imagine his way into the sexually safe castrated haven of Benjy's mind and, like Quentin, to imagine what it would be like not ever to have had sexual urges; he concludes that "you," his libidinous self, his id, his constant interlocutor, needs castrating.[1] In the second passage he proposes "two more" that need cutting: and the "one of them . . . not over a mile away" has to be his father, whom he still will not locate verbally in the cemetery. The other, closer, can only be himself.

Thus it is not for nothing that Faulkner very carefully plants the charged word "complex" deep in the heart of Jason's final paragraph. Mother and sexuality are as essentially the subtext of his monologue as of his brothers'—mother and sexuality and all the related substitutions and evasions that spiral outward from Oedipal guilt: shame, self-loathing, the need for expiative punishment: castration and death. No less than Quentin, Jason longs for a strong father, long since dead, who will force upon the world a moral center around which all the fragmentation of his psychic life can cohere. If he is, as Carvel Collins argued long ago ("Interior Monologues"), Faulkner's version of Freud's punitive super-ego, he also manifests his brother Quentin's essential Oedipal conflicts and expresses the identical fears, though in him they emerge as rage, mostly at himself. He is a cauldron, a veritable inferno, of Oedipal conflicts, containing within himself a raging id that has to deal with a bedridden mother whom it both desires and revolts from in shame and whom it cannot evade by substituting an absent Caddy or even the ever-present and insatiable daughter of Caddy; he must contend with a draconian super-ego that insists upon controlling the world, and his own libido, by punishing it appropriately—by killing it or at least castrating it; and with a surprisingly fragile ego, which no less than brother Quentin's both fears and desires castration—and death as the ultimate castration—as an appropriate punishment for one who has sinned as he has. He is therefore not so much a "negative" image of Quentin (Bleikasten,

1. See Lester's interesting discussion of this passage ("From Place to Place" 149–51).

Most Splendid Failure 152) as a complete replication of his brothers, both of whom he contains within himself, along with the raging, punishing Father he so desperately longs for. This may be why he does indeed inspire in the reader the most complex response of any of the brothers (Bleikasten, *Most Splendid Failure* 148–49).

Shegog

One of the most interesting aspects of Faulkner's treatment of language in *The Sound and the Fury* is his depiction of dialect. Representing speech in writing is tricky in English because of the range of acceptable phonemes that can be represented by a single vowel and several consonants: I don't mean just regional variations, but the difference between short and long vowels, for example. Consider idiolects, and it's easy to understand the nightmare any writer faces in attempting to render the sounds that characters make when pronouncing the words. Linguists have a very precise method of transcribing speech sounds, but fiction writers rely on less objective methods of representing speech, and they have different reasons for doing so. Because pronunciation is so varied, even within a single region, the notion of a "standard" is a pedantic one which implies a "correctness" against which variations become at worst "erroneous" and at best "curious" or "charming" or "regional" or even "sinister" or "pretentious," depending on the class and character of the person whose speech is being rendered.

Thus writers consciously or unconsciously depict a speaker's class and character in the degree to which they render speech as standard or variant (Ross 104–05). This is true when the writer represents differences in vocabulary and pronunciation—Versh's "rinktum" for "rectum" (70), for example, or something like "ribber" for "river"—but it is most noticeable in the use of eye-dialect, wherein the spelling changes not the pronunciation of a word but merely the way it looks on the page: "ov" instead of "of" or "bekaws" instead of "because". The difference, the nonstandard variance, is, like the Caddy/caddie of the novel's opening page, like Jason's "dam" instead of "damn," and like the "watter" or "watter-milyuns" that Quentin and Jason use when quoting a black character, something available only to a reader, a literate person, not to the hearer or the speaker who, in being assigned a nonstandard written form, is being depicted as non-literate and so as different from, other than, the reader and the writer. Linguistic distinctions are those of class, of cultural and psychological otherness; dialect becomes a sure way to place a character regionally, culturally, and socially, and authors can invest characters with respect or condescension, with sameness or otherness, through the representation of speech. All authors have to choose how much dialect to use, how much is enough to suggest the flavor of region and class, how much will distract from other, more important things in the fiction: George Washington Harris's *Sut Lovingood Yarns*, for example, uses an eye-dialect so heavy as to be virtually a different written language altogether (Ross 99).

Faulkner tends to work at the other end of the scale from Harris; in *The Sound and the Fury* he uses very little eye-dialect. Nearly all of the dialect spellings offer variant pronunciation, and Faulkner is usually much more interested in suggesting variant pronunciation than in rendering it precisely. Benjy's non-verbal narrative records more black speech than either of his brothers, and, given that he has often been taken as a camera and a tape recorder, it seems natural to assume that he would *hear* and so record their pronunciation in the fullness of their dialect. This is not the case. Curiously, Faulkner represents black speech in Benjy's section almost completely in standard English. When dialect spellings do occur in the Benjy section, they are seldom more complicated than Luster's "Whooey. Git up that tree. Look here at this squirl, Benjy" (6) and Versh's famous "ahun [iron] gate" (6). In effect, just as he lets his reader be confused over Caddy/caddie, Faulkner for the most part again refuses to tell us what Benjy *hears* through dialect spellings, and even refuses more than just a tiny bit of the flavor of dialect, including eye-dialect. Surely Benjy does not *hear* Dilsey say "Yes, sir" to his father, as Faulkner records it, but rather something more like "Yassuh" or the "Yes, suh" that black characters use in the other sections. When he does record dialect, he only very gently suggests variance—as when Dilsey talks about "the Lawd's own time" (26)—a device, perhaps, to keep the reader visually reminded of time and place, of social and cultural realities that Benjy cannot be aware of. In thus divesting Dilsey and other black characters of heavy dialect in Benjy's aural register, then, Faulkner invests them with sameness rather than otherness, and so reflects Benjy's sense of the Gibsons as central to his experience, the degree to which they define normality for him.

Not so Quentin and Jason, who are intensely aware of those social and cultural realities, and whose conscious rendering of black language does indeed reflect their assumptions about class and race. Quentin, trying to come to terms with black-white relations at home as he observes black-white behavior in Cambridge, reports the speech of the black man at the railroad crossing in Virginia with moderate dialect: "Yes, suh. . . . Thanky, young marster. Thanky" (87), and he notes that Deacon switches his language to suit his audience. When Quentin interrupts his conversation with another group of students, Deacon says to them, "See you again, fellows. . . . glad to have chatted with you"; turning to address Quentin, he gives the Southerner what he, Deacon, thinks the Southerner expects and wants, and Quentin registers his speech in ways that capture Deacon's exaggerated Southern dialect: "Yes, suh. Right dis way, young marster, hyer we is. . . . Hyer, boy, come hyer and git dese grips. . . . Now, den, dont you drap hit. Yes, suh, young marster, jes give de old nigger yo room number, and hit'll be done got cold dar when you arrives" (97). Quentin understands completely what Deacon is doing, and renders his dialect with some appreciation of Deacon's comic act, a timorous celebration of Deacon's otherness which all the while recognizes his impending and worrisome sameness.

On the other hand, Quentin treats Jefferson's Louis Hatcher, whose otherness is firmly fixed and nonthreatening, very paternalistically, and reports his speech with very condescending humor:

Watter kin git des ez high en wet in Jefferson ez hit kin in Pennsylvaney, I reckon. Hit's de folks dat says de high watter cant git dis fur dat

> comes floatin out on de ridge-pole, too. . . . I cleant dat lantun and me
> and her sot de balance of de night on top o dat knoll back de graveyard.
> En ef I'd a knowed of aihy one higher, we'd a been on hit instead. (114)

Quentin does not, of course, hear Louis Hatcher say *watter* instead
of *water*, any more than Benjy hears Dilsey say *Yes, sir*; but Faulkner
writes it this way, one of the very few examples of eye-dialect in the
novel, to suggest some things about Quentin's attitude toward
Hatcher. Later, Faulkner turns Quentin's condescension around on
him, invests *him* with otherness, when, after Quentin's conversation
with the swimming boys outside of Cambridge in absolutely standard
English, Quentin hears one of them observe that Quentin "talks like
a colored man" (120)! Quentin does not comment on this irony, if he
recognizes it.

Quentin's rendering of black pronunciation is mild compared to
Jason's: old Job, Jason reports, is going to the carnival in spite of
Jason's ridicule:

> "I dont begridge um. I kin sho afford my two bits."
>
> . . .
>
> "Dat's de troof," he says. "Well, ef I lives twell night hit's gwine to
> be two bits mo dey takin out of town, dat's sho." (231)

But even Jason is capable of distinctions, and so Dilsey, much closer
to him than Job, gets a dialect a good deal less heavy than Job's:
" 'And whar else do she belong?' Dilsey says. 'Who else gwine raise
her cep me? Aint I raised ev'y one of y'all?' " (198). Thus the non-
verbal Benjy, so frequently assumed to be an objective tape recorder
of sorts, makes no claim on verisimilar reproduction of what is clearly
the non-standard sounds of his black keepers' speech; each of the
two oral brothers does make such claims and, as we have seen, their
rendering of dialect pronunciation changes according to their attitudes toward and relationships with the speakers being quoted.

By far the heaviest dialect in *The Sound and the Fury*, however,
occurs in the decidedly *written* and consciously *literary* fourth section,
whose only pretense at orality is in the characters who are quoted
and especially in the central oral narrative of section four, Reverend
Shegog's Easter Sunday sermon. The writer-narrator of the fourth

section uses a visual representation of Dilsey's language that strives for greater verisimilitude than even Jason's monologue does, and so moves toward a written language near that of George Washington Harris:

"I'll have de fire gwine in a minute, en de water hot in two mo.
. . . "Luster overslep dis mawnin, up half de night at dat show. I gwine build de fire myself. Go on now, so you wont wake de others twell I ready." (268)

"Whut you doin in de cellar?" she said. "Dont stand dar in de rain, fool," she said.
. . .
"Dont you dare come in dis do widout a armful of wood," she said. "Here I done had to tote yo wood en build yo fire bofe. Didn't I tole you not to leave dis place last night befo dat woodbox wus full to de top?" (269)

The verisimilitude threatens to reduce Dilsey and other black characters in the novel to the plastic black characters of Joel Chandler Harris, those of the popular imagination, in ways that Benjy's narrative does not. The farther the point of view distances us from her, the stranger Dilsey appears to us. It's a striking illustration of just how "other" Dilsey is to Quentin and Jason, to the "narrator" of this section, and to us as we read it.

Thus as the novel moves toward more and more consciously and self-consciously "narrated," that is, written, materials—from Benjy's simple registering of sense impressions, through his brothers' much more complex sense of a psychic or social audience, to this narrator's more traditional audience of readers—the closer we come to a complete breakdown in the representation of words, and so in the capacity of words themselves to convey meaning. The movement is completely parallel to the way Quentin's mechanical control over his language gradually breaks down as he loses psychic control of his life.

It is also completely parallel to the linguistic movement of Shegog's sermon which, at the center of the fourth section, is the novel's fourth oral narrative. It is precisely Shegog's purpose to invest this life with meaning, to make it signify something instead of nothing in the midst of all the sound and fury. He locates this meaning in the life and death of Jesus Christ, and his sermon is a ritualistic incantation of that meaning for the assembled congregation, a meaning in which the congregation participates, though not in words: "Mmmmmmmmmm-mmmmmmm!" they say, "Jesus! Little Jesus!" (296), and they do this "without words, like bubbles rising in water" (296). They are rapt; they lose themselves and become a collective not in or because of his words, but because of his voice: they seem "to watch him," in a passage many commentators have noted, "with its own eyes while the voice consumed him, until he was nothing and they were nothing and there was not even a voice but instead their hearts were speaking to one another in chanting measures *beyond the need for words*" (294; my italics).

But that *meaning* is not, for Shegog or the congregation, an articulatable one; it is *beyond words*, and he understands that no matter how much he tries to say, he and his communicants cannot communicate when they share signifiers alone, which shrivel away linguistically to nothing—their "Mmmmmmmmmmm" is very close to Benjy's wordless moaning—but only when they share the signified itself. That is, since they share the ricklickshun and de blood, they need not refer to it at all. Like Deacon, Shegog reads his audience accurately, senses quickly that his very proper Northern diction will not do for this group of Southerners, and he moves immediately from the standard "brethren," with which he first addresses his hearers in a "level and cold" voice (293), directly into heavy dialect:

> Breddren en sistuhn. . . . I got de ricklickshun en de blood of de Lamb!
> . . . . Wus a rich man: whar he now, O breddren? Wus a po man: whar he now, O sistuhn? Oh I tells you, ef you aint got de milk en de dew of de old salvation when de long, cold years rolls away! (295)

His sermon is a hodgepodge of pseudo-eloquence and non sequitur and nonsense theology—he speaks of the "widowed God" (296), for example, and lapses in to Benjy's synesthesia when he speaks of "*seeing*" "de golden horns shoutin down de glory" (297)—which perhaps move by some sort of fluid stream-of-conscious associations in Shegog's mind, perhaps not: his rhetorical need, like Jason's, is to keep himself and his congregation wrapped up in his voice, which takes them "into itself" (295; Ross 40–45), to keep the sound at such a pitch that there will be no time, no reason, for his congregation to think or articulate or explain. The closer he gets to meaning, then, the farther he gets from standard language, from the signification of words, either written or oral.

At the center of his sermon, at the center of his meaning, framed by all this oral non-sense, is the image of a motionless, silent *pietà*: the Logos, the very Word itself in the arms of a mother who cannot protect it from danger. Shegog's meaning, then, cannot be evoked by the normal signifiers of their language but by ritualistic communal incantations which evoke the visual icons of their belief. That is, like Benjy—it is not incidental that he is sitting in their midst; in a linguistic sense, here the novel comes full circle—they bypass the obfuscation of signifiers and go, with Shegog, to a direct, unmediated experience of the signified. They can only do this when language breaks completely down, and they don't need to rely on it for the communication of their deepest beliefs. Jesus, in this frame, is in effect a signified which *cannot have* a sufficient signifier. They call him "Jesus," but no one believes that that mere sound carries the full significance of that image any more than the sounds "Caddy" or "caddie" or "*[kædI]*" *contain* for Benjy the full significance of his sister.

In this context we can understand how words are, indeed, "sound and fury, signifying nothing." In this ecstatic moment, Benjy's fellow worshippers don't need *to say* because they share, because they believe: here they absolve themselves of time and place, of social and cultural circumstance, of deep psychic wounds and urges, of guilt and recrimination, of all complexity. They can do this only for a brief respite, and only by focusing their hearts on the Word-less image of an idealized maternal love, of salvation and resurrection and hope that Shegog's sermon evokes. For the moment that is enough, and that is why the scene, with all its loud clashing and clanging, stands nevertheless so powerfully peaceful, almost serene, in contrast to the verbal armageddons of the Compson brothers' monologues, where articulation and meaning always meet as ruthless and inexhaustible antagonists.

The Artist as Cuckold

In order to believe that Thomas Sutpen rejects Charles Bon because he has black blood, readers have blithely been willing to do a good deal of fancy footwork around some significant obstacles. First, you have to believe that Sutpen is far more race-conscious than he proves himself to be in any other place in the novel. Second, you have to believe that Bon at birth had physical characteristics—skin pigmentation, hair texture, lip thickness: something—that identified him as black, but which disappeared as he got older so that he could enroll at the University of Mississippi and pass as white all of his life. Third, if you believe that Sutpen was worried about dynasty, traditional problems of primogeniture, you have to overlook the Mississippi law that forbade a black son to inherit a father's estate.

Nevertheless, Bon's "blackness" overwhelms discussions of *Absalom, Absalom!*, because it provides the novel's character-narrators, after many trials and errors, with a motive that allows them to explain why Henry Sutpen kills Charles Bon at the gates of Sutpen's Hundred. But Quentin and Shreve posit Bon's blackness very late, toward the end of chapter 8, in the scene they create together in which Sutpen summons Henry to his tent on the eve of battle and informs him about Bon's racial heritage (AA 283). Sutpen's revelation provides a focus, a release, a renewed energy, for the narrative quagmire they have been in. From this moment, the narrative becomes a sort of endgame. The preforeordestinated scene at the gate of Sutpen's Hundred toward which the narrative has been moving becomes, finally, inevitable: the novel relaxes from its hems and haws, its stops and starts, its proffered and then rejected explanations. In three pages Charles Bon is dead: Henry has kilt him dead as a beef.

But Sutpen's revelation asks a major question that the boys, in their headlong rush toward climax, simply beg. Why should the strong, imperious, even demonic father give the responsibility for stopping an incestuous and miscegenous union to the son? Why not stop it by killing Bon himself or by whisking Judith away to a nunnery, say, since obviously just forbidding the marriage is not going to work? The answer lies first in the fact that Quentin and Shreve know from the beginning that Henry and not Sutpen kills Bon, and their narration must move toward that act, which is the narrative nub of the novel. Moreover, and more importantly, Sutpen's relegation of that responsibility to his son reaffirms to the reader how specifically *Absalom* is a son's story and not a father's. *Absalom* insists throughout that the source of its narration is also its focus: thus the responsibility that this fictionally-created father hands to this fictionally-created son is very much at *Absalom*'s center. What finally pushes Henry over the edge is not any affirmation that blood may not marry blood, but that black blood may not mingle with white: the ultimate white horror is not just Thomas Sutpen's ace in the hole, but Quentin's and Shreve's as well.

We should be suspicious of the suddenness and the sufficiency with which the race card provides a solution for the boys' narrative convolutions. Of course, it's been a long cold night in the Harvard dorm, and they may simply want to get to bed. But in a novel which questions *everything*, it is very curious that they do not question anything in this scene. They simply accept race as the one piece of acceptable information that allows their Hamlet-hero Henry finally to act. I repeat: in this reading, incest, by itself, is not enough. Race replaces incest as the key concern; indeed, the narrators specifically pare incest away from the terms of the climactic confrontation: "*So it's the miscegenation, not the incest, which you cant bear*" (293), Bon taunts Henry. I'm not your brother, he continues: "*I'm the nigger that's going to sleep with your sister*" (294).

Sutpen's race card, then, overwhelms both *Absalom*'s narrators and its critics. For the most part, even critics who have pursued other themes—history, culture, gender, language, and narrative theory, for example—have accepted race's centrality to *Absalom*, and Bon's black blood has become the still point around which the world of *Absalom* and its critics turns. I insist, however, that Sutpen's race card must be understood as Quentin's and Shreve's narrative ace, offered so late not because other explanations for Henry's murder of Bon would not do but rather because the other explanations are rife with issues that Quentin and Shreve do not want to deal with directly. Race is, in *Absalom* and in Faulkner generally, a mask for very serious matters of sexuality and gender.

Indeed, to question Bon's black blood requires us also to question Sutpen's reasons for putting away his Haitian wife, reasons which readers have always and consistently assumed to be that that wife was part Negro, and that her blackness was the fact she and her family deliberately kept from him. But nowhere in anything Sutpen is reported as saying is there any justification for accepting this as fact. The only "evidence" of Bon's racial makeup is in the novel's Chronology, which bears a very problematic relationship to the novel (Polk, "Where the Comma Goes"; Ferrer). But Quentin and Shreve do not have access to that chronology: they know only what they hear or make up.

Our most direct evidence about Sutpen's Haiti days comes from the story Sutpen tells General Compson in the intervals between their chase of the escaped Paris architect. Nothing Sutpen says about his wife and child has to do with race; the only thing approaching a reason for putting them away has to do with his virginity:

> On this night I am speaking of (and until my first marriage, I might add) I was still a virgin. You will probably not believe that, and if I were to try to explain it you would disbelieve me more than ever. So I will only say that that too was a part of the design which I had in my mind. (205)

I'm much less astonished to believe that Sutpen was a virgin than to discover that his virginity was a part of his much-discussed "design," and I'm forced to ask: if *his* virginity was an important part of his design, how much *more* important to that design—to the design, to his sense of himself as a man—would be the virginity of the woman he chose as wife? I would, then, like to argue that the reason Thomas

Sutpen puts away his Haitian family has nothing to do with Negro blood, but with his belated discovery, after the birth of the baby, of his wife's previous marriage and/or previous sexual experience. Others have suggested this possibility (Brooks, Schoenberg, Kuyk), but dismiss it as quickly as they raise it, in order to get back to race as the novel's defining issue. But it is worth considerably more than a passing glance, both for the possibilities it raises for understanding the novel differently, and for the ways in which it allows us a new understanding of *Absalom*'s place in one of the larger arcs of Faulkner's career.

If Sutpen rejects the Haitian wife because she did not come to him as a virgin, we may ask several new questions, and perhaps offer different answers to questions we have asked for the nearly sixty years of this novel's life. We may first suppose that Bon was either not Sutpen's son or that he feared that Bon was not his, feared that he would then be raising someone else's child as his own. Thus the novel raises not just legal and cultural questions of primogeniture, which we regularly discuss, but also, and perhaps more importantly, assumptions residing historically in the male psyche about every male's "right" to his own virgin; more of this shortly. Second, if we accept Sutpen's betrayal in Haiti as a sexual one, we may better understand why he is so hell-bent on marrying Ellen Coldfield, the daughter of the most righteous Methodist steward in Jefferson: where else than in such a "righteous," repressive home could he have more hopes of finding the virgin of his design? Third, if we accept that Bon might not be a Sutpen at all, black or white, or that Sutpen fears that he is not, we open the way to question what other issues besides bigamy or incest or concubinage or race may have been at work on the infamous Christmas eve in the Sutpen parlor. Perhaps Sutpen simply doesn't like this foppish young man. Perhaps Sutpen discovered something in New Orleans other than Bon's background. Perhaps it's as simple as that Judith, for her own reasons, has asked her father to send him away. Perhaps, perhaps, perhaps.

Perhaps Bon and Henry confess to or in some way display a homosexual relationship; that would certainly be enough for Sutpen to reject Bon and for Henry to reject Sutpen and ride away with Bon. Other narrators have insinuated the possibility; throughout, Quentin's father has given us—and Quentin—an effeminate and foppish Bon, a Henry dazzled by the sophisticated cosmopolite. In one oft-noted passage he articulates a very specific sense of the triangulation among the principals that works equally well for both *The Sound and the Fury* and *Absalom, Absalom!*:

> In fact, perhaps this is the pure and perfect incest: the brother realising that the sister's virginity must be destroyed in order to have existed at all, taking that virginity in the person of the brother-in-law, the man whom he would be if he could become, metamorphose into, the lover, the husband; by whom he would be despoiled, choose for despoiler, if he could become, metamorphose into the sister, the mistress, the bride. (80)

Both *Absalom* and *The Sound and the Fury* hint broadly and unsubtly about the homoerotic tension between Quentin and Shreve. The triangle comprised of Bon, Henry, and Judith specifically replicates, in a slightly more obvious manner, that triangle made up of Quentin, Caddy, and Dalton Ames in the earlier novel (Irwin).

Finally, it is very much worth noting that none of the narrators in *Absalom*, least of all Quentin, proposes that Henry kills Bon for the same reason that Quentin wants to kill Dalton Ames, though it would seem natural: not to prevent incest or miscegenation, but to preserve that part of family honor resident in his sister's maidenhead. To put it another way, like Quentin, Henry may just want to control his sister's body, to try to contain Judith's sexuality, as other Faulkner males have done. I believe that we have not explored this possibility because we have heretofore, in *Absalom*, been so completely caught up in race, and I'd suggest, as an aside, that our collective failure, as Faulkner readers, to face the gender problematics of *Absalom* stems from the same collective need to evade the issue as Quentin and Shreve evince: that is, for Faulknerians, race seems to be easier to deal with than gender.

I'd like to push this meditation upon *Absalom* just a bit further in order to ground this magnificent novel in the complex of Oedipal relationships that I have argued for some time now is central to Faulkner ("Children"). Thomas Sutpen's curious and fatal relationship with Wash Jones supplies us with all the evidence we need. Briefly, Wash Jones is a surrogate replication of Thomas Sutpen's worthless white trash father, the author of all the chaos and misery of Sutpen's early years in the Virginia/West Virginia mountains, which he describes to General Compson so vividly, even if with such detachment. It is a childhood completely consonant with other childhoods in the Faulkner of this period, including Rosa Coldfield's: Sutpen's childhood is a living hell of instability, alcoholism, and paternal ruthlessness (178–96).

In my reading of his conflict with Wash Jones, Sutpen has now gained ascendancy over his own father, an ascendancy symbolized by the reversal of their positions: he the rich planter in the hammock, his surrogate father the servant who brings the jug, admires him unconditionally, and does exactly what Sutpen tells him. If Wash Jones is Sutpen's father, the unfortunate Millie, Wash's granddaughter, is Sutpen's surrogate daughter or sister, their union and their child incestuous. Thus it is perfectly appropriate, in this Freudian schema, that Wash kills Sutpen with that rusty scythe. Provoked, Wash transforms himself not merely into Father Time, as this scene has nearly always been read, but into the avenging, punishing father; the scythe is his castrating knife. What more appropriate punishment, in Faulkner as in Freud, for the crime of incest? Sutpen both commits the incest that Quentin cannot commit *and* forces his own father to punish him—what Quentin tries but also fails to do. In Quentin's reconstruction of *Absalom*'s narrative, then, *both* Sutpen and Henry perform the very acts that in *The Sound and the Fury* he, Quentin, cannot. Thus *Absalom, Absalom!* is, among other things, Quentin's fantasy in which he simultaneously enacts the preservation of his sister's honor and the destruction of the darker impulses toward incest and homoeroticism that he cannot face.

♂ ♀

I've begun with this little excursus on *Absalom* in order to introduce a theme in Faulkner as constant as words and to suggest its potential significance for Faulkner studies. It is a theme charged with various layers of meaning throughout his art and perhaps in his life.

The cuckold is a major player in Faulkner's fiction, a figure who recurs time and again in a wide variety of formulations: the weak husband or lover, the impotent, the voyeur, the pimp. The obsessive frequency in the fiction of the cuckold and the triangular relationships created by cuckoldry argues that they are a high priority in Faulkner's fiction, an astonishing amount of which directly explores the ways in which men deal with the real or imagined sexual lives of wives or partners which they cannot, or fear they cannot, control; often in Faulkner men create the conditions of their own cuckolding as perhaps the only alternative to losing control completely of their wives' or partners' sexual lives: to pimp is, after all, to control female sexuality. Thomas Sutpen's "design" is but one manifestation of Faulkner's career-long preoccupation with the problems of female sexuality's place in the economy of male desire. In Sutpen's case, as in many others in Faulkner, male desire requires control not just of a female's sexual present and future, but, as we shall see, of her sexual history as well.

The fourteenth way of looking at this very complex blackbird, then, lies in the lens provided by *Absalom*'s implied double triangle—Quentin-Caddy-Dalton; Henry-Judith-Bon—triangles replicated throughout Faulkner's fiction, triangles rife with homo- and hetero-erotic implications for the characters and, perhaps, for the author. This triangle of desire is specifically Oedipal and, considered quantitatively, it is more important to Faulkner's fiction, by a long shot, than race. Consider that only four of Faulkner's novels—*Light in August, Absalom, Absalom!, Go Down, Moses* and *Intruder in the Dust*—and that at most three of well over a hundred short stories—"Sunset," "That Evening Sun" and "Dry September"—are in any way "about" race, and you will have some sense of how relatively little of his work Faulkner invested in race-consciousness. On the other hand, gender problematics drip from nearly every line he ever wrote, and even *Light in*

August, Absalom, Go Down, Moses and "Dry September" are arguably more centrally concerned with gender than with race. Race has also, I suspect, provided a mask for the mostly white male or male-identified critics who have worked on Faulkner; it must be easier to deal with race than with gender, whose problems are much closer, much harder to find a language to understand with, because we are much more intimately complicit with the repressive structures of gender hierarchy. Notwithstanding Eric Sundquist's contention that race more or less defines Faulkner's greatness, I believe that race is in fact a mask for gender throughout Faulkner.

Along with Freud, the most useful contexts for thinking along these lines are those provided by René Girard, who frames a theory of desire in *Deceit, Desire, and the Novel*; Eve Kosofsky Sedgwick, who expands upon and provides a brilliant new context for Girard's ideas in *Between Men*; and Tony Tanner, also to a certain extent building from Girard, who deals with cuckoldry in *Adultery and the Novel*. Girard proposes that desire is always triangular, that it is never original or spontaneous and that it therefore always involves a mediator: we can only desire what somebody else desires first. Moreover, in the triangle of desire the most important relationship is that between the subject and the mediator, not that between the subject and the object, and varying degrees of tension in the triangle are directly tied to the distance between the subject and the mediator and to the obstacles that the mediator puts in the way of the subject's merging with either the mediator or the object.

Faulkner's wonderfully funny short story of 1942, "A Courtship," a deliberate frolicking in Freudian fields, is a conscious illustration of the dynamics of this triangle of desire. In "A Courtship," David Hogganbeck and Ikkemotubbe become competitors for the hand of a Eula Varner-like maiden who has no name but merely a designation as "Herman Basket's Sister." They eventually engage in a race and agree that whoever wins the race gets the girl; Herman Basket's Sister, whom they do not consult in any of their arrangements of her future, appears indifferent.

They race, naked, 130 miles to a ceremonial cave, an ominously vaginal "black hole" where "boys from among all the People would go . . . to prove if they had the courage to become men" (CS 374). But the victory is not just to the swiftest. In a typical Faulknerian complication, the first to arrive must enter the cave and shoot a pistol: if the cave does not collapse on him, he wins; if it does, of course, he loses a good deal more than Herman Basket's sister. The two friends race not at all as fierce competitors out to win the maiden's hand at all cost, however; during the course of the race they bond completely with each other, and by race's end they are both thinking of "that damned sister of Herman Basket's" (CS 376), who, being the presumed object of their mutual desire, had gotten them into their complicated situation. Subject and mediator merge.

Ikkemotubbe gets to the cave first, enters, and fires: *"Aihee. It comes"* (CS 377), he thinks, as he hears the Cave rumble down on him. David Hogganbeck, outside, hears the rumble too, and fearing for Ikkemotubbe, thrusts himself half-way into the Cave's vaginal opening and supports it on his back while Ikkemotubbe crawls under him and out. But he cannot back out himself, and Ikkemotubbe contemplates his friend's "buttocks and legs pink in the sunrise" (CS 377) while he tries to decide what to do. He first gets a long pole and thrusts it into the cave, to try to pry the roof off of David Hogganbeck's back. When that doesn't work, he grasps David Hogganbeck "by the meat" (CS 377) and pulls him backward to safety, as the cave collapses. They have thus shared the same orifice and given birth to each other; they are each the other's brother and father. Even while enacting a ritualistic macho competition for the woman's hand, they have in fact rescued each other from the feminine; clearly, the athletic competition is a thin, a veritably gossamer, veil for the homoerotic or at least homosocial elements in their friendship. They prefer each other's company; they do not really want Herman Basket's Sister, indeed, they fear that primal cave, but feel compelled by their culture to compete for her, to dare and conquer "it," anyway.

Back home, they discover that while they were racing, Herman Basket's sister has married an artist, a harmonica player with the Freudian name of Log-in-the-Creek. David Hogganbeck and Ikkemotubbe console each other, while the narrator projects forward a bit to Ikkemotubbe's future: he gives up love and begins to desire power instead; his mediator becomes the slave-holding civilization of the United States, and he learns how to kill "anything . . . which happened to stand between [him] and what he wanted" (CS 379).

♂ ♀

One of the staple assumptions of American literary study is that Faulkner drew heavily on his own family and region for a good deal of his fiction. We know how he exploited family legends about the old cunnel and the young cunnel, how Oxford became Jefferson and Ben Wasson and/or Phil Stone became Horace Benbow, and how Faulkner transmuted all these relatively external and more or less documentable materials into his art. More recent work, especially since the publication of Joseph Blotner's massive biography in 1974 (although there was plenty of it before that time), has been interested in Faulkner's internal life, in the kinds of things we can learn about Faulkner's mind from his works, and about his works from his mind. This is a perilous enterprise: in thinking and writing about Faulkner and Freud, for example, I have generally been content to use Freud as a source, as others have taken the Bible, Homer, and other works of literature and philosophy as sources. There are in Faulkner's fiction innumerable scenes, tableaux, characters, and situations which fit various important Freudian paradigms in what seem indisputable ways. There are also in Faulkner's life, especially in his relationships to women, the same kinds of scenes, characters, and situations that fit those same Freudian paradigms in precisely the same seemingly indisputable ways. Does the fact that Faulkner's mother resembles in a few external and apparently superficial ways many of the mothers and grandmothers in the fiction suggest that under the surface of a seemingly absolute devotion to her there was a great deal of hostility? Are such correspondences coincidental (Martin)? It would be very easy, I think, to make too much of certain of these correspondences, and equally easy not to make enough. They are, in any event, endlessly fascinating.

One of the most remarkable documents in Blotner's one-volume revision and update of his two-volume biography is an astonishing letter that Faulkner wrote to his publisher Hal Smith, probably in the very late spring of 1929, just after he had finished writing *Sanctuary*, asking to borrow $500. "Hal," he wrote:

> I want $500.00. I am going to be married. Both want to and have to.
> THIS PART IS CONFIDENTIAL, UTTERLY. For my honor and the sanity—I believe life—of a woman. This is not bunk; neither am I being sucked in. We grew up together and I dont think she could fool me in this way; that is, make me believe that her mental condition, her nerves, are this far gone. And no question of pregnancy: that would hardly move me: no one can face his own bastard with more equanimity than I, having had some practice. Neither is it a matter of a promise on my part; we have known one another long enough to pay no attention to our promises. It's a situation which I engendered and permitted to ripen which has become unbearable, and I am tired of running from devilment I bring about. This sounds a little insane, but I'm not in any shape to write letters now.

He would give Smith

> a note with ten percent. interest or whatever you wish, due the first of next March, with the reversion of all accruing royalty on the two novels of mine you have in case I die, and I will promise in writing to deliver you a third novel before that date; if it fails to please you, the note and interest to be paid on the above date. . . . I need not say this is confidential—the reasons, I mean—and urgent. I believe it will be the last time I'll bother you for money before time, because from now on I'll have to work. And I work well under pressure—and a wife will be pressure enough for me. (Blotner [1984] 240)

Apparently Smith did lend him the money, for Faulkner dedicated *As I Lay Dying*, his next novel, to him.

This is a remarkable letter: first, for Faulkner's claim of having fathered an illegitimate child—though this, of course, may be more brag than anything else. And second, for the letter's confirmation of our suspicions about Faulkner's marriage. We know from numerous sources that it was a stormy relationship that caused both Faulkner and Estelle much unhappiness over the years. This letter suggests that it was a marriage which he did not want to make, one he went into with considerable resentment, even desperation.

Faulkner and Estelle Oldham had been childhood sweethearts. Her parents disapproved strongly of Faulkner and had pushed her into a marriage with a more promising young man, Cornell Franklin. Although Faulkner urged her to elope with him, Estelle somewhat languidly acquiesced to her parents' decision and married Franklin in 1918. The Franklins moved to Shanghai and had two children, while Faulkner continued to burn a torch for her throughout the twenties: he wrote and bound for her a pamphlet of poems, *Vision in Spring*, and saw her whenever she returned from Shanghai on furlough. He was also, and very practically, pursuing other women at the same time, notably Helen Baird. At about the same time he was writing and binding *Vision in Spring* for Estelle, he was inscribing another little hand-printed book, *Mayday*, to Helen. In the spring of 1926, when Estelle was actually making arrangements to divorce Cornell, Faulkner was preparing yet another such booklet, *Helen: A Courtship*, for Helen, and in September of that year he finished *Mosquitoes* and dedicated it to Helen. In late October, however, he made for Estelle a pamphlet of his New Orleans Sketches which included a new one, a monologue by one Hong Li, a Chinese gentleman trying to come to terms with a lost love ("Hong Li").

Faulkner's desperate letter to Smith allows us to infer that during the times that Estelle and children came home on furlough from Shanghai, she and Faulkner took up more or less where they had left off, doubtless Faulkner more or less sincerely promising how wonderful their lives could be if only she weren't married.[1] Obviously when she began making plans in 1926 to get that divorce, Faulkner was somewhat shaken, and as the papers were filed and the divorce proceedings actually instituted, he began to understand what he had done. We may get some sense of his deepest feelings about his upcoming marriage and about his upcoming wife when we read, in *Sanc-*

---

1. Throughout the 1930s and 1940s Faulkner refused to divorce Estelle in order to marry Meta Carpenter because, he told Meta, Estelle would not give him custody of Jill (Wilde and Borsten).

tuary, that Temple Drake wears an expensive Chinese robe while she lives in Miss Reba's whorehouse, and when we note that he specifies June 20, *his wedding day*, as the day on which Lee Goodwin's trial begins—the trial during which Temple's testimony protects her original ravisher and causes an innocent man's death. Given, then, the frequency with which cuckolding is a central force throughout Faulkner's fiction, it is a provocative question whether at some psychological level Faulkner ever forgave Estelle for having cuckolded him—or *pre*-cuckolded him, rather—before they were married.

Sometime between 1925 and 1928, at about the time Estelle told Faulkner she was getting a divorce, Faulkner began but did not finish a patently autobiographical piece entitled "And Now What's To Do?" The narrator of this fragment outlines a background similar to Faulkner's family life and adolescent preoccupations in Oxford, then notes how his happy childhood had been upset by the onset of desire, "his changing body." He began watching the girls, "watching their forming legs, imagining their blossoming thighs, with a feeling of defiant inferiority"—an interesting and significant phrase for a man so physically small and delicate as Faulkner: "There was a giant in him, but the giant was muscle-bound." He sees the girls "with their ripening thighs and their mouths that keep you awake at night with unnameable things—shame of lost integrity, manhood's pride, desire like a drug. The body is tarnished, soiled in its pride, now. But what is it for, anyway?" He notes, ambiguously: "A girl got in trouble," but he does not clarify whether he himself is responsible. He then describes his escape on the train, and continues with a revealing meditation on the nature of women and of men, and on what was apparently his first sexual experience:

> Nothing to girls. Dividing legs dividing receptive. He had known all about it before, but the reality was like reading a story and then seeing it in the movies, with music and all. Soft things. Secretive, but like traps. Like going after something you wanted, and getting into a nest of spider webs. You got the thing, then you had to pick the webs off, and every time you touched one, it stuck to you. Even after you didn't want the thing anymore, the webs clung to you. Until after a while you

remembered the way the webs itched and you wanted the thing again, just thinking of how the webs itched. No. Quicksand. That was it. Wade through once, then go on. But a man wont. He wants to go all the way through, somehow; break out on the other side. Everything incomplete somehow. Having to back off, with webs clinging to you. Christ, you have to tell them so much. You cant think of it fast enough. And they never forget when you do and when you dont. What do they want, anyway? ("And Now" 147)

"And Now What's To Do?", then, provides an early autobiographical background for the sorts of problems that plague so many of his male characters: the fear and loathing of women, the shame and filth associated with sexuality, the immutability of desire, and the absolute inextricability of the desire and the shame.

Over and over again, as nearly all critics have noted, male characters in Faulkner have problems that are traceable to sour relationships with and attitudes toward and expectations of women; even women characters have problems traceable to sour relationships with other women, and it is undeniable that much of Faulkner's work is marked by gynophobia if not always by outright misogyny. Women in his fiction are nearly always associated not just with sex and shame but also with filth, excrement, pain, and death. And in the years following Estelle's announcement that she was getting a divorce, we may locate the beginnings of several themes in his work that equate women with whores and shame and betrayal and prison and other assorted traps.

In the years immediately following Faulkner's marriage, these concerns become extremely intense in the fiction. In *As I Lay Dying*, Faulkner's first novel after his marriage—and the novel he offered Hal Smith as security for the loan—Cash Bundren says of Jewel, when he thinks Jewel is having at it with a married woman, "A fellow kind of hates to see [a young boy] wallowing in somebody else's mire" (AILD 85). Soon after his marriage Faulkner wrote a series of short stories centered around very curious ménages à trois, several stories in which husbands allow, encourage, permit, or are powerless to prevent, their wives to be sexually serviced by other men. Of the twenty-five stories we know he sent out between January 23, 1930, and

March 16, 1931, at least a dozen explore this kind of relationship,[2] and it recurs again and again as a central motif in, for example, the relationship between Popeye and Red in *Sanctuary*; between Byron Bunch and Lucas Burch and between Gail Hightower and his wife's lovers in *Light in August*; between Roger Schuman and Jack Holmes in *Pylon*; between Rat Rittenmeyer and Harry Wilbourne and between the tall convict and the father of his lady's baby in *If I Forget Thee, Jerusalem*; and between Flem Snopes and Manfred de Spain in *The Town*.

In *The Hamlet*, Mink Snopes makes the homoerotic component of this triangulation very specific; as he makes love with his wife, the former "lord of the harem" in which he found her, he is constantly

> surrounded by the loud soundless invisible shades of the nameless and numberless men—that body which . . . was anterior even to the two-dollar marriage which had not sanctified but sanctioned them, which each time he approached it, it was not garments intervening but the cuckolding shades which had become a part of his past too, as if he and not she had been their prone recipient. (H 938).

In marrying such a woman, Mink feels he has been denied the one thing that every man holds sacred, the right to his own virgin. He approaches sex with his wife in terms that sound very like those of Faulkner's protagonist in "And Now What's To Do?": "he would contemplate [her used body] even from the cold starless night-periphery beyond both hatred and desire and tell himself: It's like drink. It's like dope to me" (H 938). Mink's feelings, with their complex combination of hetero- and homo-eroticism, may well be those of numerous men in Faulkner.

The extent to which these husbands reflect Faulkner's own state of mind during this time is, of course, highly problematical. But the external evidence of his life suggests plenty for him to be angry, nervous, and frustrated about. If he clearly was not enthusiastic about his marriage, doubtless neither was Estelle completely happy. She spent

---

2. See, for example, "Mistral," "Idyll in the Desert," "The Brooch," "Fox Hunt," "A Dangerous Man," "Honor," "Hair," "Divorce in Naples," "A Justice."

a good deal of their honeymoon drinking heavily and either tried at one point actually to commit suicide or made a dramatic gesture in that direction. After all, she had left a relatively affluent and glamorous life in Shanghai to marry a poor and unsuccessful novelist whose future could not have inspired much confidence. Doubtless she also sensed her new husband's lack of enthusiasm, and so felt no less trapped and desperate then he. Estelle's daughter Cho-Cho told Joseph Blotner years later that she thought that Estelle regretted marrying Faulkner and that she "believed that somehow Cornell would come back to her" (Blotner [1984] 245).[3] Estelle must have felt considerable tension between herself and her new mother-in-law, who apparently disapproved of her because she drank too much and thereby encouaraged Billy to do the same. Faulkner must have felt caught in the tension between his problematic new wife and a domineering mother who had, according to Phil Stone, tied her sons to her in such a way as to cause them to resent her; she was in part responsible, Stone thought, "for an animosity toward women" in Faulkner (Blotner [1984] 246). The birth and premature death of his and Estelle's baby daughter, Alabama, in January, 1931, must have seemed to the tragedian some sort of cosmic symbol of the destructive nature of his marriage.

In the works of this period, these elements and many related others from the external world of Faulkner's life in Oxford appear in an astonishing variety of combinations and permutations. Whether Faulkner's use of this material from his own life was conscious or unconscious is, of course, the question, to which I'd suggest a simple, even simplistic, answer: if it was not conscious use at first, over the course of the several novels and the dozen stories, he became very conscious indeed of how he, the quintessentially private person, had worked his own life into his fiction. This increasing awareness in its turn created its own problems that he, as usual, began to deal with in the fiction.

3. There is some evidence that Faulkner liked Estelle's first husband, Cornell, very much. According to Malcolm, he would drive the family, Estelle and Estelle's children, to Columbus for visits with Cornell.

Two stories he wrote in the first quarter of 1931 illustrate. He wrote "Artist at Home" before March 16, 1931. It is about Roger Howes, whose name is clearly a pun on "house." Howes is a writer who assists in the violation of the home of the story's title. He gets married and moves, like Sherwood Anderson, to rural Virginia on the proceeds from the sales of his first novel; there he writes another, less successful novel, and becomes more and more lethargic about his career, until he finally stops writing altogether. He and his wife are fairly cut off from other people except for a stream of New York bohemian/artist types who come, with or without invitations, to sponge off of them. His wife Anne resents their coming very much, but she becomes infatuated with a particularly obnoxious and fey young poet named John Blair, who is remarkably similar to a fey young poet named Faulkner in *Mosquitoes,* and to a similar young poet named David in Sherwood Anderson's "A Meeting South." Anne's and Blair's first embrace comes in the garden; they are both surprised when Roger suddenly emerges from behind a bush where he has been watching. But Roger is not at all upset, and we learn that he has both anticipated and even hoped for something of this sort to happen; he has, indeed, invited Blair to Virginia. During the next few days he finds ways to throw them together, encouraging their relationship.

As the affair develops, Roger begins to write again, starts to work on his long-delayed third novel. The lovers' trysts are punctuated by the sound of Roger's typewriter, a sound the narrator connects more than once with a "bull market" in typewriting. "And what was it he [was] writing?" the narrator asks: "Him, and Anne, and the poet. Word for word, between the waiting spells to find out what to write down next, with a few changes here and there, of course, because live people do not make good copy, the most interesting copy being gossip, since it mostly is not true" (CS 644). The story, then, turns on Roger's deliberate exploitation of his wife's infidelity and of his own part in the triangle. We do not know what Roger writes and we do not know what, if anything, he *feels* about Anne and John, whether he feels anything at all about his cuckolding, or whether it is difficult to control those feelings in order to channel them into his fiction. But clearly his creative juices respond directly to the erotic tension of his voyeurism, which is itself not always direct but triangulated through his writing. During this time, John Blair writes a poem, published in a non-paying small magazine, which Roger, but not Anne, likes. Roger sells his novel and with his royalties buys Anne a fur coat, which she rejects, refusing to accept financial benefit from her part in the triangle. She gives it to a neighbor woman, who has accidentally seen John swimming naked, and been properly horrified at her accidental vision of the spectacle.

Sedgwick, Tanner, Girard, and others who have written on this and related subjects, have a good deal of interest to say on the subject of cuckoldry. But they deal almost exclusively with writers before the twentieth century and so do not explore the modernist sensibility. For centuries, the cuckold was the clown, the object of ridicule, and was a culturally acceptable figure of fun because, as Tanner argues, cuckolding a clown, cuckoldry in general, no matter how rife, didn't threaten the institution of marriage. In the nineteenth century, fiction's interest in marriage takes a decided turn, and we may generally say that in large measure nineteenth century fiction's towering (even if reclining) and defining figures are its adulterous heroines: Anna Karenina, Emma Bovary, Hester Prynne, and Edna Pontellier. In the twentieth century, however, the defining figures of modernist fiction—at least in our current but rapidly changing sense of literary history—tend to be the men for whom all things sexual and personal are universally problematic: Prufrock's "overwhelming question." In the twentieth century the cuckold is neither a comic nor a tragic figure, but a pathetic one whose sexual sensibilities define his sense of self and his world view, a world view that he imposes on others as a "universal" view. This is true of both characters and authors: in nothing do William Faulkner and James Joyce resemble each other more particularly than in their relationships with their wives and in the significance of the figures of the cuckold and adulterous wives of their fiction.

At first glance the title, "Artist at Home," merely describes the creator in domestic surroundings; a second look invokes the Victorian

sense of "at home" as meaning "ready to receive." An even closer
look may suggest that the title in fact describes an active creator *of*
home, One Who Arranges Things or Creates Situations at Home
in Pleasurable or Profitable Patterns. Whichever meaning Faulkner
intended, perhaps all three, the title and what we know of the external
circumstances of Faulkner's life invite us to believe that at least at one
level the story springs from a conscious recognition of the ways in
which he had been exploiting his own psychic life in his fiction. If we
may legitimately make such inferences from the story, we may make
ourselves privy to some form of confession that Faulkner, at least in
the early years of his marriage, felt himself, as artist, to be at best a
voyeur, perhaps at worst a pimp. It is very easy, perhaps *too* easy, to
invoke *Sanctuary*'s Popeye, and to remember the several ways in
which Faulkner, both more and less humorously, identified himself
with this most vicious and impotent and voyeuristic of all his characters.

Another story of this early period is also worth our attention. Faulkner apparently wrote a version of "The Brooch" in January of 1930,
under the title "Fire and Clock," which is now lost. He had revised
it by January 29, 1931 as "The Brooch," but did not sell it until he
revised it again and expanded it five years later. This story concerns
Harry Boyd, a wimpish sort of Mama's boy all his life—Fauntleroy
suits and all, as a fatherless and sissified child—Harry Boyd (whose
name puns on the "airy void" that is his life), his gray-haired invalid
mother who dominates him and his wife Amy, whom his mother does
not like because she hears reports of Amy's behavior and reputation
from her friends. The similarities between this triangle and the
Faulkner-mother-new bride triangle I described a moment ago seems
so clear as not to need elaborate comment.

To get to their room Harry and Amy must pass his mother's bedroom at the bottom of the stairs, from which vantage she monitors
ingress and egress and keeps tabs on everything that goes on in the
house. There is constant tension among all three of them, especially
between Harry and Amy. Amy wants Harry to leave the house so they
can start their own life, but he refuses to leave his mother: "She'll be

dead soon," he argues, paraphrasing yet another problematic mother in Faulkner. For a while they go out together at night. After the death of their 9-month old baby, however, Harry loses all interest, all volition, and begins to encourage Amy to go out by herself. He soon becomes aware that she is not just dancing at the Country Club, but having sexual liaisons with other men, and he not only allows this to happen, but actively cooperates in it by escorting Amy loudly down the stairs past his mother's bedroom as if they are both going out, then sneaking quietly back upstairs until time for Amy to return, at which time he reverses the process, helping his unfaithful wife to deceive not himself but his mother. This impossible state of affairs ends when a complication regarding Amy's carelessness with the brooch Mrs. Boyd had given her exposes the charade to Mrs. Boyd. The story ends somewhat limply when Amy crumples to the floor in despair: "My little baby," she says. "My dear little baby," while Harry prods "clumsily" at the fire with a sadly phallic poker (WFMS 24:266).

The emphasis in the first known version of this story is on the debilitating effects of the baby's death on their marriage, as if that death were indeed, for Amy at least, the final straw. Faulkner's and Estelle's own baby daughter, Alabama, died at the age of 9 days, not 9 months, on January 20. He sent out the revised version by January 29, so it is almost impossible not to think of this story as one he wrote or rewrote in the wake of Alabama's death, as a sort of *cri de coeur* arising from the total picture of his own complicated physical and psychic circumstances, but it seems to be primarily a specific response to his heartbreak over the loss of Alabama. We can only imagine what Alabama's death meant to him or to Estelle or to his fiction, but knowing what we know we can hardly help but wince when we read in *The Hamlet* that as Flem Snopes and his brand new wife, Eula, who is pregnant by another man, leave Frenchman's Bend for their honeymoon, Flem holds their "straw suitcase on his knees like the coffin of a baby's funeral" (H 865). In *The Hamlet* Faulkner associates the dead baby with Flem Snopes, another cuckolded husband who has shared, and will share, his wife with another man, who will raise yet another man's child, and who will deliberately profit from his wife's infidelity. This is hardly an image Faulkner could have used without knowing exactly where it came from, since he himself carried Alabama's coffin on his knees to the cemetery (Blotner [1984] 274); whether he made a conscious association between Flem and himself in this regard, we cannot know, but Flem, like Roger Howes in "Artist at Home"—and perhaps like Faulkner too—also exploits his own cuckolding to economic and social advantage.

Faulkner revised "The Brooch" again in the late fall of 1935, during a break from his work on *Absalom, Absalom!*. The revised story is over twice as long. He left the narrative elements of the first part of the story mostly alone, although he developed parts of it at more length. But in the revision he de-emphasizes Amy and the baby, though retaining the early version's closing scene, and focuses on Harry, in this version named Howard. The revised story ends as Howard allows Amy to leave home for good. He turns to reading W. H. Hudson's *Green Mansions*, and understands, finally, that in marrying Amy in the first place he was searching for an ideal woman, *who does not exist.* This epiphany causes him to commit a very symbolical suicide; he takes a pistol and the "down coverlet" from his wife's bed to his bathroom, which is also very symbolically "detached from the house proper," the symbol of his mother, "and the whole depth [of the house] from his mother's room." He stuffs the edge of his wife's coverlet under the door to muffle the sound, wraps himself like a baby in the rest of the coverlet, puts the gun barrel in his mouth as he would a mother's nipple, and pulls the trigger (CS 664–65).

Any critic must see how urgently the revised version of this story insists upon a Freudian reading, but I do not know what we can infer from such evidence about Faulkner's inner life, if anything at all. I don't know whether Howard's suicide, any more than Quentin Compson's, might be Faulkner's conscious or unconscious death wish, whether it was a conscious literary borrowing from Freud, or whether we can learn anything at all from any of the stories and novels about Faulkner's relationship with women. Yet as I've noted, the cuckold is as persistent a character or character type in Faulkner's fiction as the Woman as Whore, and I'm forced to wonder about the next twenty years of Faulkner's life, which found him increasingly miserable at home, and looking for solace and comfort in the arms of various other younger, more beautiful women, whom he romanticized and whom he *would not marry*, although promising at least one that he would marry her if not for his daughter Jill (Wilde). It may be too easy to think of all the women in Faulkner's life not as the objects of his desire, but rather as revolving and replaceable avatars of *Green Mansion*'s Rima, the ideal woman, who does not exist (Hult).

Estelle must have been as miserable and insecure as Faulkner, and for many of the same reasons. *Requiem for a Nun* in 1951 provides some evidence of Faulkner's growing understanding of the situation his sensibilities about women had largely created. In *Requiem*, Faulkner seems finally to recognize the inherent unfairness in any man's holding any woman culpable for her sexual life before marriage. Up to *Requiem*, Faulkner's concern had been almost exclusively with the cuckold's attempts to deal with a wife who had betrayed him with another man—"betrayed" would be the man's term for her past, not hers. In *Requiem*, Faulkner literally dramatizes the internal dynamic of a marriage that has cuckoldry at its center: Temple Drake, resurrected from *Sanctuary*, is forced to admit her culpability to her husband, Gowan Stevens. But Faulkner raises the stakes here considerably. By allowing County Attorney Gavin Stevens, Gowan's uncle, to conduct the interrogation, which is really an elaborate accusation, Faulkner makes it clear that it is not just her husband's claim on her sexual history that is at stake, but the culture's too.

Requiem for a Nun runs in two directions. It is precisely about Temple's attempt to rescue herself from her husband Gowan, who, under the guise of forgiving her for her past in the whorehouse, manages to keep her always reminded of and so ashamed of that past; he expects large measures of gratitude from her for his generosity in forgiving her—a forgiveness which in fact he never quite manages. Second, *Requiem* is about the culture's concerted efforts to bring her to judgment for her sexual history. The culture is personified in the ruthless figure of Gavin Stevens, who is not just a surrogate for Gowan but for the culture itself. Indeed, Stevens drags her to the Mississippi

Governor's office for her confession, and in the name of the patriarchy that that office symbolizes, does not merely insist that Temple repent for *having* a sexual history, but demands that she accept and recite its version of her sexual history, admit that her sexual history is directly responsible for the death of her baby, and use its language in doing so—"loved it" indeed (Wondra). The patriarchy inscribes her history on her very life no less deliberately than the punishers in Kafka's Penal Colony inscribe sins on the bodies of the guilty and condemned.

No one seriously tries to hold Gowan responsible for their baby's murder, although he created the situation which put her in Popeye's, and therefore Pete's, grasp. In *Sanctuary* Gowan Stevens abandons Temple at the Old Frenchman place, leaving her to her own devices to deal with Popeye and the Memphis underworld; Popeye rapes her with a corncob at the Old Frenchman place, then takes her to Miss Reba's. Temple's *Requiem for a Nun* version of her time at Miss Reba's is that her tenure there was relatively chaste—it "was worse than being the wealthy ward of the most indulgent trust or insurance company: carried to Memphis and shut up in that Manuel Street sporting house like a ten-year-old bride in a Spanish convent, with the madam herself more eagle-eyed than any mama" (568)—until she fell in love with Red, the cuckolding lover Popeye brought in to make love to Temple while he watched.

Gowan's version of Temple's past, even though he was not there, is that she spent time in a Memphis whorehouse and, being a woman, of course, reverted to woman's natural whorishness and "loved it." He assumes that she became one of the girls, even though she engaged in sex with nobody but Red; there is some evidence that she was in love with Red, and plenty more that she had very little choice in the matter. Nevertheless, after Temple's rescue and the trial, Gowan marries her, out of his own sense of guilt over having abandoned her, and out of some sense of honor. Gowan's Uncle Gavin analyses the husband this way:

And when I say 'past,' I mean that part of it which the husband knows. . . . Because it was not long before she discovered, realised, that she was going to spend a good part of the rest of her days (nights too) being forgiven for it; in being not only constantly reminded . . . but say made—kept—aware of it in order to be forgiven for it so that she might be grateful to the forgiver, but in having to employ more and more of what tact she had . . . to make the gratitude . . . acceptable to meet with, match, the high standards of the forgiver. But she was not too concerned. Her husband . . . had made what he probably considered the supreme sacrifice to expiate his part in her past; she had no doubts of her capacity to continue to supply whatever increasing degree of gratitude the increasing appetite—or capacity—of its addict would demand, in return for the sacrifice which, so she believed, she had accepted for the same reason of gratitude. (581–82)

Temple had earlier described their marriage as a plan for redemption gone awry:

And then maybe there would be the love this time—the peace, the quiet, the no shame . . . Love, but more than love too: not depending on just love to hold two people together, make them better than either one would have been alone, but tragedy, suffering, having suffered and caused grief; having something to have to live with even when, because, you knew both of you could never forget it. And then I began to believe something even more than that: that there was something even better, stronger, than tragedy to hold two people together: forgiveness. Only, that seemed to be wrong. Only maybe it wasn't the forgiveness that was wrong, but the gratitude; and maybe the only thing worse than having to give gratitude constantly all the time, is having to accept it— (577)

Precisely, I think.

In *Sanctuary* Temple is a victim, of a variety of forces, including her own youth and inexperience, but she *is* a victim. By the time of *Requiem* she is an eight-year-married woman with two children who has spent a long time trying to live down a past that her husband and her culture have conspired to make her feel responsible for, guilty for, ashamed of, and in need of forgiveness for. But Gavin Stevens, patriarchy's advocate and chief prosecutor, is mired in Temple's sexual past, moves through it deliciously, voyeuristically concerned with Temple's sexual pathologies. It is the burden of the *present*, not that of the past, that forces Temple to try to escape from her marriage, which attempt in turn precipitates the central crisis of the novel, the murder of one of her children by their black servant.

Faulkner's sympathy for Temple is unmistakable, and the novel's ending, with her return to Gowan, is unambiguously bleak in offering her the rest of her life with a husband who has not learned anything, who is still mired in selfpity and in loathing of her sexual past, and who will doubtless add her more recent sins to the list of things he has to be honorable about and that she will have to be grateful for being forgiven for. But Faulkner perhaps had learned something, by looking at the problem from the woman's point of view, and in fact his final novel, *The Reivers*, may represent a resolution of many of his own problems about such matters. In *The Reivers*, Faulkner returns yet again to Miss Reba's whorehouse, looks at that world through eyeglasses deliberately rose-colored, and sees the same *Sanctuary*'s unstable world of whores, of voyeurists, of sexual shame and of impending violence, but denuded here of the shame and the terror, the nightmare, that was the essence of *Sanctuary*'s vision. In *The Reivers* Boon Hogganbeck extracts Everbe Corinthia from her employment at Miss Reba's in order to marry her. He goes to her in the whorehouse, accepts her for what she is, and marries her for what she is going to be: there is no recrimination for her past, no troublesome ghosts of that legion of other men. Forgiveness for her past is not an issue between them (though to be sure Boon is furious with Corrie when he learns that she has reverted to her old profession in order to get him and Lucius out of jail). The baby they have at the end of the novel indicates that they will not build their future upon the unsteady vacillation of forgiveness and gratitude, but rather upon a solid base of love, mutual respect, and mutual acceptance of each other's past, present, and future.

♂ ♀

The early Faulkner is the Artist as Cuckold, disguising his various sexual neuroses and frustrations and fears and resentments of women as intensely tragic fiction. By the last decade of his life he is the Artist at Home, older, cooler, more thoughtful; his later work grows out of a more reflective sense of humor about the neuroses that had so antagonized his youth. The last three novels offer a softening of his intensity about women, a mellowing of his sense of sexuality as something shameful, a considerable abatement of his sense of women and of domesticity as middle-class traps, and a larger, more generous sense of women as complete human beings, as something other than genital: as something more than spittoon for men who only want to chew.

Eula Varner Snopes, her daughter Linda, and Maggie Mallison, in *The Town* and *The Mansion*, are three completely different, but equally magnificent women. In *The Town*, Faulkner's most domestic novel, Eula Varner Snopes lives almost completely outside the respectable. She is an adulteress, one who has, like Estelle, brought into their marriage a child which is not her husband's. She has continued the cuckolding, more or less publicly, through her affair with her husband's employer for eighteen years, a length of time which indicates that the relationship has more than just sex going for it: compared to this infidelity, Temple Drake's liaison with Red at Miss Reba's is little more than a one-night stand. If we believe Chick Mallison, everybody in the town knows of Eula's adultery. Eula knows that the town has conspired to support the sham in the name of respectability. She who is so completely out of the range of the ordinary lives a lie for eighteen years, staying with an impotent husband in an unsatisfying sterile marriage, then commits suicide suddenly when her illicit relation threatens to become in fact public.

The town itself, the community of men and women too, is the cuckold in *The Town*, the desiring subject, and Major de Spain the mediator. In its collective imagination Jefferson invests Eula with its own fantasies to titillate its respectably repressed libido. She is at once the wife of a banker and a deacon; at the same time, with their voyeuristic cooperation, she violates the most sacred of their mores. The town *creates* her; then, through its mouthy representative, Gavin Stevens, it exploits her, even in her death, by erecting a marble monument over her grave. In idealizing her in her death, the community makes her the mediator in a triangle in which the object of desire is respectability—wholeness bought with a lie. After following her sexual exploits over the years, at her death the town remakes her into a monument to its virtue, forgiving her, and themselves, for their sexual shame: they have revelled in the titillation she has brought them, but refuse at last to let her be what she was. Stevens and Ratliff conclude that she committed suicide because she was bored. Perhaps they are right. As Dawn Trouard puts it,

> Eula arrives where she has always been heading. By the time of *The Town*, Faulkner's sympathies and understanding of what male-female relationships have done to women allow him to get the image right, and in putting a marble nymph in the Jefferson cemetery, he may be offering us his profoundest and most moving rendering of what it must be like to be a sexual female in such as Yoknapatawpha. The marble faun of 1924 looks out over a fructive garden whose vital life he cannot participate in; the marble nymph—perhaps a more tragically apt symbol of the twentieth century's wasteland than a marble male faun—looks out over a dead dead world of men, and women too, who cannot either accept what she has to offer, sexual or otherwise, or reconcile themselves to their failure of her, and so must force her to join them in the cemetery. ("Eula's Plot" 294–95)

Eula, like Temple Drake, was in an impossible situation. I rather suspect that Faulkner learned something in writing *The Town* about the bind that he and all masculine others have put all women in. It may have been in some ways liberating for him, for as Hee Kang has convincingly demonstrated, in *The Mansion* he constructs a "radically creative and unprecedentedly modern feminine" in the figure of Linda Snopes Kohl, Eula's daughter:

> Refusing to surrender herself as a victim of the patriarchy, Linda, in her deaf voice, defiantly breaks the "vault of silence," conceives her own seductive yet threatening feminine desire by interrogating men's logic, and finally undoes and subverts the patriarchal authority, law, and language. . . . In *The Mansion* Faulkner, through Linda, changes the landscape of woman's space in his fictional world, tracing a trajec-

tory from the space of victimization, betrayal, and death to a newly
configured feminine space of desire, autonomy, and freedom. (Kang
21–22)

From this point of view, perhaps it is possible to see *The Reivers*, its
rose-colored overview of his misogynist world, as a deliberate reins-
cription of the scene of the primal crime in his work, in which Faulkner quietly elides from it the sexual shame and the sexual terror, the
fear and loathing of women that mar so many of his characters. Thus
The Reivers may be a kind of implicit message to his grandchildren, to
whom the novel is dedicated, and to us, that there are enough things
in this world to loath and be fearful of without seeking them out in
the unoffending spaces of our wives', mothers', and sisters' sexual
lives and sexual histories.

I do not mean to argue a "happy ending" for Faulkner the artist or
Faulkner the citizen. Nor do I absolve him of the misery he, as artist,
as cuckold, created in his own home. I doubt very seriously that as a
result of writing *The Town* or *The Mansion* or *The Reivers* he altered
very many of his social presumptions about male-female relations.
And yet it seems to me demonstrable that at least part of his political
engagement with racial problems during the fifties was a direct response to the racial morality of, say, *Go Down, Moses* and *Intruder in
the Dust*. I believe it would be very difficult to write such novels and
not learn *something* from the process of confronting the narrative materials of those books. Whether his aging, his mellowing, his renewed
fictional understanding of gender problematics would ever have
prompted him to a similar social and political engagement is of course
impossible to say. But the change in his fictional treatments of gender
problems from his earliest books to his latest is undeniable.

In his late career, Faulkner seems to understand that men cannot
claim their own histories until women can claim theirs, too, and tell it
themselves, if they choose, in their own voices, in their own language,
without yielding to the cultural narrative that binds us all to a singular
narrative that is so frequently reducible to sexual pathology. Like

Faulkner's, and like Jefferson's, a good deal of the specific energy of our own cultural narratives is based in our voyeuristic fascination with the supreme primal cracked foul oozing unscratchable chaste and utterly insatiable uterus. Faulkner knew this, I think. He knew more about desire than René Girard and Eve Sedgwick, and more about adultery than Tony Tanner and Emma Bovary. He knew that for male communities to place women on the pedestals of their desire is to be cuckolded by death—whom we, like Quentin, prefer above all else.

Ratliff's Buggies

The Hamlet begins with a blurring of geographical, temporal, and political boundaries. Though Frenchman's Bend lies "twenty miles southeast of Jefferson," it is "Hill-cradled and remote, definite yet without boundaries, straddling into two counties and owning allegiance to neither"; the old Frenchman's mansion is still known as the Old Frenchman place, but "the original boundaries now existed only on old faded records in the Chancery Clerk's office in the county court house in Jefferson, and even some of the once-fertile fields had long since reverted to the cane-and-cypress jungle from which their first master had hewed them." But this "master" was only master for a time, and those who came after him have "almost obliterated all trace of his sojourn" (731). Even the old Frenchman's name has been forgotten; it now has "nothing to do with any once-living man at all"; his legend is "but the stubborn tale of the money he buried somewhere" (732).

Presiding, omnipotent, over this cosmos is Will Varner,

the chief man of the country. He was the largest landholder and beat supervisor in one county and Justice of the Peace in the next and election commissioner in both, and hence the fountainhead if not of law at least of advice and suggestion to a countryside which would have repudiated the term constituency if they had ever heard it. . . . He was a farmer, a usurer, a veterinarian; Judge Benbow of Jefferson once said of him that a milder mannered man never bled a mule or stuffed a ballot box. He owned most of the good land in the country and held mortgages on most of the rest. He owned the store and the cotton gin and the combined grist mill and blacksmith shop in the village proper and it was considered, to put it mildly, bad luck for a man of the neighborhood to do his trading or gin his cotton or grind his meal or shoe his stock anywhere else. He was thin as a fence rail and almost as long, with reddish-gray hair and moustaches and little hard bright innocently blue eyes; he looked like a Methodist Sunday School superintendent who on week days conducted a railroad passenger train or vice versa and who owned the church or perhaps the railroad or perhaps both. He was shrewd secret and merry, of a Rabelaisian turn of mind and very probably still sexually lusty . . . . (733)

Will Varner doesn't have to worry about boundaries: boundaries have to worry about him. Like the 800-pound gorilla, he can sit anywhere he wants to. If he read Schopenhauer he might well subscribe to the philosophy that The World is Will's, and Ideal. He has appropriated, by hook or by crook obtained, all of the accoutrements of Frenchman's Bend's political, legal, economic, religious, and social power. In controlling *everything* in Frenchman's Bend so completely, he is as much a parody of white male power in Western culture as his daughter, Eula, is a parody of the Western idealization of female sexuality.

More specifically, Eula is a parody of the male imaginary's idealization of all things female. Like her father, she, too, refuses boundaries (Trouard, "Eula's Plot"). But whereas he owns them, she simply disregards them, as having nothing to do with her. Nothing can contain her, not the perambulator that Will has made for her when she is a baby, not the undergarments Jody insists that she wear, not the dresses that should cover her long dangling legs when she rides behind Jody on the horse; she constantly spills over and out of whatever restrictions her brother and her father try to force upon her. But Will's disregard of boundaries for himself merely puts them more firmly in place for others. By his will he makes of himself the central and singular head of the local hierchate—patriarch, totem, and locus.

Where all things move toward a center there is no need for outward boundary. Eula is a threat in Frenchman's Bend precisely because she is so completely indifferent to the patriarchal order that her father represents. At Labove's school, she is

neither at the head nor at the foot of her class, not because she declined to study on the one hand and not because she was Varner's daughter

on the other and Varner ran the school, but because the class she was
in ceased to have either head or foot twenty-four hours after she entered it. Within the year there even ceased to be any lower class for her
to be promoted from, for the reason that she would never be at either
end of anything in which blood ran. It would have but one point, like a
swarm of bees, and she would be that point, that center, swarmed over
and importuned yet serene and intact and apparently even oblivious,
tranquilly abrogating the whole long sum of human thinking and suffering which is called knowledge, education, wisdom, at once supremely unchaste and inviolable: the queen, the matrix. (836–37)

Eula's challenge to Will's centrality, then, lies not at all in ambition,
but rather in the complete indifference to masculine hierarchy and
tradition that her manifest femaleness represents, even in its passivity.
Eula creates problems for all the males in Frenchman's Bend (except
one, Flem Snopes, because he makes of her not a problem but an
opportunity). On the one hand, she is supremely desirable; on the
other, as we shall see, she is all that the men of Frenchman's Bend
want to escape. In that simultaneous attraction and repulsion lies the
specific energy of a great deal of *The Hamlet*'s actions and themes.

In appropriating the Old Frenchman place, Will possesses the classic Western tradition of male privilege and power. Not that he understands that tradition, of course. Though he kinglily sits in the flour-
barrel throne (734), he does not have the imagination to conjure any
sense of the Old Frenchman's "magnificence" (731); his primary response to the building is a puzzled sense of wonderment at "what it
must have felt like to be the fool that would need all this . . . just to
eat and sleep in" (734). The practical non-idealistic Will is exactly
right to believe that the Old Frenchman place contains more room
than anybody should *need*, but he completely misses the point of such
a structure because he's thinking like the proletarian he believes himself to be and not like the bourgeois that he actually is. Thus he does
not at all understand the tradition of male kingship and power. But it
isn't necessary to understand the tradition of power and privilege in
order to inherit it or to exercise it or to cash in on it, and if anybody
wanted to argue that one of the redeeming features of that tradition

was the extent of the magnificence it created—the castles, the cathedrals, the mansions—it would follow that Will Varner, in trading the Old Frenchman place for his daughter's and his own good name, has debased that tradition even more completely than have the Frenchman's Bend's folk who have been pulling it apart for years, using its lumber for firewood. But we cannot overlook the fact that the tradition's magnificence was based upon the ruthless exploitation of a laboring underclass, so that in eventually using the Old Frenchman place to purchase respectability for his family Varner is not debasing the Old Frenchman place at all but rather in fact restoring that magnificence to its original debased use: the flashy exterior, the magnificence, was but the glamourous façade to hide a corrupt and corrupting system of white and male power and privilege.

The Old Frenchman place, then, aptly symbolizes the tradition Will has inherited and is so querulously trying to understand. It is a multi-layered and complex symbol that each major male character in *The Hamlet*—Varner, Flem Snopes, and V.K. Ratliff—appropriates to his own meanings. For Will Varner, it is a puzzle of dimensions. For Flem, it is a means to an end. For Ratliff it is more complicated because for him, more complex and thoughtful, the Old Frenchman place's various meanings become fused with his more problematic responses to Eula Varner and to all things feminine. Though Eula becomes directly involved with Flem's and Will's determination of the Old Frenchman place's value, for Ratliff, Eula and the Old Frenchman place become symbols of the price of domesticity, the cost of heterosexuality.

House and domesticity, woman and economics, then, are inextricably linked in the symbolic structure of *The Hamlet*. Will Varner and the Old Frenchman place stand together at the center of the boundaryless economic and political unit called Frenchman's Bend, rooted and permanent. Ratliff is a roving vicar of Varner's economic tradition if not specifically of his empire. Moreover, though Ratliff insists upon mobility above all—he is constantly seen riding or sitting in his buckboard—he carries with him on his buckboard a reducto absurdum of the Old Frenchman place and its many significations. By that symbol,

Ratliff metaphorically tethers himself to Varner's economic center and he in effect moves Frenchman's Bend's very elastic boundaries with him wherever he goes.

Ratliff is a sewing machine salesman, and he keeps a demonstrator model in the bed of his buckboard in a "dog-kennel . . . painted to resemble a house, in each painted window of which a painted woman's face simpered above a painted sewing-machine" (740). Ratliff's kennel-house, then, is an iconic crystallization of the economic and cultural traditions the Old Frenchman place represents; it is thus an apt and complex symbol of the economic relations between men on the one hand, and between men and women on the other—of the system's entrapment of women in the domestic: the painted simpering woman in the window of Ratliff's kennel-house makes one with the dozens of other women in Faulkner iconically framed in windows of the houses in which they are trapped (Polk, "Children of the Dark House"). Even the most dazzling mansion is little more than a social and economic prison for women, who both propel and are pulled along by the male economic vehicle. Indeed, powerful men might answer Will's question quite simply: we need all this room to keep it from looking like the prison it is. But it is also a prison for those men who don't own such a mansion but who feel compelled to desire the symbol of masculine power that owning it would invest them with, as though the symbol would bring with it the actual power.

For all of Eula Varner's overwhelming female presence, *The Hamlet* is pre-eminently a novel about relations among men: her alienage from both male and female in Frenchman's Bend and her value as a commodity in the male exchange system set the men's separation from the feminine into severe, if sometimes pathetic, sometimes tragic, sometimes comic, relief. It also confirms them in their relations with each other. Even those men who putatively compete for Eula's "hand" compete not at all for sexual pleasure or even for sexual conquest but rather for the sign of conquest, the reputation, the affirmation among their peers of sexual conquest, that "having"—owning—Eula or any other woman would produce. They calibrate their own worth in terms of how much of what they have other men want, and what other men will trade or do in order to get it. Even Labove eagerly awaits the beating, the killing, he assumes Jody will give him as a public sign of the conquest that he has not made. Each of the young men who leaves Frenchman's Bend after Eula turns up pregnant is running mostly in the hope that everybody will think that he is the guilty party.

Men who run from the feminine usually run to each other, and in Frenchman's Bend they congregate on the front porch of Varner's store, talking and ogling and staying away from home, where their wives are privately doing the sort of backbreaking work that Mrs. Littlejohn does so publicly. The men's constant relationships with each other become sublimated into various forms of competition — horsetrading, for example — that galvanize them together into a community that does not, cannot, admit women: Eula — woman — is, in Ratliff's terms, an "unscalable sierra, the rosy virginal mother of barricades for no man to conquer scot-free or even to conquer at all, but on the contrary to be hurled back and down, leaving no scar, no mark of himself" (877). *The Hamlet*, then, defines masculinity in terms of its opposition to and, finally, its fear of the feminine.

Specifically, *The Hamlet* defines masculinity as a retreat from the maternal, from that "rosy virginal mother of barricades," from the "supreme primal uterus" (835). Frenchman's Bend's retreat from the feminine may best be understood in the terms that Nancy Chodorow has used to describe the phenomenon in *The Reproduction of Mothering*. Indeed, as Ilsa Lind was among the first to note (32–39), Chodorow's discussion throws a good deal of light on the general problematics of mothers (Polk, "Children") and on the sources of gender problems in Faulkner. Chodorow traces many of the socialized gender differences to children's differing relations with their parents. In traditional family structures, the father is almost always nominally absent, so the mother becomes the familiar against which children's egos must function in order to define themselves.

> Because all children identify first with their mother, a girl's gender and gender role identification processes are continuous with her earli-

est identifications and a boy's are not. A girl's oedipal identification with her mother, for instance, is continuous with her earliest primary identification (and also in the context of her early dependence and attachment). The boy's oedipal crisis, however, is supposed to enable him to shift in favor of an identification with his father. He gives up, in addition to his oedipal and preoedipal attachment to his mother, his primary identification with her.

What is true specifically for oedipal identification is equally true for more general gender identification and gender role learning. A boy, in order to feel himself adequately masculine, must distinguish and differentiate himself from others in a way that a girl need not—must categorize himself as someone apart. Moreover, he defines masculinity negatively as that which is not feminine and/or connected to women, rather than positively. This is another way boys come to deny and repress relation and connection in the process of growing up. (174)

Because the father is nominally absent, or minimally present, masculinity is presented to boys as less available and therefore more desirable. Because it is more desirable, the culture idealizes the masculine; a boy therefore perforce "represses those qualities he takes to be feminine inside himself"—those qualities of connectedness— "and rejects and devalues women and whatever he considers to be feminine in the social world" (181). Yet Western culture, like that of Yoknapatawpha County, assumes heterosexual domesticity, or at least its trappings, as its core value so that males must define masculinity in terms other than the domestic. According to Chodorow,

> it becomes important for masculine identity that certain social activities are defined as masculine and superior, and that women are believed unable to do many of the things defined as socially important. It becomes important to think that women's economic and social contributions cannot equal men's. The secure possession of certain realms, and the insistence that these realms are superior to the maternal world of youth, become crucial both to the definition of masculinity and to a particular boy's own masculine gender identification. (182)

These external, non-domestic, "realms" become the sites of what Eve Kosofsky Sedgwick calls the "homosocial," where protective

bonding takes place and where relations between men, though putatively based in some form of competition, are structured to allow men
both to dominate and to escape the domestic:

> The phrase "A man's home is his castle" offers a nicely condensed
> example of ideological construction [of the necessary relations between
> men and domesticity]. It reaches *back* to an emptied-out image of mas-
> tery and integration under feudalism in order to propel the male wage-
> earner *forward* to further feats of alienated labor, in the service of a now
> atomized and embattled, but all the more intensively idealized home.
> The man who has this home is a different person from the lord who
> has a castle; and the forms of property implied in the two possessives
> (his [mortgaged] home/his [inherited] castle) are not only different, but
> . . . mutually contradictory. The contradiction is assuaged and filled in
> by transferring the lord's political and economic control over the *envi-
> rons* of his castle to an image of the father's personal control over the
> *inmates* of his house. (473)

Men's deepest needs for self- and gender-identity lead them away
from the feminine and toward each other, into the homosocial and,
one might assume, easily into the overtly homosexual. But since the
culture actively demands heterosexuality, it necessarily produces in
homosocial men an intense and relentless homophobia (Sedgwick)
that is at least as strong as the fear of the feminine. Thus men who
cannot find comfort or ease in either homosexual or heterosexual
worlds revert to the sexually neutered (but not neutral) world of the
homosocial, from which vantage they can both escape and control
the women, the domestic, that threaten them, and where they find
acceptable, non-threatening community in the company of other men.
Women who encroach or even seem to encroach upon any of these
"masculine" realms create anxiety in the men precisely because their
attractiveness threatens their sense of self. At the same time that boys
are developing a "dread" of the mother, they nevertheless still find
her seductive and attractive, so that even the eventual substitution of
a heterosexual partner for the mother does little to resolve the tense
ambiguities, the complications, of a heterosexual life. There is no
more chilling demonstration of the homosocial at work in French-

man's Bend than the scene on the front porch of Varner's store when Mrs. Armstid comes to try to get back from Flem the money, her money, that Henry has in effect stolen from her in order to buy one of the spotted ponies at the auction. The men of Frenchman's Bend, including Ratliff, witness her humiliation. As she walks away, the small bag of candy clutched in her hand, the Snopes clerk exclaims: "By God . . . you cant beat him" (1028). We do not, of course, know what the other men think or how they react to what they have just witnessed, but they are solid in their conspiracy to watch her humiliation in silence.

Not every bear-hug or pat on the butt on the football field or in the locker room, perhaps not even many of them, is an overtly homosexual act, but each one is a publicly acceptable affirmation of gender solidarity and identity between the patter and the pattee and the surround of men who cheer them on in approval. The culture will not approve the next step, into homosexuality, but clearly that step is a logical extension of the range of possibilities that the homosocial allows and even encourages, but does not permit.

ii.

Chodorow and Sedgwick could have asked for no better illustration of their arguments than *The Hamlet*. V. K. Ratliff, Faulkner's ubiquitous, loquacious, genial alter-ego, is the most complex vehicle for understanding the homosocial in Frenchman's Bend. Ratliff's complex meditations on Eula and on domesticity, along with his attempts to connive the Old Frenchman place away from Flem, are the novel's central articulations of the problematics, for men, of heterosexuality and domesticity. In the remainder of this essay I want to follow Ratliff's meditations on the furor that is Eula, and to do so in a sort of free association that will in effect follow his own associative train of thought. For, as I say, Ratliff is in all ways tethered to the Old Frenchman place and to the cultural economy. His meditations, his running commentary on the developing saga of Flem and Eula, which he can interpret out of his own core experience of domesticity, provides us with the novel's, and Faulkner's, most profound analysis of the complexities of American gender structures. Though he owns a house in Jefferson, Ratliff is utterly mobile, economically bound to his buckboard. But his load, his baggage—that simpering face in the window of the dog kennel on the back of his buckboard—is what interests us.

To look at Ratliff thus, however, will require us to challenge outright our traditional critical sense of him as the "hero" of *The Hamlet*, as the premier opponent of Snopesism; as simultaneously *at*-tached and *de*-tached observer and commentator; as shrewd gamester and tradesman; as genial homespun humorist and philosopher; and as the fairly stable moral center of Frenchman's Bend and environs. In many ways he is all of these things. Yet he is much more than even the sum of all these things, and something less too. He is, at any rate, something richer and more complicated than a mere straightforward, if fallible, hero in the struggle against Snopesism.

Ratliff ought to have made us more uncomfortable than he has when we generalize about the novel's themes. If we condemn the materialistic Snopeses, as earliest critics did, for leaving the land to become merchants, we must ignore or explain away Ratliff's background, almost identical to Flem's, and his own defection from the plow to the sewing machine business. If we want to make Ratliff the hero of a novel which bemoans the failure of masculinity in Frenchman's Bend (Broughton), we must likewise ignore or explain away certain of Ratliff's essential characteristics—his occupation as sewing machine salesman, his preoccupation with gossip, his sewing of his own shirts, his perennial bachelorhood, and others that we shall momentarily explore—that associate him more nearly with the women of Frenchman's Bend than with any definition of masculinity the men of *The Hamlet* might accept. For all of Ratliff's contrapositions to Flem—his garrulity, his neighborliness, his easy membership in and access to the community, his general humanity, his manifest humanness—we in fact know very little more about him than we do about Flem, and there are ways in which he is as big an enigma as his archrival. But that, in a Faulkner novel, should not be so surprising.

Faulkner repeatedly describes Ratliff as "absolutely pleasant, easy, inscrutable" (816), as "faint, quizzical, quiet" (811), as "pleasant and quizzical" (803); as speaking in a "tone of absolutely creamlike innocence" (742), and as having a "shrewd" face "bland and smooth . . . beneath the shrewd impenetrable eyes" (742). His "blandness and inscrutability" might merely be that of a seasoned trader or poker player, but Faulkner insists upon these characteristics so frequently that we might well suspect that they are at least partly a façade, a deliberate construct behind which Ratliff for the most part successfully hides some anxieties, some emotional baggage.

Book II of *The Hamlet*, "Eula," is framed by the events of Books I and III. Book I chronicles the time from Flem's entrance into the community as a pauper to his accession to Will Varner's throne at the Old Frenchman place, as virtual prince of the surrounding countryside. He is in more ways than one Will's heir apparent. His rise is marked by changes in his mode of transportation. Flem first walks to Varner's store to work, then rides a mule. Before long he has taken Jody's place not only in the store but also on his roan horse and at Will's side as they make their daily rounds over Will's demesne. Very soon, too soon, Flem moves into the Varner house, where he watches Eula's courtship by the neighborhood boys; a month later Will buys a "new runabout buggy with bright red wheels and a fringed parasol top" (814), to which are harnessed Will's white horse and Jody's roan, which Will and Flem, sitting "side by side in outrageous paradox" (814), drive their rounds in. Months later Flem gives this runabout to Buck Hipps, after the horse auction, for Buck to get back to Texas in. Buck is not so sure about being seen in public in what he considers a sissified vehicle: "Only I ought to have a powder puff or at least a mandolin to ride it with," he objects. "I wouldn't get past the first Texas saloon without starting the vigilance committee," he says, and then wants to know "What's the short way to New York from here?" (1009).

This curious runabout triggers some interesting and significant questions about Will's and Flem's relationship—about, if you will, the "vehicle" of Flem's rise up Varner's corporate ladder. Flem's advent into Frenchman's Bend is directly a result of Jody's temporizing with Ab Snopes. Flem's job in Varner's store is a form of "fire insurance," Jody's fearful effort to keep Flem's barnburning father placated. Jody, Will's son and presumptive heir to the Varner estates and privileges, ceases to be a major player after Eula's pregnancy. Flem completely supplants him.

Faulkner initially presents Jody as yet another of his male siblings, like Quentin Compson, who is overly concerned with a sister's virginity: he overreacts to Eula's long and casually-displayed thighs as he rides behind her on the way to school and constantly gropes at her to see whether she's wearing her confining undergarments. Jody is "not only unmarried," he emanates "a quality of invincible and inviolable bachelordom," a "quality of invincible bachelorhood"; he is "the perennial and immortal Best Man, the apotheosis of the masculine Singular" (734, 735). Since he is not likely to continue the genetic Varner line and so its name, all he has as a claim on the Varner fortune is his economic competence, but he proves himself incompetent here too: even as a trader and merchant he is no worthy scion. The bad bargain he makes with Ab Snopes that permits Flem's entrance into the game is also the bargain by which he moves himself out. As Flem becomes more powerful, Jody gradually recedes in power and influence and, indeed, almost completely disappears from the novel as soon as Eula gets pregnant—a sure sign that he has also failed as protective brother and, more, failed to prove himself a scion worthy of the patriarchal tradition he stands to inherit. Faulkner suggests the degree of his failure later in the novel when he writes that Jody, perennial bachelor though he be, will one day be an old man "who at about sixty-five would be caught and married by a creature not yet seventeen probably, who would for the rest of his life continue to take revenge upon him for her whole sex" (1029).

That is, though Jody initially seems as thoroughly committed to the "tradition" of female purity as Quentin Compson and Horace Benbow are, Jody's story makes it clear that there's much more at stake in *The Hamlet*—and, reading backward, perhaps also in *The Sound and the Fury* and *Absalom, Absalom!*—than just the preservation of a sister's maidenhead. At issue is not at all its preservation but rather its appropriation by a male economy. All the obsession with incest in *The Sound and the Fury* and *Absalom, Absalom!* may be at least partially a scion's fantasy of despoiling the sexual merchandise — rendering her unmarketable by destroying that which makes her a valuable commodity — by which he fends off in advance his own pre-emption by a brother-in-law who might successfully compete not just for the father's affection but for his kingdom too. Thus a sister's virginity is not just a commodity in the exogamic market; it is also, as the son sees it, a central value in the relationship between father and son, and therefore central to the maintenance of his own right to inherit. Flem does not claim Eula's maidenhead, but he certainly controls its value, so that he, and neither Jody nor Ratliff, is the rightful heir to Varner's position at the top of the totem pole.

Faulkner does not dwell on Jody, for in the larger, perhaps Darwinian, survival scheme, the patriarchy simply discards those who who are not worthy of it. And, to be sure, Faulkner had already explored the inner workings of Jody's spiritual cousins in *The Sound and the Fury* and *Absalom, Absalom!* at considerable lengths and in *The Hamlet* moves deliberately away from such intensely internal, solipsistic explorations of sexual pathologies, toward a more open, social view of such characters.

But even Jody's protuberant incompetence as son, protector, and trader does not explain why Will in effect adopts Flem, long before Eula gets pregnant, moves him not just into Jody's position in the store, at the gin, and by his own side as they make rounds but also, astonishingly, into his own house. Flem doesn't even have to usurp Jody's place: Will hands it to him on a platter — or on a sissy runabout, rather. But why? Fire insurance? I doubt it.

How does Flem come to own "some two hundred acres of land, with buildings"? (797). This is the portion of Jack Houston's land that Will has foreclosed on and that Flem, the new owner, has rented to Mink, who in turn now believes that Flem will be vulnerable to threats against his own barn. Perhaps he buys it: he is a sharp trader and shrewd, and there's no reason to think he has not made enough money to buy it from Will, though he would have to have worked very fast. But even if he buys the land from Will, there are more important questions: why does Will take up with Flem after Flem goes to work in the store, spending Sunday afternoons and evenings with him, in the wooden hammock, he Thomas Sutpen to Flem's Wash Jones, while Flem squats beside the tree and watches Eula being courted by the other young bucks in the county? (896). There is no evidence that Flem is a scintillating conversationalist, nor any that Will needs somebody to talk to. If Flem must live in town, why not at Mrs. Littlejohn's boardinghouse? At whose invitation, then, does Flem come to live in the Varner household? Will Varner is the only one who could have issued such an invitation. Further, why does Will agree to ride around the countryside with Flem in that sissified runabout? It may be easy to understand why Will marries Eula to Flem instead of to anybody else, but is it so easy to understand why Will gives him the Old Frenchman place to boot as dowry? Could he not have found any number of other young bucks to take Eula by herself? Are we to understand that Flem refuses to take Eula unless Will includes the Old Frenchman place in the deal? Is he *that* desirable a son-in-law? What gives him such bargaining power? What, in short, is the relationship between Flem and Will Varner?

We have no direct answers to any of these questions, which, to my knowledge, have never been asked. But we may approach an answer indirectly. Just after Flem has come to work at the store, Ratliff meets Varner at the Old Frenchman place. Varner, who is still riding his white horse at this point in Flem's advent, proposes that he and Ratliff change places: "I want to sit down and ride," he says. Ratliff suggests they tie the horse behind and ride together in the buckboard, but Varner refuses: "You ride the horse," he says. "That's close as I want you right now. Sometimes you are a little too smart to suit me" (753). Though there's plenty of room for both of them to ride in the buckboard, Varner refuses to be so close to Ratliff—afraid he'll discover something?—though he doesn't mind sitting with Flem in the runabout; perhaps it's just a whim, of course, and Will is certainly entitled to his whims. They proceed to town talking about the new employee and his family, Varner in the buckboard, Ratliff on the horse. The scene ends with Ratliff's proffered compliment to Will, that "there aint but two men I know can risk fooling with them folks. And just one of them is named Varner and his front name aint Jody" (755). Although Varner is polite enough to ask, and Ratliff shrewd enough not to answer, each knows who the one not named Varner is, and they part with this modest, muted, and mutual ratification of each other's skill as traders.

A related scene, at the beginning of Book III, occurs three years later, just after Flem and Eula have gone to Texas and, more specifically, just as Ratliff emerges from his fantasy about Flem in hell. Awaking and, as usual, "sitting in the halted buckboard" (875), Ratliff once again meets Varner, who is now, Ratliff observes, again riding the white horse "which, with the exception of the three-year runabout interval, [he] had bestridden . . . , the same saddle between them, for twenty-five years" (877). "He's got to straddle his legs at least once to keep on moving," Ratliff continues thinking. "So he had to pay that too. Not only the deed to the land and the two-dollar wedding license and them two tickets to Texas and the cash, but" — and somehow this seems more important to Ratliff at the moment than the mere money and the land — "but the riding in that new buggy with somebody to do the driving, to get that patented necktie out of his store and out of his house." The seriousness with which Ratliff views *this* change, and Will's loss of the Old Frenchman place, is suggested by Faulkner's description of him as Varner approaches: Ratliff sits in the buckboard "neat, decorous, and grave like a caller in a house of death" (875).

Significantly, Ratliff is more upset about Varner's loss of the Old Frenchman place than about what nearly everybody in *The Hamlet* would call Eula's shame, at least partly because the loss involves Ratliff's disillusionment about Varner's invincibility as a trader. After a brief conversation, Varner rides off toward town, and Ratliff, from his buckboard, watches as Varner's horse begins to make his automatic turn toward the Old Frenchman place. Varner "haul(s) it roughly back" (878). The "roughly" suggests some agitation on Varner's part, some irritable reaction against his former castle, now that Flem owns it, which in turn implies that he too feels he is no longer the man Ratliff and others believe him to be. Losing the Old Frenchman place, he has lost status with Ratliff, with other men, and with himself. Moreover, the gesture makes it clear that he, and they, believe that he has gotten snookered in the deal, gotten beaten so badly that he has good reason to feel humiliated.

Again I ask: what are the terms of Will's and Flem's deal? What does Will get in exchange for his daughter and his ruined mansion? Ratliff's is a simple answer: fire insurance, an unburned barn. A considerably more complicated answer asks us to understand that, like Ratliff in the goat deal, Will has been beaten because Flem had a sight draft that he, but not Will, was willing to cash in.

Not to put too fine a point on it, I propose that there is some form of homosexual relationship, overt or latent, between Will and Flem. I grant, of course, that there is no proof of any sort of sexual liaison between Flem and Will, but the indicators are so numerous that we must at least see the possibility both as a logical extension of the extreme homosocial atmosphere in the novel and as an explanation of the more than curious external features of their developing relationship. The possibility also provides interesting resonances for other incidentals in the text. One cannot, for example, avoid Bookwright's vituperative speech early in Book III, in which he associates Will with Snopeses in a very curious way:

> Snopes can come and Snopes can go, but Will Varner looks like he is fixing to snopes forever. Or Varner will Snopes forever—take your pick. What is it the fellow says? off with the old and on with the new; the old job at the old stand, maybe a new fellow doing the jobbing but it's the same old stern getting reamed out? (879–80)

A man who gets beaten at a deal is said to get screwed; one beaten *very* badly is said to get screwed in the ass. Under the circumstances, then, we cannot help but wonder whether Will wants to ride in Ratliff's buggy instead of on his horse simply because, well, he is sore—

and doesn't want to sit that close to Ratliff because of whatever shame he feels, or the fear of being discovered somehow, perhaps by revealing himself in his physical and/or psychic discomfort. Of course what works on him is not any rational worry that he will reveal himself, but rather the quite irrational fear of what he knows about himself.

Flem's sight draft is not necessarily economic or social, then, but psychological: given Will's economic and social power, he could dismiss any accusation of homosexuality as being simply unbelievable, and there is no reason to doubt that Will could survive a public confrontation over such issues. It is, then, the private confrontation that he cannot survive, the admission perhaps not even of overt homosexual acts but of the mere inclination toward them, and so he avoids the issue by yielding to Flem's threats, which may be only implied rather than real. In a novel so completely "about" compromised male sexuality in a homosocial world, a novel in which Flem regularly exploits the idealized masculinity of so many of Frenchman's Bend men, it should not be surprising to find homosexuality a significant part of the whole, as it is in many other of Faulkner's novels, or to find it a point upon which the novel's most overtly successful and "masculine" character should be vulnerable.

iii.

Ratliff's thoughts at the beginning of Book III are not exclusively of the lost Old Frenchman place, however; they become very personal and revelatory. As Varner rides off, Ratliff's meditations move by fluid association from Varner's horse to his and Flem's sissified runabout to the wagons and buggies of the young bucks who had courted Eula to Eula herself to Eula's baby then to himself and to what he calls his own past's "tom-catting's heyday" (877), then to Flem and the waste that Eula's marriage to him represents. At precisely the point in Ratliff's meditations when he reaches Eula, Will reaches the lane going to the Old Frenchman place, jerks his horse "roughly" away from the turn, and Ratliff himself moves on. It is a *very* curious scene, and I think it can best be understood as the second part of a longer meditation that occurs in the minutes just before Ratliff's fantasy in which Flem out-trades the Prince of Darkness himself, at the end of Book II. Indeed, Flem's negotiations with the Prince emerge directly out of Ratliff's meditations here, so that in effect Ratliff's single meditation on a variety of things connected with Eula and buggies is interrupted by his vision of Flem in hell, by the change from Book II to Book III, and by his conversation with Will Varner. His elegiac cadenza on Eula tells us a good deal about himself and about the complex of reasons that govern men's homosocial retreat from women. These reasons are, I believe, here as in so many others of Faulkner's work, grounded in family structures that can best be understood in terms of Freudian Oedipal theory.

Book II is entitled "Eula," but like Caddy Compson in an earlier novel, Eula is primarily depicted in terms of the way men respond to her: those on the porch at her father's store; her erstwhile suitors; the drummer; her brother Jody; Labove; her father; Hoake McCarron; Flem. To this list I would add Ratliff, who makes his appearance in Book II very late, just in time to watch Eula, Flem, and Varner in Jefferson going from bank to courthouse to Chancery Clerk to Circuit Clerk. "He did not need" to see them married, so he goes straight ahead to the station "an hour before the train was due" to wait to watch them board and depart; at the station he sees her virtually in the same terms as the simpering woman in the window of the kennel on his buggy: he sees "the calm beautiful mask beneath the Sunday hat once more beyond a moving window, looking at nothing, and that was all" (867). His vision of that face "beyond a moving window" reminds us of *our* first vision of her, in the opening paragraph of Book II, as one who existed "in a teeming vacuum in which her days followed one another as though behind sound-proof glass, where she seemed to listen in sullen bemusement, with a weary wisdom heired of all mammalian maturity, to the enlarging of her own organs" (817). Now, as she leaves on her honeymoon, pregnant, her organs are enlarging indeed. Her face is wonder-full to Ratliff; it is all he sees, and his responses to that face suggest a range of things Ratliff associates with Eula and her environs. Frenchman's Bend is "a little lost village, nameless, without grace, forsaken, yet which wombed once by chance and accident one blind seed of the spendthrift Olympian ejaculation and did not even know it" (867). Like Labove, Ratliff knows how extraordinary Eula is. And that is the rub.

What follows is a magnificent, complicated passage, unlike anything else in Faulkner. After he places Eula in that "little lost village," Ratliff almost immediately notes the "three fairly well-horsed buggies" of the boys who courted her, buggies which disappeared after word spread that she was pregnant. He names the principal actors in this drama, then describes the reactions of various categories of people in Frenchman's Bend to Eula and her hasty marriage and departure in terms of the gossip that flies "from cabin to cabin above the washing pots and the sewing, from wagon to horseman in roads and lanes or from rider to halted plow in field furrows." Among the gossipy men are

> the young who only dreamed yet of the ruins they were still incapable of; the sick and the maimed sweating in sleepless beds, impotent for the harm they willed to do; the old, now-glandless earth-creeping, the very buds and blossoms, the garlands of whose yellowed triumphs had long fallen into the profitless dust, embalmed now and no more dead to the living world if they were sealed in buried vaults.

These "buried vaults" are, significantly, located "behind the impregnable matronly calico of others' grandchildren's grandmothers" (868). Hidden in that mouthful—"the impregnable matronly calico of others' grandchildren's grandmothers"—is the word "cuckold," the known fact of it in Flem's case and, I'd suggest, the fear of it in the minds and mouths of those men who talk about Flem and Eula.

The fear of being cuckolded, then, is the unspeakable terror at the heart of male heterosexuality. Though frequently invoked nervously as a topic of vulgar jokes, that terror always operates as an aggression, a sweeping indictment of all women, older than Chaucer, that admits all men's vulnerability to the cuckold's horns, which will publicly proclaim their own heterosexual insufficiency. This terror is especially real to the men of Frenchman's Bend, who know that Will Varner himself is very active in the bushes with other sharecroppers', and perhaps their own, wives. Even the proudly virile Mink Snopes can never rid himself of the phantoms of those bodies which had preceded him to his wife's bed (952–53).

From cuckoldry Ratliff abruptly moves back to Eula, or to the magnificence, the plenty, that Eula represents. And which best, he wonders: "to have that word, that dream and hope for future, or to have had need to flee that word and dream, for past" (868). Ratliff wants to know whether it is better to have and hold the physical Eula from now on, to live with her in the sorry, imperfect, unbeautiful, mundane give and take of domestic life, to watch her fade and grow old — perhaps, probably, to know that you will not be enough for her, that she *will be* unfaithful? or to have had her once, as Labove wants her, to have had the passion but not the problematics of possession, then to be free of her except as the grandest of perfect and unchanging memories? Ratliff answers his own question indirectly by thinking yet again about the buggies the boys courted Eula in: "Even one of the actual buggies remained. Ratliff was to see it, discovered a few months afterward, standing empty and with propped shafts in a stable shed a few miles from the village." Ratliff then evokes, predicts, that buggy's future: no longer new and shining, it will gather dust; chickens will roost upon it and their droppings will streak and mar its once pristine finish. It will undergo a series of changes of ownership in a steady decline,

> while its new owner married and began to get a family and then turn gray, spilling children, no longer glittering, its wheels wired upright in succession by crossed barrel staves until staves and delicate wheels both vanished, translated, apparently in motion at some point into stout, not new, slightly smaller wagon wheels, giving it a list, the list too interchangeable, ranging from quarter to quarter between two of its passing appearance behind a succession of spavined and bony horses and mules in wire- and rope-patched harness, as if its owner had horsed it ten minutes ago out of a secret boneyard for this particular final swan-song's apotheosis which, woefully misinformed as to its own capacities, was each time not the last. (868–69)

This buggy's biography becomes, in Ratliff's imagination, an extended trope for marriage: the bright promise of youthful passion gradually destroyed by time and familiarity and use: domestication. For Ratliff, mutability (among many other anxieties, sexual and otherwise) casts its pall even over passion, and his answer to the question whether it is better to marry your goddess and have her reality or to forgo the reality in order to maintain her perfect memory is certainly suggested when, later in the trilogy, in *The Mansion*, we learn that he keeps a shrine to Eula in his house in Jefferson. Clearly, no less than Labove is Raliff overwhelmed by Eula. But for the moment he evades that realization, and focuses once more on "the calm beautiful mask seen once more beyond a moving pane of glass, then gone." But he jerks himself back from admitting what that face, that woman, means to him with the melancholy and unconvincing assertion — and we suspect that he is mostly arguing with himself — that it was "all right, it was just meat, just galmeat . . . and God knows there was a plenty of that, yesterday and tomorrow too. Of course," his other self counters, "there was the waste, not wasted on Snopes but on all of them, himself included — Except," he argues back, "was it waste?" Can anything that dangerous, he wonders, be worth having? Behind that face, he tells himself, there lurks "only another mortal natural enemy of the masculine race. And beautiful: but then, so did the highwayman's daggers and pistols make a pretty shine on him" (869). And as he remembers Eula's unforgettable, dangerous, face moving off toward Texas behind the train's soundproof glass, he shifts gears a bit to imagine Flem in hell. Perhaps Ratliff's sympathies for Flem in this comic Faustian revery are stronger than critics have allowed: after all, in outtrading the Prince, what Flem gains is not heaven; in outtrading Will Varner, what he gains, by analogy, is, to the men of Frenchman's Bend, perhaps no different from hell itself: wife, mansion, domesticity.

As Book III opens, Ratliff is still sitting in his buggy. Varner approaches, and the scene ensues that I noted a moment ago. As he watches Varner ride away, Ratliff thinks again about those courting buggies, which, as we now know, evoke in Ratliff all of youth's dangerous passion. He is fixated on those buggies. He imagines he sees them still tied to the fence around Varner's yard: "those buggies were still there. He could see them, sense them. Something was [there]; it was too much to have vanished that quickly and completely." The air is "polluted and rich and fine which had flowed over and shaped that abundance and munificence." "Polluted" is the operative word here. It evokes the connection between sexuality and corruption that is so common in Faulkner's work. But the buggies, Ratliff finally understands, are "merely a part of the whole, a minor and trivial adjunct, like the buttons on her clothing," compared to Eula herself: "so why," he wonders, "should not that body at the last have been the unscalable sierra, the rosy virginal mother of barricades for no man to conquer scot-free or even to conquer at all, but on the contrary to be hurled back and down, leaving no scar, no mark of himself." Ratliff almost reproaches himself for not having made his own desperate and futile attempt on that height, even one time, at no matter what cost. But that—the passionate and injurious assault on such an "unscalable sierra—*that*, he concludes, "would never have been for him," he admits, "not even . . . of what he and Varner both would have called his tom-catting's heyday." The phrasing—"what he and Varner both *would have called*"—argues that Ratliff's "tomcatting heyday" wasn't, as he might put it, no great shakes of a heyday. "He knew," Faulkner tells us, "that without regret or grief, he would not have wanted it to be [i.e., for him to assail that height]."

Ratliff has, then, simply opted out of sexual life. He tries to explain to himself his inadequacy before the likes of Eula—before Woman: "It would have been like giving me a pipe organ, that never had and never would know any more than how to wind up the second-hand music-box I had just swapped a mail-box for, he thought." He is not jealous of Flem, though, he thinks, because he knows that "regardless of whatever Snopes had expected or would have called what it was he now had, it would not be victory." He is wrong, of course, as we shall see, because he thinks that Flem's relationship to Eula is based in the same sexual anxieties that plague him and the other Frenchman's Bend men. He thinks that Flem wants the same thing out of marriage that the men of the Bend do, but he clearly doesn't. From all we can tell from *The Hamlet* and *The Town*, Flem accepts his cuckolding as a part of Eula's exchange value: what he must pay to possess her, to have her long enough to trade her, as he trades the Old Frenchman place, for whatever he wants to own next.

Ratliff believes that even Eula will grow old and, growing old, fail to measure up to his and every other man's dream of her; at best Flem's marriage, like all others, will succumb to the ordinary; at worst, marriage will be for Flem the same domestic trap it is for every other man. So whatever Flem thinks he has won, Ratliff believes, Flem will soon know it as loss. But this thought, in its turn, prompts the admission from Ratliff, less self-deceptive than before, that Eula has indeed been wasted.

> What he felt was outrage at the waste, the useless squandering; at a situation intrinsically and inherently wrong by any economy, like building a log dead-fall and baiting it with a freshened heifer to catch a rat; or no, worse: as though the gods themselves had funnelled all the concentrated bright wet-slanted unparadised June onto a dung-heap, breeding pismires. (877–78)

This is a bitter tirade against such waste as he has just witnessed, but he is less concerned with how Eula is being wasted on Flem than with how she is being wasted on such a stinking, corrupt world as he, Ratliff, lives in. What grim joke would put the physical embodiment of all passion's perfection into the world so as to challenge man, to befuddle him and, worse, to force him to have to make excuses for himself, after all his dreaming and hoping and sweating?

When Ratliff decides to buy the Old Frenchman place, he locates Flem on a drive in the country with his Varner family and invites him to drive with him back to Frenchman's Bend; he thus negotiates his "deal" to buy the Old Frenchman place while moving in his buckboard. As they negotiate, they pass the schoolhouse and Ratliff is reminded, as in a premonition of disaster, of the vanquished schoolmaster: "That fellow, that teacher you had three-four years ago. Labove. Did anybody ever hear what become of him?" (1063). Even if neither Ratliff nor Flem knows exactly why Labove left the country, Ratliff's question is Faulkner's reminder to the reader of Ratliff's kinship with Labove: the teacher already, and Ratliff about to be, vanquished by Eula.

iv.

Thus Ratliff is no less vanquished by Eula than Labove; he is so thoroughly unwomanned and unwomanable that we may well say that he has been pre-vanquished by all women. Faulkner tells us that though they share many similarities, Ratliff and Jody Varner have one "unbridgeable difference": Jody, as I noted a moment ago, will marry late and be unhappy. "Ratliff, never" (1029). Why? What quality of sexuality or domesticity impels Ratliff to abjure the womanned state? We do not know for sure, of course, because Ratliff is reticent. But neither do we know how Labove knows what love is—"That's it," he tells Eula when she resists him: "Fight it. Fight it. That's what it is: a man and a woman fighting each other. The hating" (842)—but we can reasonably suspect that some experience of his own parents' marriage is his inspiration: where else?

We know that Ratliff listens to a lot of women talk, and that he learns a lot from them. But we can usefully turn once again to his own buckboard and to the "sheet-iron box the size and shape of a dog-kennel and painted to resemble a house, in each painted window of which a painted woman's face simpered above a painted sewing-machine" (740) in which he keeps his demonstrator sewing machine. These women smile at him in "fixed and sightless invitation" (797), though whether they are sirens or merely customers we do not know for sure. Those faces, however, are haunting vestiges from many of Faulkner's works, in which a face in the window invariably connotes some repression of the sexual life, some Oedipal strife, and it seems reasonably clear that that miniature house on Ratliff's buggy represents some emotional baggage from his childhood that has made him a constantly moving refugee from the feminine.

In Chodorow's terms, Ratliff can only define himself in terms of his resistance to, his separation from, his mother: hence his insistence upon mobility, unattachment. In Freudian terms, consistent with Chodorow's argument, Ratliff cannot separate himself from the Oedipal attachments that have controlled him from the beginning of his life. In this he is like many, many of Faulkner's characters. As we have already noted, he seems to share Quentin Compson's sense that sexuality and corruption are inextricable. Like Horace Benbow, Ratliff owns a house in Jefferson in which he lives with his widowed sister and her children; like Horace, he brings into that home the prostitute wife of a man in that same Jefferson jail awaiting trial for murder; like Horace, he is fascinated by the hands of the accused as they grip the bars of the window of his jail cell.

When Ratliff and Varner part at the beginning of Book III, Ratliff first has that recriminatory vision of how wasted Eula has been on such a world as this, then drives directly to Varner's store, where, genial raconteur again, he begins a voyeuristic tale in which Flem and a Negro girl have sex against the back wall of Varner's store. Lump Snopes interrupts him when the word comes that Ike Snopes is about ready to perform with his paramour cow; all the real voyeurs rush across the street to the fence that Lump has prepared for viewing, and Ratliff finishes his story while walking with the men to the barn lot. Ratliff shuts the peep show down, but his initial response to what he sees is utterly astonishing: "He knew not only what he was going to see but that, like Bookwright, he did not want to see it, yet, unlike Bookwright, he was going to look." It may be easy to understand why he doesn't want to see it. It's not so easy to understand why is he determined nevertheless to look.

> He did look, leaning his face in between two other heads; and it was as though it were himself inside the stall with the cow, himself looking out of the blasted tongueless face at the row of faces watching him who had been given the wordless passions but not the specious words. (913)

Incredibly, Ratliff identifies with Isaac: he sees *himself* caught in the shameful act of stockdiddling. Why? His reaction to Isaac's activity is, *must be*, based in a sense of sex as something bestial and unclean, and doubtless in an intense sense of guilt and shame over his own sexual, doubtless Oedipal, perhaps homosexual, impulses. He would not, as we know, be the only male in Faulkner with such impulses, and such a pathology would be perfectly consonant with the Freudian scheme that hangs so heavily over Faulkner's other works.

Ratliff does not participate in the spotted horse auction, not even as a witness or commentator, and has contempt for those who do. But in one of the novel's funniest scenes, one of the ponies chases into Mrs. Littlejohn's boarding house and on into Ratliff's very room, where he stands in his nightshirt, preparing for bed; he and the pony see each other at the same time, each is equally frightened of the other. The horse backs out the door, and Ratliff, running even from this diminutive masculine force, jumps out the window. Mrs. Littlejohn simply hits the unruly pony on the head with her washboard and tells him, as she might a husband, "Get out of here, you son of a bitch" (1014). Ratliff's and the horse's reaction to each other is just about as funny, and of the same order, as the scene in "Was" when Uncle Buck inadvertently gets into Miss Sophonsiba's bed. Funny as the scene is, however, it leaves no doubt about Ratliff's sexual anxieties.

Amidst the swirling force of those ponies Buck Hipps is trying to sell, wagons and buckboards—not the courting buggies or sissy runabouts—represent a degree of security: the men run to the wagon when they feel threatened by the horses and find in the wagon bed a timid solidarity above that symbolically sexual and putatively masculine maelstrom, even if their security is as illusory and transient as the innocence that seems to protect Eck Snopes's son as he wanders about among the chaotic and dangerous ponies. One pony attacks Tull's wagon, which is loaded with himself and his womenfolks—Tull is, Faulkner tells us, so domesticated and tamed as to be "the eldest daughter" of his own wife (737)—and convulses the family as comically as Lucy Pate's stallion's attack upon her is tragic. Likewise, Tull's valiant but ineffective attempt to protect his family by standing up in the seat and beating the spotted pony with his whip also reminds us of Hoake McCarron's identical but more succesful defense of his possession of Eula against his competition. It is therefore also worth noting that Hoake, too, for all his vaunted masculinity, is, like Tull, crippled during that attack, and that he, too, can consummate his sexual union, even with the Earth Mother—especially with the Earth Mother—*only* with her active assistance: she must support him, actually hold him up, so that he can perform (860). It is, then, a serious question with me whether Hoake runs from Will and Jody Varner's wrath or from his fear at having touched the grandeur and terror that woman represents to the homosocial male.

Ratliff wants nothing to do with those wild if diminutive symbols of chaotic masculinity that simultaneously attract and elude the other men of Frenchman's Bend. He in effect already owns two: pulling his buckboard are not powerful stallions such as Jack Houston gives Lucy Pate, nor even a mismatched pair like Jody's roan and Will's white, which are yoked togther to pull Flem's sissy runabout. His team is rather, in point of fact, a pair of "shaggy ponies as wild and active-looking as mountain goats and almost as small" (740). If they are not Texas spotted ponies, they are at least second or third cousins. Ratliff's ponies, then, are, to use Jack Houston's phrase, symbols of his own "bitted masculinity."

More specifically, like the spotted ponies, they symbolize heterosexual desire, the powerful and destructive Oedipal impulse toward the seductive mother: toward domestication, toward entrapment, toward engulfment by the supreme primal uterus in any of its substitute or surrogate avatars. Indeed, what can the "supreme primal uterus," to which we are all prostrate, be, but Mama? This is why they want them and why they can't even catch them, much less handle them. For men, the unbearable paradox is that to get the prize, the public affirmation of their masculinity, is to be stuck forever with a constant challenge to it: to win is therefore not just to lose, but to be lost.

The men of Frenchman's Bend are thus forever caught in suspension between heterosexuality and outright impotence. Their only safeplace is the economic shield of the homosocial provided by the dusty distance between the front porch of Varner's store and the barn lot where Buck Hipps auctions those forever elusive ponies.

Flem brings those ponies with him from Texas, along with Eula and Eula's baby; he is firmly in possession of all he needs to publicly establish his masculinity. He can afford, now, to discard, must get rid of, the sissified fringed runabout that symbolizes, even more than the Old Frenchman place, his victory over Will Varner, a victory he gains because he knows that sexuality, too, is rather a medium of exchange than an activity by which one defines one's *self.* He leaves Frenchman's Bend not in the runabout, but in a buckboard, much like Ratliff's, and drives three miles out of his way, Eula and baby in the wagon with him, in order to go past the Old Frenchman place, where the crazed Henry Armstid is still digging: for no other reason than to gloat, to proclaim his final victory over Ratliff himself, which is also a victory over Varner, over the symbolic order of things, of which he has now become master.

His victory over Varner and Ratliff is also a victory over the feminine that lies less in his having parleyed the Old Frenchman place into Ratliff's share of the Jefferson cafe where he and Eula will move than in his appropriating from all the Frenchman's Bend men the visible signs of the same mastery over the domestic that they have long admired in Will Varner. Flem and Eula and the baby are in their own wagon, transporting their load of

> furniture and . . . trunks and . . . boxes . . . and small crocks and hermetic jars of fruit and vegetables . . . the dismantled bed, the dresser, the washstand with its flowered matching bowl and ewer and slop-jar and chamber-pot, the trunk which doubtless contained the wife's and the child's clothing, the wooden box which the women at least knew doubtless contained dishes and cutlery and cooking vessels

and the tent they will live in behind the cafe (1070, 1071): no shabby merchandizing symbol here of any sexual anxieties but rather a symbol, in all its domestic fullness, of Flem's absolute mastery of the patriarchal tradition.

Thus Ratliff is no worthier an heir of Varner's tradition than Jody, and he too is vanquished, not because he is more likeable and more human than anybody else in Frenchman's Bend—being *liked* has nothing to do with the tradition's maintenance of itself—but because like Jody he fails to demonstrate the necessary business acumen and to acquire the equally essential signs of mastery over a castle.

Ratliff prides himself on being a sharp trader, but there's in fact not much evidence of it in *The Hamlet*, certainly none in his dealings with Flem. Flem's entrance into the Frenchman's Bend economy and his growing reputation as a trader become a challenge that Ratliff cannot avoid but that he cannot win. In fact, though Ratliff makes one with the men on Varner's front porch, he doesn't do any business with them, and has carefully staked out a market in which he doesn't even have to compete with Will Varner. As a sewing machine sales-man, he naturally deals more often, and more safely, with their wom-enfolks, and he can be no less cold-blooded in dealing with women than Flem can be in dealing with either gender. To engineer the goat deal, recall, Ratliff "mistakenly" delivers a sewing machine to Mink Snopes's wife: he thus uses her to play upon Mink's desire for owner-ship as skillfully as Buck Hipps sells those worthless spotted ponies to the men, and she and Mink want the sewing machine for the same reason that the others want those spotted ponies.

Thus Ratliff's relationship to women is no less completely based in economics than Flem's is; perhaps it is more so. For the most part he seems content to remain seated on his floating buckboard island, the reins of control always firmly in his hand, deliberately restraining his own sexual energies and fears, and carrying safely behind him a woman—any woman: all women: his mother, Eula—carefully locked away in a dog kennel-house on the back of his buckboard, a woman eternally simpering, eternally looking at him in "fixed and sightless invitation," though offering him no more of a challenge than the sim-per. These painted women, no less than Eula herself, no less than other women in Faulkner, are untouchable, unknowable, dangerous: the primal uterus's primal terror's very self. Ratliff, men, render them harmless, voiceless, impotent, and so safe: trapped like Eula in a vacuum behind a moving window made of soundproof glass, trapped in their very iconicity and so contained at last not at all by man's courage but by his retreat; not by his sexual mastery but by his impotence; not by his love but by his economic power.

Woman and the Feminine
in *A Fable*

At almost the exact dead center of *A Fable* occurs one of those characteristic Faulknerian scenes that abrupt into the narrative, encounter one or more of the plot's central characters or elements, then disappear as abruptly. By 1954 this was so well-established an aspect of Faulkner's technique—the most famous example being the "Notes on a Horsethief" section of *A Fable* itself—that we ought to know to take such scenes' very disruptiveness as the measure of their significance to the larger work. The scene I refer to here occurs on Wednesday evening, as precisely at the center of this "Passion Week" as at the center of the novel, following the dispersal of the crowd that has gathered to watch the arrival of the mutinous troops.

In the almost empty road the corporal's wife, who for some un-known reason has been separated from the corporal's sisters, her travelling companions, encounters "an old man and three women, one of them carrying a child" (863). Two of the women are the corporal's sisters, Marya and Marthe. Marthe is carrying a child that is not hers: this fact has such significance that seventeen times within the four pages of the scene the narrator identifies her as "the woman carrying the child"; she is only once in these four pages identified in other terms. The second woman is Marya, Marthe's gentle but "wit-less" sister. The third, apparently though not certainly the mother of the child, is blind. The man is a cripple. They approach, the old man "on a single crutch and carrying a small cloth-knotted bundle and leaning on the arm of an old woman who appeared to be blind." Though blind, the woman sees everything; she anticipates move-ments; she knows before anybody else when the old man drops his knotted bundle; she strikes down a hand that Marthe reaches out to touch her with; she reaches out and grabs the crippled man with "sightless unerring aim" (866).

Thus at the center of the novel is an omniscient blind woman who leads a crippled man and allows—or forces: we do not know— someone else to "carry" her child. She pushes and pulls the man, "dragg[ing] him, holding [him] up," and "jerking him" after her when she departs (864–66). The man is obviously more than physically crippled; the one time he speaks he does so in a "thin quavering disused voice," and the blind woman pays no attention to him (865). Her name, which the old man utters once in pathetic remonstrance to her harshness, is grimly ironic: Angélique, *like an angel* (865). Unlike the angels of our dreams and our theology, however, Angélique is bitter, excoriatingly moralistic and contemptuous; she condemns both the "anarchist" corporal, for causing the deaths of so many, and the woman they have just encountered, whom Marthe has identified as the corporal's wife: "His whore, maybe you mean," she says. "Maybe you can fool them that dont have anything but eyes, and nothing to do but believe everything they look at. But not me" (865). At the conclusion of the encounter Angélique moves "unerring as light" toward the child Marthe is carrying and "snatche[s]" it away from her. She then leads the crippled man away from the three women and out of the book; they never reappear. This scene has little or nothing to do with the novel's central narrative, but it is a significant scene, and by no means pointless. In it are sounded several chords that resonate throughout the work, and it stands as an emblem for the entire novel, even, in some ways, for Faulkner's entire fictional oeuvre: a contemptuous, condemning, domineering blind woman leading a crippled man, a woman who "carries" another woman's child, and a child victimized by the harsh caprices of its mother.

A Fable is thus not so far distant from Yoknapatawpha County as most readers have thought, nor are its thematic concerns so very far removed from Faulkner's better-known fiction. In fact, underlying *A Fable*'s overt historical and theological scaffolding is a structure directly related to Faulkner's earlier work; it is in an important sense

but one link in a long series of novels exploring parent-child relationships—in particular Oedipal relationships—and the pressures and
anxieties that are the heritage of those victims of too-strong or too-
weak or absent parents. Three of the major male characters in *A Fable*
are orphans, all are fatherless, and over and over again men in *A Fable*
respond to the present reality of World War I in the terms of their
problematic relationships with their parents: over and over again soldiers, even—and in particular, the old general—are described as, are
treated like, or act like children.

Not just women characters, but images of women, of the feminine,
occur regularly throughout this novel about men at war, imbuing the
narrative with a sexual presence that is as fierce and as fundamental
to its structure and significances as that in *The Sound and the Fury*, *As
I Lay Dying*, *Light in August*, and *Absalom, Absalom!* The feminine in
A Fable is a dark ferocious quantity which resolutely insists, on page
after page, that the battlegrounds of *A Fable* are far larger than the
fields of northern France and that the casualty lists include those
maimed and destroyed by something other than howitzers. Two of
the major battles of World War I occurred at the Chemin des Dames
(the women's way), a large area just northeast of Paris along the Aisne
River. The second battle there was a bloody confrontation for both
sides (Cruttwell 522ff) and a resounding defeat for the Germans in
the late spring of 1918, approximately the time of the events of *A
Fable*. They who lost, General Gragnon thinks, lost because they
"thought the Chemin des Dames would be vulnerable, having a female name" (692). The boche underestimates the strength of the
feminine; few of the Allies are capable of making *that* error.

It is doubtless too much to argue that World War I is in *A Fable*
merely a metaphor for sexual conflict, but we may glean some sense
of the relationship between war and sex in the novel by noting one of
the images used by the unillusioned old general when he attempts to
convince his corporal son that martyrdom is futile and pointless. The
war will end soon anyway, he argues, whether he, the corporal, dies
or not: the Germans, "the best soldiers on earth today or in two thou-

sand years," have not stopped since they crossed the Belgian border.
They will "win perhaps two or even three more [battles]," he says,

> and then will have to surrender because the phenomenon of war is its
> hermaphroditism: the principles of victory and of defeat inhabit the
> same body and the necessary opponent, enemy, is merely the bed they
> self-exhaust each other on: a vice only the more terrible and fatal be-
> cause there is no intervening breast or division between to frustrate
> them into health by simple normal distance and lack of opportunity for
> the copulation from which even orgasm cannot free them. (984–5)

Of the war his meaning is reasonably clear. War is the human condition; peace is not a condition of either victory or defeat, and neither
victory nor defeat can stop war permanently. Of the sexual basis for
the old general's figure the meaning is perhaps not quite so clear, but
it does seem to derive from a sensibility very like that of the school-
teacher Labove in *The Hamlet*, for whom sex is clearly some sort of
savage battlefield: "That's it," he tells Eula, when she resists his ad-
vances: "Fight it. Fight it. That's what it is: a man and a woman
fighting each other. The hating. To kill, only to do it in such a way
that the other will have to know for ever afterward he or she is
dead" (842).

The old general's principle of hermaphroditism is at work throughout the novel in language that constantly defines war and sex in terms
of each other. The Air Force David Levine joins, for example, is not
the old Royal Flying Corps of his dreams; his uniform is "not the
universal tunic with RFC badges superposed on the remnants of old
regimental insigne which veteran transfers wore," but rather a newer
and to his eyes sissified uniform "not only unmartial but even a little
epicene." It looks to him like "the coat of the adult leader of a neo-
Christian boys' club" and on the hat are "modest dull gold pin[s
that look] like lingerie-clips" (746). His flight commander is Major
Bridesman, whose succinctly hermaphroditic name is appropriate for
one who can herd his military children through all the peculiarly masculine pursuits of military life—battle and drinking and whoring—
and then mother them back into sobriety and responsibility: "he could

carry the whole squadron through a binge night, through exuberance and pandemonium and then, with none realising it until afterward, back into sufficient sobriety to cope with the morrow's work" (748). Several times the narrative calls Levine a "child" and at least once calls their squadron "the nursery" (752). Levine is not only a "child" here, however; he is also, in the metaphor of hermaphroditism, the bride-to-be: his training consists of three weeks at the aerodrome and "one carefully chaperoned trip" to the front line with Bridesman. The flight he is assigned on this Monday, Levine thinks, might well be called "the valedictory of his maidenhood" (748); on this assignment he does indeed lose his innocence, when he discovers that his guns have been loaded with blanks and that the entire maneuver is a ruse to get the German general past the Allied lines. Levine's suicide follows hard upon his disillusionment.

At home Levine has obviously been a mama's boy: for ten years his mother has been a widow and he her only child. We extrapolate some sense of their relationship from her continual presence in his thoughts and from the fragments of the letter he has written to her (760). We may gather a great deal indeed from his desire to write these letters at all. At one level, his need to have a "last letter" for his mother to find among his effects after he is killed in battle is a sentimental aping of a cliché of popular war stories. Just beneath the surface of this cliché, however, lie Oedipal attractions and antagonisms that stem from her ten-year widowhood and from what we readily see is her overprotection, her overnurturing, of her only child. She has, we are told, used her "mother's unrational frantic heart fiercely and irrevocably immune to glory" (747) to make him promise not to enlist until he is eighteen: he is thus a year late, and too late for the glory—since the war, he thinks, is over—because of his "inability to say no to a woman's tears" (747).

Part of why he, like other men in the novel, goes to war, then, is to escape his mother, to escape the obviously suffocating security and domesticity she forces upon him. Like the men in the infantry, he goes to war seeking "unsafeness" (777); he deliberately flouts his mother's proffered security and he clearly hopes through his death to hurt her somehow. He "asked only that the need for the unsafeness . . . be held by the nations . . . immune and unchallengeable above all save brave victory itself and as brave defeat" (777). He asks of his government, which he calls the "motherland," that it continue wars so as to keep constant the supply of opportunities for "unsafeness" — for freedom, that is, from those mother's tears even if it is only the freedom to die. But the tears prevail, and just as mother has betrayed him into impotence, so has motherland betrayed him right back into the security he has been hell-bent upon escaping, by putting him into Bridesman's nursery, by sending him on a phony mission, and by rendering his bullets hollow: "those who had invented for him the lingerie pins" (747) have filled his guns with blanks.

David Levine's story is complemented by that of Charles Gragnon, the commander of the mutinous regiment, whose life has significant parallels with Levine's, from the Monday of this Passion Week when both at nearly the same time become disillusioned with and betrayed by their respective governments, through the Thursday evening when both die — Levine at his own hands, Gragnon at the hands of the three American soldiers, but no less a suicide all the same. The similarities between them are instructive, the differences no less so. Both men are equally betrayed by their countries, by their dreams, and by the feminine. Levine's mother and motherland betray him, keep him safe in spite of himself; Gragnon's lack of parents and of any sort of political or military connections get him equally betrayed, in spite of his long years of loyal, dedicated military service: in *A Fable* having or not having a mother is all the same. Levine kills himself in despair, a gesture of spite toward his mother. Gragnon is executed by the military hierarchy he has served all his life precisely because he insists upon enforcing the very rules that hierarchy has taught him: he goes to his death likewise spiting his surrogate mother, Mama Bidet, refusing from first to last to participate in the sham he and the military want him to cooperate with.

Gragnon is an orphan, reared at a Pyrenean orphanage run by Catholic nuns. This is a fact of no little importance to him for, partly making a virtue out of a fact, he believes his orphanhood makes him the perfect soldier, since he is therefore "pastless, unhampered, and complete" (684)—that is, free of the emotional baggage that others have, free of folks back home to worry about, and free to live his life, or give it, as he wants. He has no mother's tears to keep him from enlisting. Until now he has appeared splendidly competent and tough, perfectly in control of a career he has nurtured without any of the familial or political connections that have made military careers easier for others. To the crisis of mutiny around which *A Fable* turns, Gragnon responds with characteristic bull-headed rigidity; lacking other resources, he falls back on what he knows best. He walks through the scene of defeat as he always has: "chop-striding, bull-chested, virile, in appearance impervious and indestructible, starred and exalted and, within this particular eye-range of earth, supreme and omnipotent" (700).

But his apparent strength is, we know, a façade. The sisters at the orphanage try to comfort him by telling him that "the Mother of Christ, the Mother of all, is your mother." But this is not enough for the orphan, "because he didn't want the mother of all nor the mother of Christ either: he wanted the mother of One" (704). At two very poignant moments in the novel Gragnon evokes memories from his Pyrenean childhood by sitting in the grass of northern France, nestling close to the earth, whispering "the one word"—obviously "mother"—to the "noon-fierce stone under his face," and listening for the northern sister of the Pyrenean cicada, which gives him his only comfort; that sound is for him "a purring sound such as he imagined might be made by the sleeping untoothed mouth itself around the sleeping nipple" (705). He thus longs for the very comfort, the very security, that Levine has rejected.

Gragnon's story, too, is rendered in the language of sexuality. But if Levine's Air Force is a "nursery" wherein the children are "chaperoned" by a loving Major Bridesman, who nurtures and encourages their childhood dreams of pleasing mama, Gragnon's infantry is a grimly adult world of men who accept the muck and ooze of the trenches as a fair price to pay for the chance to escape the dull routine of domesticity. It is a military world which not only seeks to escape the feminine but also actively fights back, if not at the feminine itself, then at least at certain symbols of femininity which linger around the battlefield.

Levine has his Major Bridesman, Gragnon has a group commander whom the troops, not with affection, have nicknamed "Mama Bidet." Like "Bridesman," "Mama Bidet" is a hermaphroditic epithet.[1] Like other officers, Mama Bidet has taken over an abandoned château for his field headquarters. When Gragnon goes from the battlefield to demand that the troops be executed, he must step over a conspicuous "pile of horse-droppings" that desecrate "the terrace beside the door" (711), and he must pass through a "shabby cluttered cubicle" that has been "notched" into the château like a "rusted spur in a bride's cake" (694).

But if the feminine in *A Fable* is under attack, it is by no means powerless to defend itself. Even though war deliberately upsets and disrupts the domestic, violates the feminine, by converting the châteaux to military use, the men who inhabit these domestic settings are invariably drawn to and are in important ways defined by the symbols of femininity, the symbols of their own impotence. Gragnon's headquarters are also in an abandoned château, one built by a self-made millionaire specifically for an "Argentine mistress" (705). Gragnon's bedroom is the millionaire's "gunroom . . . containing a shotgun which had never been fired and a mounted stag's head (not a very good one) and a stuffed trout, both bought in the same shop with the gun" (706). More pertinently, when Gragnon goes to Mama Bidet for the second time, he gets ushered into Bidet's bedroom by candlelight, and he is received by the group commander, who remains in bed. Faulkner thus depicts Mama Bidet in this scene in terms that connect him unmistakably with the gray-headed bespectacled women—mothers, grandmothers, sisters, lovers, and aunts—whom I have identified as being at the epicenter of nearly all of Faulkner's fiction between *Flags in the Dust* and *Light in August*—who recur in

1. The *OED* suggests that a "bidet" was, in slightly archaic French, a small horse. Apparently the lavatory was so named because of the riding position astraddle it one must assume in order to use it.

various avatars as a decidedly feminine punitive superego watching over the activities of such emasculates as Quentin Compson and Horace Benbow. In her most condemnatory, Medusa-like avatar, this woman is in bed, her graying hair splayed out against the pillow, sitting in judgment on her children (Polk, "Children of the Dark House").

Gragnon's meeting with Mama Bidet, then, reenacts a classic Faulknerian tableau: the condemning maternal fury in bed, the son at the foot of the bed, hopelessly yet respectfully suppliant. Levine, who has a similar scene at the foot of Bridesman's bed (755ff), despairs that his motherland has failed him: *"What had I done for motherland's glory,"* he thinks, *"had motherland but matched me with her need"* (747). Mama Bidet tells Gragnon that one could stop wars by effacing from memory a single word. When Gragnon admits that he does not know what that word is, Mama Bidet sneers: "fatherland" (716). This may merely be Mama's contempt for father; however, if Bidet is correct in assuming the love of *"father*land" to be the main cause of war, the sexual implications of his contempt are large indeed.

Levine, Gragnon, and Mama Bidet are relatively minor characters in *A Fable*, but the terms in which their stories get told help us to understand something of what is at stake in the central conflict between the old general and the Christ-corporal, his illegitimate son, since so much of what is at stake in their confrontation is likewise shaped by their attempts to deal with the feminine in their own lives.

The old general's and the corporal's stories are not just shaped by the feminine, large parts of them are actually narrated by Marthe, the avenging fury who has dragged the corporal and her older, witless sister from their Tibetan home to Beirut and thence westward to France for the sole purpose of confronting the old general with the fruit of his mountaintop dalliance. In her lifelong hatred of the old general for what she calls his betrayal of their mother, she bears many resemblances to Rosa Coldfield, and her narrative of the old general's abrupt advent into their lives in that remote Tibetan village makes him in important ways an avatar of Thomas Sutpen; Marthe even tells the old general's story in terms of his "design."

She is so full of hatred, however, that we can no more accept her story completely than we can accept Rosa's demonization of Sutpen as the complete truth. Like Rosa, Marthe tells the tale of a monster; but as in *Absalom, Absalom!*, Faulkner in *A Fable* gives us enough other information about the old general's career to suggest that the story is much more complex than Marthe's maniacal recital allows.

Like Gragnon, the old general is an orphan; unlike Gragnon, however, who is reared in a rural orphanage, the old general is reared by an aunt and uncle in Paris. They give him social and political and military and financial connections which, combined with his own talent, promise to make him the most fabulous of the fabulous, and which guarantee not only that his military career can be pursued with relative ease in Paris but that Paris itself can be his for the taking. His classmates at St. Cyr—both his supporters, like the quartermaster general-to-be, who believe that he will save humanity, and his critics, who believe that his success is guaranteed by his political connections—are astonished to learn that upon graduation the old general heads not for Paris but for the most remote and primitive outpost he can find, in desert Africa, "a place really remote, not even passively isolate but actively and even aggressively private . . . a small outpost not only five hundred kilometres from anything resembling a civilised stronghold . . . but sixty and more from its nearest support" (900). His critics believe that this retreat is merely a gesture, that he is off to do some time in the ranks, noblesse oblige, before accepting all the splendor of his heritage; the quartermaster general, the old general's John the Baptist, sees it as his desert trial before returning to save humanity. But the old general foils both critics and supporters when he leaves that African outpost to go to an even more remote location. He heads to the top of the Himalayan Mountains to a Tibetan lamasery, where he meets the woman whom he will make the corporal's mother, and he spends an unspecified amount of time there before coming back to Paris, finally, to accept the old general's baton.

The curious orbit of his career is strange, indeed, but not inexplicable. For his life, too, is described in terms that reflect the peculiarly feminine nature of his experience. We don't know much about his childhood with his aunt and uncle in Paris or what, if anything, he knows of his parents. We do know that when he enters St. Cyr he wears a locket containing two pictures, one a picture of his mother, and that he wears this locket "on a chain about his neck *like a crucifix*" (893, my emphasis); the connection between mother and crucifix is provocative. We know that he had a "secluded and guarded childhood," that he was "an orphan, an only child" (893). The narrator tells us numerous times that he is a small, fragile creature, like a child *and* like a girl; he is "still girlish-looking even after two years of African sun and solitude, still frail and fragile in the same way that adolescent girls appear incredibly delicate yet at the same time invincibly durable" (899). At dinner during the week of the mutiny, the old general, the supreme high commander of the Allied armies in Europe and so one of the most powerful men on earth, sits in a chair

> whose high carven back topped him like the back of a throne, his hands hidden below the rich tremendous table which concealed most of the rest of him too and apparently not only immobile but immobilised beneath the mass and glitter of his braid and stars and buttons, he resembled a boy, a child, crouching amid the golden debris of the tomb not of a knight or bishop ravished in darkness but (perhaps the mummy itself) of a sultan or pharaoh violated by Christians in broad afternoon. (884–85)

His own headquarters is a château which had been "a boudoir back in the time of its dead duchess or marquise" (876); he employs a "handsome young personal aide" (878), a batman who was "hardly larger than a child . . . rosy and blemishless . . . pink as an infant" (891–92). More ominously, he employs as his chauffeur a "six-and-a-half foot Basque with the face of a murderer of female children" (878). Though it is hardly possible to say with complete certainty what can be inferred about him from these associates, from the kind of men he surrounds himself with, together they suggest the degree to which he is not so very different from other men in the novel, especially in his relation to the feminine.

The old general's career takes the direction it does because he wants most of all to escape Paris, the Paris of his powerful aunt and uncle, and all that Paris symbolizes. Paris is here, as always in Faulkner, a rich, foul, rank, fecund, feminine presence which all men in the novel *except the old general* aspire to—the eternal symbol of opulence and satiation: "of all cities it was supreme, dreamed after and adored by all men" (895). It is

> the desired, the civilised world's inviolate and forever unchaste, virgin barren and insatiable: the mistress who renewed her barren virginity in the very act of each barren recordless promiscuity, Eve and Lilith both to every man in his youth so fortunate and blessed as to be permitted within her omnivorous insatiable orbit. (895)

Levine wants to lay his glory before his mother and his motherland; French men want otherwise. Paris is "barren"; it "had no sons: they were her lovers, and when they went to war, it was for glory to lay before the altar of that unchaste unstale bed" (896). That Paris has no sons, but only lovers, is part of its attraction.

This Paris and its heritage are the old general's, if he wants them. Yet, unlike every other man in the novel, he runs as far away from Paris as he can possibly get. Why? We can only suppose from what the novel tells us that he is running from something in his opulent, lonely childhood that has made the feminine repellent: he joins the army, a peculiarly male institution, and takes his first commission as far into the heart of desert Africa as he can manage, to a post of foreign legionnaires "recruited from the gutter-sweepings of all Europe and South America and the Levant," a post where "troops were sent as punishment or, incorrigibles, for segregation until heat and monotony on top of their natural and acquired vices divorced them permanently from mankind" (900). Even in this remote, preternaturally unwomanned spot, however, he finds his life complicated by the sexual, by a crime involving the disappearance of a woman and a camel from a tribe of natives in the neighborhood: he coldbloodedly sacrifices the man of his regiment who is responsible, a man indeed who is at that post because eighteen years earlier he had "corrupted and diseased and then betrayed into prostitution and at last murdered" (903) a Marseilles woman. The old general deals professionally with the situation, but he responds personally to it by retreating even further into what he thinks is an even more impenetrable masculine world. He goes to Tibet, to a lamasery.

The rest of his story we know from Marthe, who recounts it to the old general himself as a reproach. What emerges from her recital, however, is a story as much about herself as about the old general, and as much about the corporal as about either.

But the general cannot escape the feminine, even in Tibet. Indeed, if we believe Marthe he runs headlong into femininity's quintessence, for there he encounters a mountain Eula Varner, a woman, Marthe says, "who had something in her . . . which did not belong in that village—that village? in all our mountains, all that country" (931). Marthe describes her mother as a "weak and vulnerable [and] beautiful" woman (931) and claims that the old general came to their peaceful mountain village "just to destroy her home, her husband's faith, her children's peace, and at last her life,—to drive her husband to repudiate her just to leave her children fatherless, then her to die in childbirth in a cow-byre behind a roadside inn just to leave them orphans" (931). According to Marthe, this mountain Eula has the decency to spare her cuckolded husband the shame she has caused him and so leaves, taking her two daughters and her swollen belly with her. As she dies in childbirth she gives Marthe the locket that Marthe brings to the old general, extracting from Marthe the promise that she will take care of her new brother and her older, idiot sister, a promise much like that Ellen Sutpen extracts from Rosa Coldfield when she dies.

Marthe would have it that the old general seduces and abandons her mother and family; she accuses him of believing "that people are to be bought and used empty and then thrown away" (936). But her hatred is so intense and so long sustained that we cannot simply accept her story as the whole truth; besides, as a nine-year-old at the time, she surely could not have known or understood all that happened between her father and mother and between her mother and the old general, or even the limitations and perhaps frustrations of her mother's life in that small village, which we may imagine to be not so different from lives such as hers in the Southern small towns of Faulkner's Yoknapatawpha fiction. Loyal to her father, she has no sufficient imagination, no sufficient experience of life, to wonder whether her mother, far from being a victim of the old general's cynical manipulations, may rather have embraced this outland stranger as a way out of a lonely and frustrated life in that isolated mountain Eden—her release, perhaps, from an unsatisfying marriage. We who have watched the old general run in undeviating retreat from the feminine may also question whether he is likely to be the aggressor; indeed, she seems to be the strong one in the relationships with the men in her life, and it is at least possible that she has seduced and abandoned him, rather than, as Marthe would have it, the other way around. Tucked away in an earlier conversation between the old general and an American officer is a curious exchange. As he explains some detail of his experience with the corporal, the American stumbles into an awkward moment: "I just happened to have found out by accident the last night before we left because a girl had stood me up and I thought I knew why," the American says: "I mean, who it was, who the guy was. And you know how it is: you think of all the things to do to get even, make her sorry; you lying dead right there where she's got to step over you to pass, and it's too late now and boy, wont that fix her—" He stops suddenly as the old general interrupts: "Yes," he says. "I know." "Sir?" the captain repeats, and the old general reiterates: "I know that too" (923). It is a very quick exchange, but Faulkner doesn't want us to miss it, I think, or to believe that the old general is lying or simply being nice so the American will get on with the story. Though this conversation occurs in the book several pages before we learn of his relationship with the corporal's mother, it of course occurs chronologically years after his time in Tibet, and it is obviously to that episode that he refers when he interrupts the captain; his comment, then, seems to be an admission that that mountain girl somehow had hurt him deeply and that he, like other men in the novel, had responded to that hurt with that impulse to do himself harm just to spite the offending woman. Unlike Levine, however, he refrains. Like L. Q. C. McCaslin, he leaves the child a legacy of money—a stake if it is a boy, a dowry if it is a girl—that Marthe uses instead to bring herself and her sister and the boy to Beirut and then to France. The old general has kept up with them; without interfering in their lives more than he already has, he has never allowed himself to forget what he has done, though whether from fear or simple guilt we do not know.

At the conclusion of her tirade, Marthe throws at him a locket her dying mother gave her, containing two miniature portraits on ivory: one is identified as his mother. This is obviously the locket his St. Cyr coevals had noticed so many years ago, the one he wore around his neck "like a crucifix." We do not know whose is the second portrait, but he has apparently given the locket to his mountain lover, as some sort of token, a gesture of despair or love. When Marthe throws it back to him, the "crucifix" indeed comes home to roost; but in one important sense it has never left his neck.

We must be careful to be sympathetic with Marthe. Like Rosa Coldfield, she is herself a victim, one of Faulkner's abused children, and her life, if not perfectly parallel with Rosa's, does bear many resonances with it. At nine years old, she is hoicked by her pregnant mother out of her home, taken away from her father and forced to wander, homeless and for all she knew destinationless, accepting handouts of food and shelter, to watch her mother die in childbirth in the straw of a dark stable:

> I remember only the straw, the dark stable and the cold, nor whether it was Marya or I who ran back through the snow to beat on the closed kitchen door until someone came—only the light at last, the lantern, the strange and alien faces crowding downward above us, then the blood and lymph and wet: I, a child of nine and an eleven-year-old idiot sister trying to hide into what privacy we could that outraged betrayed abandon[ed] and forsaken nakedness. (935)

Because of this traumatic experience, she, at nine years old, must accept her mother's charge to care for her sister and her new brother: an innocent child herself, like so many children in Faulkner, she must suffer for sins she is not guilty of, assume burdens not of her own making. As Rosa Coldfield is consumed with hatred of Thomas Sutpen, so is Marthe consumed by hatred of the old general, whom, rightly or wrongly, she blames for her miseries.

All we know about the corporal's early life we know from Marthe's diatribe. She assumes that the corporal is as outraged by his father's defection as she is, and no doubt over the years she has filled him as full of his father's faults as Rosa Coldfield fills Quentin full of Thomas Sutpen's. But what clearly emerges from her monologue is the extent to which he, like Levine, wants only to escape his "mother's" clutches. By her own unwitting testimony, Marthe is very like blind Angélique, with whom she is associated at her first appearance in the book, who bullies and drives the men in her life and has no concern for what they need or want or think. The matter of his marriage is instructive: "We had long ago designed marriage for him," Marthe tells the old general; "he was free, grown, a man. . . . Except that he refused twice, declined twice the candidates virtuous and solvent and suitable which we picked for him." She claims she does not know whether "it was the girl he said no to or the institution." "Perhaps [he said no to] both," she charges the old general, "being your son. . . . [T]he repudiation of the institution since his own origin had done without it" (942). She thus claims that the corporal rejected marriage and solvency just to spite the old general, his father. But his subsequent marriage to a girl of his own choice, a Marseilles whore who has neither money nor respectability, is so direct a contravention of *her* preferences that he seems clearly to have made the match to spite Marthe rather than his absent father. When the war begins he—like Levine, like Gragnon, like the old general—goes into the military, she says, "almost eagerly" (941): "A stranger," she says, "might have guessed it to be a young bachelor accepting even war as a last desperate cast to escape matrimony" (943). She cannot know either how completely right or completely wrong she is. The appalling irony of her narrative, as she admits, is that in her singlemindedness she herself has brought the corporal to France where he could join the French army in the first place and so be at this moment a candidate for execution. We can only speculate how much of his martyrdom, his desire to die, can be attributed to Marthe.

The Marthe-old general-corporal family relationship, then, with all its surrogates and substitutes, is yet another of the classic Faulkner triangles: a ferocious, dominating mother; a father absent or on the periphery of the family's life, having problematic relationships with women, yet potent nevertheless to doom or save; and a gentle, idealistic son burdened with such parents and so, like Quentin Compson, capable only of loving death. It may be worth remembering that Faulkner wrote the Compson Appendix, in which he described Quentin as being in love with death, in late 1945, barely two years after he had begun work on *A Fable*, and so it may not be surprising to find in the new book vestiges of his rethinking of that earlier work. My reading of *A Fable*, then, offers the Christ-corporal as yet another of Faulkner's crucified children: he is indeed the ultimate apotheosis of all outraged abandoned violated and crucified children in all of Faulkner's work, his "crucifixion" but the literal acting out of what has so often, so profoundly, appeared in Faulkner as metaphor.

Under the circumstances, we cannot help but recall that awesome moment in *The Sound and the Fury* when Reverend Shegog invokes the Virgin Mary sitting in the door with her baby on her lap. "Breddren!" he says:

> Look at dem little chillen settin dar. Jesus wus like dat once. He mammy suffered de glory en de pangs. Sometime maybe she helt him at de nightfall, whilst de angels singin him to sleep; maybe she look out de do and see de Roman po-lice passin. . . . Listen, breddren! I sees de day. Ma'y setting in de do wid Jesus on her lap, de little Jesus. Like dem chillen dar, de little Jesus. I hears de angels singin de peaceful songs en de glory; I sees de closin eyes; sees Mary jump up, sees de sojer face: We gwine to kill! We gwine to kill! We gwine to kill yo little Jesus! (SF 296)

In *A Fable* the "Roman sojers" fulfill Reverend Shegog's promise.

The image, in *The Sound and the Fury*, of that virgin mother and son may be the only portrait in Faulkner of anything resembling an ideal mother/son relationship. But there it is a relationship sealed and perfected into one transient moment. It exists on the edge of destruction and, indeed, for Faulkner's and Shegog's dramatic purposes, exists to be destroyed by the "Roman po-lice." The iconic tableau of Madonna and Christ-child is conspicuous by its absence from *A Fable*'s elaborate even if ironic reconstruction of Christ's life, but its absence is significant too. The image of the virgin who is a mother outside the intervention of a man, of the son who is a son outside the need for a father: of motherhood and childhood complete in themselves, outside the complications of time and sex and death, stands in stark contrast to the heavy weight of history and the burden of family that the characters in *A Fable* must contend with.

Marthe drags her family to a small village in France named Vienne-la-Pucelle, a name significant enough for Faulkner to have retyped a line of the final typescript in order to call it that. *Vienne* is the present subjunctive of the French verb *venir, to come*; *la Pucelle* means *the virgin*, so that, translated literally, the village's name means *if the virgin comes* or *should the virgin come*. This is the village of the corporal's youth and adolescence: "If the virgin comes," he might therefore think, "if we could have the maternal ideal, then we could have peace." The complex strands of the novel's "meanings" would appear to confirm him in this idea, but only, I think, in the sense that the image of Madonna and child represents a regression, a removal from the present difficult world to the complete safety and security of mother's bosom.

The village's name cuts quite another direction, however, for of course *la Pucelle* was what Joan of Arc called herself, and since it is Marthe who chooses the place where they settle, she may in some way want to identify herself with that warrior girl who made kings and slew men. In this case, perhaps, *if the virgin comes* she would right all wrongs, conquer all enemies, and restore peace not through motherly love but through military power. The Virgin Mary, the virgin Joan:

herein lies the hermaphroditism of war that the old general has spoken of—two opposing poles, of regression and aggression, between which poor impotent man ceaselessly moves, opposites that inhabit human beings' breasts and exhaust and renew themselves there in endless conflict. Or perhaps Mary and Joan, virgin and warrior, are not opposed at all, really, in that they offer man the same thing: peace; the one through death or, since she wields a sword, through castration, the other through regression to the near unconsciousness of that simple relationship, the eternal mouth at the eternal nipple. Recall once again how General Gragnon, early in the novel, in the midst of his troubles, in a rush of loneliness and frustration, regresses to the mother he never had; lying on the ground of the scarred and torn battlefield of his life on which he has just failed, he listens to the cicadas, which are for him "a purring sound such as he imagined might be made by the sleeping untoothed mouth itself around the sleeping nipple" (705). Breast and sword, then, equally bring desire's cessation: peace: death. *"[I]f I'd just had a mother,"* Quentin Compson pines, *"so I could say Mother Mother"* (SF 172).

Earlier in the war the British battalion runner, fatigued with striving, goes to Paris to seek his "lost youth dead fifteen years now" (802); it is for him a deliberate regression, a "pilgrimage back to when and where the lost free spirit of man once existed" (802). As he wanders through his—and, not incidentally, Faulkner's—old haunts around the Left Bank looking for his garret home—also, like Faulkner's home in Paris, in the rue Servandoni—he stumbles by accident upon the sign announcing the offices of the Reverend Tobe Sutterfield's organization: *Les Amis Myriades et Anonymes à la France de Tout le Monde.* That title, the narrator tells us, is a designation "so embracing, so richly sonorous with grandeur and faith, as to have freed itself completely from man and his agonies, majestic in empyrean, as weightless and palpless upon the anguished earth as the adumbration of a cloud" (800). The office he enters seems to him "like a dream"

(803), and he climbs the stairs to Sutterfield's office, "mounting to the uttermost airy nepenthelene pinnacle: a small chamber like a duchess's boudoir in heaven" (804).

Gone, then, to seek "the lost free spirit of man," regressed to his youth in Paris, he in fact finds not that spirit itself, but rather an acceptable and inspirational symbol of it, in a dreamlike maternal chamber profoundly removed from the concerns of earth, profoundly removed even from the present moment. From this maternal nest, the runner hears from Sutterfield the story of the fabulous three-legged racehorse that Sutterfield and the English groom and the Negro boy had raced throughout the Edenic American backwoods of the lower Mississippi Valley four years earlier. As the runner listens to Sutterfield tell the story, it is "like listening to a dream" (807). The maternal setting of the story's telling makes it possible to understand the relationship of the "horsethief" episode to the rest of the novel.

To be brief, the story is a fable about a crippled male horse that is nevertheless faster than all four-legged, completely healthy opponents. The horse and Sutterfield and the two attendants become so famous throughout the Mississippi Valley that all men in the area conspire to protect them from the law that pursues them. The runner's thrilled imagination responds to the story by romanticizing the chase in sexual terms; he sees it as

> a passion, an immolation, an apotheosis . . . the immortal pageant-piece of the tender legend which was the crowning glory of man's own legend beginning when his first paired children lost well the world and from which paired prototypes they still challenged paradise, still paired and still immortal against the chronicle's grimed and bloodstained pages. (807)

The pairs he invokes are legend's tragic lovers: Adam and Lilith, Paris and Helen, Pyramus and Thisbe, Romeo and Juliet, lovers who scorned the safe and domestic, who gave their lives to their passions (807). More violently, he associates the groom with "earth's splendid rapers" (807).

The law finally catches up with the crew of horsethieves, only to find that the groom has killed the magnificent racehorse. The ex-deputy who has followed them around believes he knows why:

> so that it could run, keep on running, keep on losing races at least, finish races at least even if it did have to run them on three legs. . . . While [its owners] would have taken it back to the Kentucky farm and shut it up in a whorehouse where it wouldn't need any legs at all. . . . Fathering colts forever more; they would have used its ballocks to geld its heart with for the rest of its life, except that you saved it because any man can be a father, but only the best, the brave— (816)

He doesn't finish the sentence, but clearly in his analysis of the killing of the horse is the same bitter rejection of both sexuality and domesticity we have seen in the rest of the novel: *They would have used its ballocks to geld his heart with for the rest of its life.* The horse, then, represents to these Americans the same thing that those wild, untameable, spotted ponies of *The Hamlet* represent to the men of Frenchman's Bend: some edge of passion, uncontrolled and potent, which they do not have, some freedom from, a mighty power over, the constrictions of the feminine. The men of *The Hamlet* find haven from their women at Varner's store; the men of this episode of *A Fable* retreat to the masculine exclusivity of their Masonic lodges.

That three-legged horse, then, is a powerful symbol of masculine resistance to the feminine, and we need only remind ourselves of Mama Bidet's château, into which the army has "notched" an entrance cubicle like a "rusted spur in a bride's cake" (694), and of the "pile of horse-droppings" on the terrace by the door (711) to get some sense of how completely the men of *A Fable* despise and fear the feminine and to understand how puny their attempts to desecrate it, how impotent their efforts to violate it, how futile their efforts to escape it. They run from it at the moment of birth, to it at the moment of death.

+ ♀ +

Executed with the corporal are two malefactors who like most men in *A Fable* only want to get to Paris and who in the process of trying to steal some money break into a house and confront an old woman in bed: "all she had to do," Lapin says, "was just tell us where the money was hidden and then behave herself, keep her mouth shut. Instead she had to lay there in the bed yelling her head off until we had to choke her or we never would have got to Paris—" (998–99). *Casse-Tête* is the name of the drooling idiot who kills this screaming mother/woman: literally, *casse-tête* means "break-head," a term used to refer to "something done with great difficulty"; it is also a club used by primitive peoples. Casse-Tête's nickname, however, gives us the final clue to the meaning of this episode: Lapin, his partner, simply calls him Horse. Both name and nickname are significant: Horse is the masculine who kills the feminine to get to Paradise—which is, paradoxically, the eternally feminine Paris.

Horse wants to get to Paris. He is almost totally libidinous about it: "Paris" is the one word he knows and he repeats it over and over again whenever he is spoken to. Lapin, the worldly rabbit, says to Horse, in his joking reassuring manner: "You found out you were going to have to go to Paris before you even found out you were going to have to have a woman, hey, Horse?" (999). It is a complicated statement which Horse can surely not understand: Lapin refers specifically to the old woman Horse has killed, but the sexual meanings of "to have a woman" are unmistakable, and so is the connection between sex and death, and that between sex and death and Paris.

Even as they are about to be shot, "Paris" is all Horse can say. "Say something to him" (1022), Lapin calls to the corporal, who responds with Faulkner's version of Christ's *This day shalt thou be with me in Paradise:* "It's all right," he tells Horse. "We're going to wait. We wont go without you" (1023). Thus if Paris, the world's courtesan, the feminine, is, in Horse's meaning, heaven, it is in the corporal's meaning, death. It is where the corporal goes when he dies, where the old general, his father, is laid to rest.

As "articulations" of "two inimical conditions" (988), father and son are one of the novel's many hermaphroditic pairs. At the close of the novel they are laid together, the two conditions they represent no longer inimical but self-exhausted on their deathbeds, the body they now inhabit that of mother earth, the Arc de Triomphe's symbolic masculine bulk rising high above them. There are two pietàs at the end of the novel—one, implied, is the martyred corporal safe and comforted at last at mother earth's breast; the other, more potent, is that of the crippled and scarred battalion runner receiving the masculine comfort of the quartermaster general—masculine idealism, or fantasy, sucking yet again at the dry breast of the military.

I have in this essay barely touched the full extent of the feminine presence in *A Fable*, or of its significance to the novel, though I dare hope that an approach to Faulkner's most misunderstood work such as I have here suggested may open up the novel to studies which will not dismiss it, as most studies do, as a pious aberration from Faulkner's other work. *A Fable* is not at all a simple-minded reenactment of Christ's passion. It is rather a tough-minded and artistically perilous attempt to invest that hollow fable of sacrifice and salvation with meanings more profoundly tied to the people of the Waste Land of the twentieth century, whose anxieties are not so easily laid to rest by any hope of ultimate peace, or dissolved so completely at any martyr's feet.

Man in the Middle

Faulkner and the Southern White Moderate

For Evans Harrington

Faulkner wrote *Intruder in the Dust* in the winter and early spring of 1948, seasons during which the Mississippi Democratic party geared itself for a vital confrontation with the national Democratic party at the summer convention in Philadelphia over the report of President Truman's Commission on Civil Rights. Truman was urging Congress "to adopt his civil rights program embodying voting rights, employment opportunities, and other provisions destined to draw fire from Southern Democrats" (Winter 141). Governor Fielding Wright called a meeting of Mississippi Democrats for February 12, Lincoln's birthday, in Jackson. All members of the legislature attended, hoping to find some way to counter in advance the proposed civil rights planks in the national party's platform. On February 22, Washington's birthday, Mississippi Democrats met with representatives from the Democratic parties of nine other Southern states to plan strategies to force upon the Democratic platform planks favoring states', rather than civil, rights. Failing to sway the national body at the August convention, the entire Mississippi delegation and part of Alabama's walked out. In a subsequent convention in Birmingham Southern delegates founded the Dixiecrat party, which nominated the fiery states' rights Governor Strom Thurmond of South Carolina for president and Mississippi's own Governor Wright for vice-president. Mississippi voted 87 percent for the Dixiecrat ticket, and was joined in the colossal losing battle by South Carolina, Louisiana, and Alabama (Winter 144). The political and emotional issues at stake in this Dixiecrat year—states' rights, anti-lynching laws, mongrelization, the future of the white race, and other associated issues—were surely not lost on William Faulkner as he wrote *Intruder* in the spring and then saw it through the press during the summer.

Intruder was published on September 27. On October 23 Edmund Wilson wrote in the *New Yorker* that *Intruder* seemed to have been at least "partly . . . stimulated by the crisis at the time of the war in the relations between Negroes and whites and by the recently proposed legislation for guaranteeing Negro rights. The book contains," Wilson went on, "a kind of counterblast to the anti-lynching bill and to the civil-rights plank in the Democratic platform." This was a line that many reviewers would take, and most commentators since have generally agreed with Wilson's assessment that "the author's ideas on this subject are apparently conveyed, in their explicit form, by the intellectual uncle, who, more and more as the story goes on, gives vent to long disquisitions that seem to become so 'editorial' in character that . . . the series may be pieced together as something in the nature of a public message delivered by the author himself" (Wilson 335–36). About the time Wilson's review appeared, Faulkner paid his first visit to the New England home of Malcolm Cowley, a friend since their collaboration on *The Portable Faulkner* of 1946. Cowley had reviewed *Intruder* for *The New Republic* along the same lines as Wilson, although he had been a bit more generous than Wilson. In writing about Faulkner's visit, Cowley reports that Faulkner discussed *Intruder* in terms that might have been an "indirect answer" to his review: "[Gavin] Stevens, he [Faulkner] explained, was not speaking for the author, but for the best type of liberal Southerners; that is how they feel about the Negroes" (Cowley 110–11).

In this comment to Cowley, Faulkner seems to be distancing himself from Stevens's views on the South's racial problems in a way that should make the average New Critic very proud, although to be sure, it is not a distance many new or old critics either have been successful at finding. Yet barely three months later, in January 1949, Faulkner sent to Robert Haas, at Random House, a two-page addition to *Intruder*, along with instructions to insert it if there were ever a second printing: it was something, he wrote, that he had "remembered . . . last year only after the book was in press" (SL 285). The addition was to Stevens's long argument that Southern blacks and whites are the only homogeneous groups left in the United States. The addition has Stevens conclude this speech with the prediction that social and political assimilation of whites and blacks will eventually result in the extinction of the black race. In the closing lines of the speech, Faulkner makes Stevens actually refer to and quote from *Absalom, Absalom!*, a book, Stevens says, by "a mild retiring little man over yonder at Oxford,"; he quotes what he calls the book's "tag line," from a conversation, he says, between a "Canadian [and a] self-lacerated Southerner in a dormitory room in a not too authentic Harvard." The "tag line" is Shreve's parting shot to Quentin on the subject of the amalgamation of the races: "I who regard you will have also sprung from the loins of African kings" (WFMS 17:719–21).

In identifying Stevens as "the best type of liberal Southerner," Faulkner was placing him in pretty good company—that of such people as Hodding Carter, P. D. East, James Silver, Frank Smith, Duncan Gray, and others who risked lives and fortunes in numerous ways during those tumultuous years. If in responding to Cowley Faulkner was distancing himself from Stevens, then, was he thereby removing himself from the company of "the best types?" If so, why did he go out of his way to inject himself into what Stevens has to say? If he were trying to distance himself, did he have in mind another category for such Southerners as himself? Was he trying to make some sort of statement about the "best type of liberal Southerner"? Was he speaking seriously to Cowley or was he simply putting on his novelist's mask of anonymity? Did he have a different opinion of this "type" of "liberal Southerner" in 1948 than he was to develop during his deliberate public identification with them during the fifties?

To be sure, it is difficult to escape a considerable sense of urgency, of "message" in Stevens's diatribe against the North, and equally difficult to resist assuming that Stevens is mouthing Faulkner's own feelings, especially given the similarity of Faulkner's rhetoric to Stevens's as his own public involvement in civil rights issues grew over the next few years. Even so, we should take seriously Faulkner's effort to distance himself from Stevens, if only because the novel itself problematizes Stevens's opinions about race; even Chick Mallison is suspicious. The garrulous lawyer is, in *Intruder* as in the other works in which he appears, more interested in talking than in doing. Three times in the novel's closing pages Faulkner describes Stevens as talking while he smokes his cob pipe:

> his uncle even struck the match to the cob pipe still talking not just through the smoke but into it with it;

> his uncle struck the match again and puffed the pipe still talking, talking through the pipe stem with the smoke as though you were watching the words themselves;

> again his uncle was striking the match, holding it to the pipe and speaking through with into the smoke. (ID 451, 454, 466)

It could hardly be clearer that in *Intruder* Gavin Stevens is largely blowing smoke—not altogether because of what he says but rather because of the relationship between what he says and what he actually does. Stevens says to the North: let the South free the black man; we owe it to him and we will pay him and we don't need anybody to interfere. Yet *Intruder* is precisely about the wrongful imprisonment of an innocent black man; given the opportunity to defend Lucas in court, or even to listen to his side of the story, Stevens—the "best type" of liberal Southerner—hastens to an assumption of Lucas's guilt that is worthy of even the reddest of Beat Four necks. Proven wrong by his nephew's impetuous trust of Lucas, Stevens elbows and mouths his way into Lucas's salvation. Much of what he has to say, then, should be taken as a vain attempt to fill up the gap between what Chick has done and what he, Stevens, with all the best intentions, has failed to do: to act in good faith with the judicial presumption of innocence.

The essence of Stevens's role in *Intruder*, then, is not the political relevance in 1948 of his diatribe against the North but rather in his inability to see past the persiflage of his own words. Stevens talks about everything but his own failure: he is defensive about the hypo-critical North, fearful of federal interference in Mississippi's affairs, worried about amalgamation of the races; he is concerned whether blacks are ready for full equality; he is bothered that they imitate the ways of the lowest class of whites (instead, obviously, of the more acceptable manners of the Gavin Stevenses of the world); he conde-scendingly concedes that the reason rednecks fear blacks is that blacks can work harder and do more with less than whites can. What he has to say is in fact very much in line with what other moderates of the forties and fifties in Mississippi had to say and not at all unlike Faulkner's public statements during the same period. But as Stevens articulates them in the dramatic context of the novel, all of these top-ics become rhetorical, sophistical, devices to evade his own particular guilt in regard to a very particular Lucas; mostly he's covering his failure to operate according to the rhetoric, at least, of his own highest moral and social standards. He is, as I say, blowing smoke to hide behind: he throws up Sambo, the condescending abstraction, to avoid Lucas, the concrete human being. This is the same Stevens, we should remember, who in *Light in August* pontificates so superfluously on Joe Christmas's ambiguous blood, and the same Stevens whose good intentions in the concluding chapter of *Go Down, Moses* are seri-ously undercut by his consternation upon confronting Molly Beau-champ's real, impenetrable grief and by the reader's simultaneous discovery of how arrogantly Stevens has presumed to know what Molly—The Negro—wanted, and of how terribly little he understood of her life: how much he talked, how little he said: how much less he did. Among the other important things Chick comes to recognize is the "significantless speciosity of his uncle's voice" (344), and his "un-cle's abnegant and rhetorical self-lacerating *which was . . . phony*" (384, my emphasis).

What is novelistically at stake in *Intruder*, then, are Chick Mallison and his efforts to find his own way through the tangle of Southern race relations. In this, Lucas and Aleck Sander and even the Gowries are his concrete experience of that tangle; Stevens is the tangle's ab-straction, the looming and ponderous weight of history, of the tradition of black-white relations as seen from the secure financial and social position of the educated aristocrats who can afford easy platitudes, can afford to be "concerned" about Sambo precisely because, unlike the rednecks in Beat Four, they do not have to compete with Sambo for what living they can muster with their own sweat.

Faulkner's attitude toward Stevens in *Intruder* seems reasonably clear from the context that the novel creates: the novel provides sufficient evidence of Stevens's shortcomings to make us wary of accepting his words at their face value. The distressing extent to which Faulkner seems to have endorsed Stevens's opinions in the series of speeches, public letters, and more formal essays of the middle 1950s, which got him more and more publicly embroiled in the problem and more and more formally associated with the moderate point of view. As with other moderates in the South, Faulkner's moderation earned him the contumely and spite of both sides—whites, including family and friends, who were outraged at his break with traditions; and blacks, who felt that such moderates were more a part of the problem than of the solution. The middle was not an easy position to hold. Faulkner gave his white neighbors and friends plenty to scream at him about and, on one occasion, gave black accusers a real reason to question his racial sensibilities.

In February of 1956 Faulkner submitted to an interview by Russell Howe. Among numerous thoughtful responses to questions in which he articulated both his abhorrence of the injustices of racial segregation and his fear that the current crisis would precipitate bloodshed, he also, according to the interviewer, said this astonishing thing:

> If I have to choose between the United States government and Mississippi, then I'll choose Mississippi. What I'm trying to do now is not have to make that decision. As long as there's a middle road, all right, I'll be on it. But if it came to fighting I'd fight for Mississippi against the United States even if it meant going out into the street and shooting Negroes. . . . I will go on saying that the Southerners are wrong and that their position is untenable, but if I have to make the same choice Robert E. Lee made then I'll make it. (LG 256)

When published, the remark created such controversy that Faulkner wrote a public letter in which he contended that the statement, as reported, was "more a misconstruction than a misquotation." Without explaining the misconstruction, he concluded that such statements were both "foolish and dangerous": "statements which no sober man would make and, it seems to me, no sane man believe" (Blotner [1974] 1599, 1601).[1]

There seems to be no question that Faulkner was accurately quoted in the interview, that he actually said he would shoot Negroes in the street to defend Mississippi. He himself did not directly deny having said it and his editor, Saxe Commins, who was present at the interview, never denied it—and one has to assume that he would have been quick to defend his author from the effects of such an admission if he could have (Blotner [1974], 1590[2]). Faulkner apologists in the matter take some comfort in his implicit admission that he was drinking during the interview, and indeed, according to Blotner's account, he had been drinking heavily during the period of the interview, responding to pressures of the mounting racial crisis in his native state and particularly to that developing at the University of Alabama. His critics suspect that, liquor or not, the statement reveals William Faulkner for what he *really* was, at heart, a white Mississippian, with all the moral and cultural and even intellectual limitations that soubriquet implies.

The episode is a significant one in Faulkner studies because in it are crystallized and intertwined all of the biographical and historical and political considerations and, radiating outward from it, a number of artistic and aesthetic considerations, that make "Faulkner and Race" a hellishly complex topic. One can hardly call his purely outrageous confession that he would shoot Negroes in the street to defend Mississippi "moderate." And yet the statement seems to be such a

1. See ESPL 226 and LG 265. Meriwether and Millgate's introduction to the Howe interview (LG 257) suggest the reasons that one must approach the interview with caution.

2. In the 1984 one-volume revision of *Faulkner: A Biography*, 617–18, Blotner omits to mention Commins's presence at the interview.

dramatic departure from the very straightforward moderate positions he had been taking during the decade of the fifties, and a far cry indeed from a more intimate view he had offered to Else Jonsson not quite a year earlier, in a letter of 12 June 1955:

> We have much tragic trouble in Mississippi now about Negroes. The Supreme Court has said that there shall be no segregation, difference in schools, voting, etc. between the two races, and there are many people in Mississippi who will go to any length, even violence, to prevent that, I am afraid. I am doing what I can. I can see the possible time when I shall have to leave my native state, something as the Jew had to flee from Germany during Hitler. I hope that wont happen of course. But at times I think that nothing but a disaster, a military defeat even perhaps, will wake America up and enable us to save ourselves, or what is left. This is a depressing letter, I know. But human beings are terrible. One must believe well in man to endure him, wait out his folly and savagery and inhumanity. (SL 381–82)

There is a very long distance between on the one hand abandoning in despair a homeland one loves and, on the other, being willing to go to armed battle against overwhelming odds in defense of the very land and people who have caused the despair that makes him consider leaving. He made his comment to Russell Howe in the context of a discussion of Autherine Lucy's attempts to enroll at the University of Alabama; he expressed a fear that she would be killed, and worried over the consequences of that eventuality. Just three months after Faulkner died, James Meredith enrolled at the University of Mississippi. I doubt very much that if he had lived he would have taken up arms alongside other Mississippians against the Federal Marshals who were posted there to keep the peace and to insure Meredith's right to an education.

I said that Faulkner's statement to Howe that he would shoot Negroes in the street *seemed* to be a departure from his more moderate statements; for if the part of his statement about shooting Negroes is an appalling contradiction of his previous positions on racial justice, his willingness to "defend Mississippi against the United States" is at the same time perfectly consistent with his often reiterated desire to hold at bay any sort of outside intervention into Mississippi's affairs. While racial matters clearly dominate Faulkner's nonfictional pronouncements of the fifties, they are not his only concerns; there are others whose relationship to the Negro question, in Faulkner's mind, or at least in his rhetoric, has not, I think, been sufficiently noted.

Part of his anxiety about the modern world was caused by the degree to which social, economic, and political phenomena seemed to be conspiring to rob the individual of the capacity to act as an individual. The very idea of collective humanity, which he found abhorrent, expressed itself politically in the post-World War II world as a product of Communism and of the American government's various welfare and support programs that, in Faulkner's view, were depriving the individual of both the capacity and the right to be independent. Socially and economically it expressed itself in Madison Avenue's aggressive enforcement of a consumer conformity through the brand new power of television advertising; psychologically, it expressed itself as an increasing dependence upon technological gadgetry to do not just our work but our thinking for us. All of these forces were causing, in Faulkner's view, a standardization of life all across the world and, particularly in America, an intolerable conformism that threatened to swallow up the individual, to render the individual human being invalid.

To be sure, many of the views on the modern world that Faulkner expresses in his nonfiction emerge from a deeply rooted political and personal conservatism. At one level, for example, he never seemed quite able to reconcile himself to many of the New Deal's welfare and assistance programs, especially those programs of farm subsidies designed to bring some sort of order and stability to farm produce markets that were increasingly involved in very complicated national and international economies that made his own implicit ideal, the Jeffersonian self-consumer, not only obsolete, but virtually impossible even to imagine except as a historical oddity. His world vision also seems to be marked by a kind of xenophobia, which can be seen in a variety of his reactions both to the international problems connected with the Cold War and, especially, to the local and national problems connected with the racial antagonisms in his home state and region.

That is, while he supported equality of opportunity for all races as the morally right thing to do, his rhetoric tended to operate along the very pragmatic lines that for the South not to solve its own problems would be to invite the federal government to intervene in its affairs. Southern whites and blacks, he argued, had more in common with each other than any Southerner had with any Northerner; therefore, Southerners, black and white, had better stick together to stave off any outsider's challenge to their way of life. By the same token, he felt, all Americans, black, white, Southern, Northern, needed to stick together in order to present a united front to combat the menace of Communism.[3] It was therefore in the best interests of the white majority to abolish the system that kept Negroes in economic and educational slavery; not to solve our own problems was to invite the federal government to solve them for us, probably in ways not to our liking. It was also in the best interests of Negroes, who had made enormous gains and who now had the political and economic power to continue the initiative, to "go slow," not to precipitate crises which would weld the white majority, including moderates like himself, into a unit in backlash resistance, precipitate violence and bloodshed, and so create the conditions for yet another kind of federal involvement, another Civil War.

Indeed, the violence and federal intervention he feared did occur. But it may also be true—how will we ever know?—that the "moderate" positions Faulkner was advocating would have delayed social and political change for many years, perhaps generations. Certainly we look back now on the words and good wishes of the "best types" of liberal Southerners with an overwhelming sense of how empty the words advocating caution, patience, and good will must have seemed to black citizens, who had practiced these virtues for generations and had gotten so little from them. Southern liberals' best intentions not-

3. See, for example, "On Fear: Deep South in Labor: Mississippi" and the "Address to the Southern Historical Association" in *Essays Speeches and Public Letters*.

withstanding, how could African Americans of the fifties not have taken admonitions to patience as yet another tactic of delay? The violence Faulkner feared had a bloody but immediate impact, and we seem now, on the other side of the chaos and misery of those awful years, to be at least some the better for it, though I, a male Mississippi WASP, may not be qualified to say how much better. It seems clear, in retrospect, that Faulkner simply underestimated the impatience of Negroes and their willingness to suffer and die for their rights as American citizens. He also overestimated the capacity of Southern whites to act in their own best interests. He *never* made this mistake in his fiction.

We should be very careful, however, not to read backwards from the public statements into the fiction, as readers have done so readily, for his attitude toward the modern world, as writer and citizen, was neither simplistic nor simple, and he was not, as he has sometimes been thought, a simple-minded reactionary retrenched against the modern world and longing sentimentally for the lost innocence of the Big Woods. He was no mid-century Miniver Cheevy, born out of his time and resenting it. No writer I know of places more value than he on the ability to cope with change — change of environment, of relationship, of historical and social circumstance. This was, from one way of looking at it, the point of his entire argument with Mississippi, certainly it was the point of his rhetoric whenever he talked publicly about race. That is, he did not try to change white Southern hearts, but only their behavior. He argued, very pragmatically, that change was inevitable and that it was in everybody's best interest, blacks and whites, North and South, for Southern whites themselves to effect that change and to learn to live with new social and political conditions. A large part of Gavin Stevens's problem in *Intruder* is that, unlike Faulkner, he is wedded, even if he does not know it, to the status quo. An even larger part of Stevens's problem is that, like other Faulkner characters, he is so completely wedded to the abstraction of justice that he does not see the concrete; he is so completely concerned with what he would call the larger picture that he does not see the details that make up that larger picture.

Readers and critics have been all too willing to accept Faulkner's post-Nobel public career, especially his engagement in the Civil Rights debate, as at worst an embarrassing mistake, at best a pious aberration, from his former artistic isolation from such battles, and borne of what Phil Stone called Faulkner's "Nobelitis of the head." We might more generously attribute his public life of the fifties to his own direct, moral response to the racial morality of *Intruder in the Dust, Go Down, Moses, Absalom, Absalom!,* and *Light in August,* and take it as a sincere effort to communicate with an audience of blue-collar citizenry he had previously more or less forsaken in his pursuit of his art's high modernism (see "Faulkner at Midcentury"). If so, it is perhaps not to be wondered at that the intellectual content of his public pronouncements is not high or that his language is more utilitarian than poetic, though to be sure in public he never grasped at such tawdry conservative clichés as he wrote in private to Else Jonsson: "I think nothing but a disaster . . . will wake America up and enable us to save ourselves" indeed!

We may indeed see many similarities between Stevens's fictional and Faulkner's public rhetoric; but Stevens's abstractions, his preference for talking instead of doing, his overriding interest in Sambo rather than in Lucas, point directly to the differences between Stevens and the public Faulkner. Faulkner's concern during the fifties was consistently with the *individual.* Even while making public and private generalizations about race that could and should be construed as racist, that could be and were construed as part of the problem rather than as part of the solution, he never lost sight of the need to make specific contributions to the solution of specific problems rather than just blow smoke. His chief concern during the crisis at the University of Alabama was for the life of Autherine Lucy, who he feared would be killed if she tried to enroll there (ESPL 108; Blotner [1974] 1591). Rather than simply declare that blacks needed more education to be worthy of equality, he took part of his Nobel Prize money to establish a scholarship fund for needy and worthy black students (Blotner [1984] 535). Malcolm Cowley reported a conversation in which Faulkner told him, probably with some exaggeration, that his own farm was run by "three Negro tenant families. . . . He lets them have the profits, if any, because—he said, speaking very softly—'The Negroes don't always get a square deal in Mississippi.' He figures that his beef costs him $5 a pound" (Cowley 111). His actions in these and doubtless other cases did not, of course, speak louder than his words, but they certainly did help alleviate racial misery in these individual cases.

Faulkner, too, was a complex combination of historical, economic, psychological, and social forces; like the rest of us he was a product of his own time and place, and it would be surprising indeed if this were not reflected in his work. It would be astonishing if, writing fifty years ago and more, he had been able to please an audience of the 1990s, who are much more sensitized to the subtleties of racial prejudice than any white person in 1920s or 1950s Mississippi, or in the entire United States either, for that matter, could possibly have been. Can we argue that Caspey and Simon Strother never existed? Can we argue that individual Negroes have never been irresponsible, have never looked like the stereotype even if they were deliberately puttin' on ol' massa? Have no Negroes ever played to their white bosses' prejudices either to save their skins or to keep their jobs? If we can allow Faulkner to describe the dark and violent underbelly of the average Mississippi redneck as he saw and tried to understand him, can we not also allow him to describe the dark and violent and unsavory underside of the blacks he saw? Is there no coin for verisimilitude or historical accuracy? Many critics have tried too hard to discover the number and kinds of things that Faulkner *did not* or *could not* do correctly in writing about race; many seem happy indeed (Taylor) to catch Faulkner in his Southern limitations—the intellectual desire to improve things at odds with ingrained racial prejudice—and this is of course fair enough. But at the same time, we should not ever overlook the magnitude of what he did attempt, over the manifest opposition of his state and region and family, and no doubt over his own fair share of those ingrained racial instincts and phobias.

In the closing scene of *Intruder* a proud, independent Lucas Beauchamp comes to Stevens's office to pay Stevens his lawyer's fee. Early in the novel, Lucas had had the dignity to refuse Chick's attempts to pay him for his hospitality after pulling him from the creek: he knows that there are some things you can't buy, some things you can't pay for. Stevens has neither that knowledge nor that dignity, so he takes Lucas's proffered coins even though he has done *nothing* to save Lucas's skin. Technically, Stevens refuses to let Lucas pay him a legal "fee"; but he does accept a trivial, two-dollar payment for his "expenses." This is a patently paternalistic ruse that can hardly be interpreted otherwise than as allowing Lucas to pay him for something he, Stevens, did not do. Stevens allows Lucas to pay for the very freedom that he, Stevens, has throughout the novel argued that the South, if left alone, would eventually give him. In this way, Stevens, the "best type of liberal Southerner"—and with what irony that phrase now rings in our ears—tries to keep Lucas obliged to him, to keep him in the bondage of gratitude. The shrewd Lucas understands what Stevens is doing, however, and in the novel's final line demands a receipt. Michael Millgate perceptively reads this scene as

> Lucas's insistence on . . . keeping affairs between himself and his white 'benefactors' on a strictly business footing, makes it clear that he does not intend his recent experience to affect his behaviour in the slightest degree and that he will not even release Charles from that indebtedness, that sense of being always at a disadvantage, which prompted the boy to his original intervention on Lucas's behalf. (220)

Lucas's demand for a receipt is his very direct way of saying that he does not trust Stevens. Thus he protects himself from any future demand Gavin Stevens and the best type of liberal Southerner might make on him. He wants proof that he is fully paid up.

Thus there is plenty of distance between Gavin Stevens and William Faulkner. I do not know certainly why Faulkner wrote that curious addition to *Intruder* four months after its publication, why he would want to associate himself with what Stevens was saying. I can only propose a partial answer that may be more ingenious than useful: even as other critics and reviewers like Edmund Wilson and Malcolm Cowley had quoted *Intruder* and others of Faulkner's novels to their own social and political purposes, making of *Intruder* an authorial polemic where no polemic was intended, so does Faulkner have Stevens quote Faulkner out of context and for his own self-justifying purposes. Like others who have quoted Faulkner on the race issue, Stevens patronizes the author—Stevens's Faulkner is "a mild retiring little man over yonder at Oxford"—and *Absalom, Absalom!* itself. Stevens, an old Harvard man, notes, just a little too archly, that Quentin and Shreve live in "a dormitory room in a not too authentic Harvard"—and he calls Shreve's flip and callous parting shot—"I who regard you will have also sprung from the loins of African kings"—the novel's "tag line" (Samway 111). He thereby glibly reduces that very complex novel to a single line. He quotes not Quentin's tortured and ambiguous testament—"*I dont hate it. I dont. I dont hate it*"—, but rather Shreve's clichéd reduction of America's race problems to a single, simple, issue. Shreve is, of course, a Canadian, an outsider with no experience of the South but what he has learned from Quentin, but who nevertheless presumes to sum up the South's problems in a clever rhetorical flourish. Faulkner, then, here makes Stevens a Faulkner critic. Like other critics, Stevens takes the words of one character more or less as Faulkner's own and, like many critics, he homes straight in on the easy, the simple, the clever, and avoids the hard and even dangerous complexities. More than Stevens have done this: more than Stevens have misunderstood *Absalom, Absalom!*, and more critics than should have have taken Stevens as Faulkner's voice.

Faulkner apparently did not pursue the insertion of the new material into new printings of *Intruder in the Dust*, and I suspect that he simply forgot about it, having written it on an impulse, perhaps even a whimsy, in response to being subjected yet again, by Wilson and even his friend Cowley, to the sort of manipulation and misunderstanding he had already had to put up with, and would increasingly have to endure during the coming decade.

II.

The question of Faulkner's racism has been operative if not explicit in a good deal of the dialogue about Faulkner and race, nearly from the first appearance of "race" as theme in his work (Taylor, Peters, Davis, Jenkins, Sundquist), and nearly all of it assume race as Faulkner's major theme, ranging from Sundquist who dismisses *The Sound and the Fury* in favor of *Absalom, Absalom!* because, he argues, Faulkner didn't find his real theme until he discovered the Negro, to Walter Taylor, who reads Faulkner's entire career as a not-so-successful attempt to work his way through his own ingrained regional attitudes toward blacks. Most readers of Faulkner would probably identify race as what Faulkner wrote "about," and indeed if you agree that *Absalom, Light in August*, and *Go Down, Moses* are major Faulkner achievements, it is hard to deny the importance of race in Faulkner's work. This is a curious circumstance of Faulkner's reputation, since only four of his nineteen novels, and barely three of his over a hundred short stories, are "about" race, even when they contain black characters. Whatever one might say about the significance of race in Faulkner's work, it is very difficult to argue that Faulkner was in any way obsessed with racial problems — more especially if there is any validity to my argument that race, in Faulkner, even in *Absalom, Light in August* and *Go Down, Moses*, is a mask for gender (see "The Artist as Cuckold") — or that in his fiction he had any sort of personal or political agenda as regards race.

The 1950s was not the first time Faulkner entered the public sphere in racial matters. On February 2, 1931, he read in the Memphis *Commercial Appeal* a letter from Mr. W. H. James, a black citizen of Starkville, Mississippi, which expressed his gratitude to the Association of Southern Women for the Prevention of Lynching for their efforts to stop lynching in Mississippi. In spite of urgent personal and family problems[4] Faulkner responded in a letter published on February 15, that was signed "William Falkner." It is an extraordinarily long letter, pointless except for its meanspiritedness, and mired in racial mythology, in which he takes the position that though he

4. He was still devastated by the death, at 9 days old, of his and Estelle's baby daughter on January 20. He was drinking heavily in his grief, and had set about to pay medical and other bills — including a gift to the Oxford hospital of an incubator (McMillen and Polk).

himself holds no brief for lynching, it is nevertheless true that lynching is mostly caused by black lawlessness, usually for raping white
women, and that the dispensers of home-made white justice are about
as discriminating as the courts, and rather more expeditious (McMillen and Polk 9–10). It's an astonishing letter, all the more so for its
curious juxtaposition to the publication, in January of 1931, of "Dry
September," in which an innocent black man is accused of and murdered for raping a white woman by a mob; in August of 1931 he
would begin writing *Light in August*, perhaps the novel *par excellence*
about the pathology of lynching. Both "Dry September" and *Light in
August*, powerful and convincing works of fiction, flatly contradict the
argument of his letter—so flatly it's hard to believe that the same man
could be responsible for all of them.

The letter thus stands with his statements in the Russell Howe
interview, a quarter century apart, as absolutely anomolous with the
novels and stories that intervened. It is easy enough to dismiss both
incidents as occurring at times of personal stress and heavy drinking,
and no less easy to argue that the stress and the alcohol indeed released a volatile racism that he otherwise mostly managed to keep
under control. It is only slightly more difficult, perhaps, to do as Neil
McMillen and I did in commenting on the 1931 letter, to allow
Faulkner to be a part of his own time and place, to recognize the
complexity of his makeup, and to allow him the contradiction—the
contradictions of genius, the contradictions of us all. That, too, is
an unsatisfactory response, because of how it nags with unanswered
questions; but it's the only one I have yet been able to devise. It would
be easier, I think, if the poles of Faulkner's racial attitudes were closer
together and therefore more morally ambiguous than the flatly unambiguous contradictions of the poles, since the ambiguity would allow
for a kind of interpretation that the contradiction forestalls. Perhaps
our—perhaps it's my—own complex and ambiguous responses to racial questions, no matter what our rhetoric or public stance, seques-
tered in the darker places of our consciousnesses, would make us
more comfortable with a Faulkner who was also more morally ambig-

uous too. It's a tough spot for those who want their heroes and sages to be morally untainted, to be somehow outside of time and place.

Was Faulkner a racist? If by "racism" one means a hatred or fear of Negroes, one can probably say No. If, however, by "racism" one means a belief in the inferiority of Negroes, one could probably answer that question with a Yes, but only by citing his numerous invocations of historical, rather than biological and genetic, circumstances as responsible for the Negro's social and economic and cultural "condition." In this, too, he was consonant with other moderate Southerners of his day. Even Hodding Carter did not generally argue for immediate social equality, perhaps not believing blacks capable of immediate social amalgamation; what he, and Faulkner, *did* confront was the issue of political and economic justice.[5]

But suppose it could be proven that in his very heart of hearts Faulkner was in fact a raging racist, that like his Southern and Mississippi brothers and sisters of the stereotype he imbibed from his mother's milk an absolute hatred of all people with black skins. Even if this were the case, shouldn't we still give him credit for the love and compassion and understanding with which he treated his black characters, his white ones too, and for the courage with which he spoke out, publicly, to try to correct a situation which his intellect, even if not his passions, found intolerable? One of his Negro characters opines that "Quality aint *is*, it's *does*." The same is true, I submit, of racism, since by certain definitions we are all racists of one sort or another: however ingrained they are, whatever their sources, whatever their objects, our prejudices and their capacity for mischief can only be measured by what they force us to *do*.

The fact is that even though a grandchild of slaveholders and a very defensive Southerner Faulkner acted quite responsibly, both in his fiction and, in the fifties, in the public forum. From beginning to end the works explode with a powerful sympathy with both the individual and the race. And his concern with the problem of Negro humanity expresses itself more eloquently and more profoundly in *Light*

5. See Carter's *Where Main Street Meets the River* and *Southern Legacy*, and David Cohn's *Where I Was Born and Raised*.

in August, Absalom, Absalom!, and *Go Down, Moses* than in any other book by any other author, written any where, at any time, ever. What more could be expected of an artist?

If in his public declarations during the fifties he expressed moderation, we must remember that he hardly seemed "moderate" to white Southerners of the day. Even if black leaders were right in perceiving the white moderates of the day as part of the problem rather than as part of the solution, we must also remember that Faulkner made his public statements at a time when it was very dangerous to do so, and did so even though it cost him the contumely of his family and of his community and of the entire state. What more could be expected of a citizen?

As a novelist, Faulkner knew that nearly all significant problems are too large and complex to be contained by any single opinion or point of view; as a novelist, he could and regularly did dramatize those problems without being obliged to solve them. As a citizen he undertook the perhaps quixotic task of solving them.

In his life, then, as in his fiction, Faulkner focuses on the individual human being. Part of the power of his depiction of black characters comes directly from his refusal to sentimentalize or simplify. What makes "That Evening Sun" remarkable is not just Mr. Compson's abandonment of his responsibility to Nancy, or of the children's inability to understand what is happening, but rather the intensity and the complexity of the relationship between Jesus and Nancy. They do, in fact, seem to love one another very much; but their relationship is thwarted by a variety of forces, some of which they have no control over, others which perhaps they do. How victimized are Nancy and Jesus? Nancy is pregnant—by a white man? Apparently so, though there is no proof; Jesus certainly appears to think so. Has Nancy been raped, forced? Apparently not, since she has at least one "customer," a Mr. Stovall. One critic tells us bluntly that Stovall has "made her his whore and got her pregnant" (Taylor 55), though there is no evidence in the story to support such a conclusion. Is Nancy perhaps here, as in *Requiem for a Nun,* a "casual prostitute"? Does she entertain Mr. Stovall, and others, for enough money just to stay alive? for her own sexual pleasure? to get back at a husband who is apparently something of a philanderer? When Mr. Compson patronizingly thinks to comfort her by telling her that Jesus won't hurt her because he has probably gone away and "got another wife by now and forgot all about you," Nancy is outraged: "If he has," she says, venomously, "I better not find out about it. . . . I'd stand there right over them, and every time he wropped her, I'd cut that arm off. I'd cut his head off and I'd slit her belly and I'd shove—" (CS 295). Jesus's love and sexual fidelity are clearly important to Nancy. Her response indicates that neither she nor her creator subscribes, as Mr. Compson obviously does, to the myths of sexual casualness among all Negroes.

Is Jesus, by the same token, more outraged at a social structure that allows a white man to come into his house, for sexual and other purposes, but refuses him the opposite privilege, or only at Nancy, for cuckolding him in the first place and then for compounding the cuckolding by publicly humiliating him when she attacked Mr. Stovall in front of the bank? Clearly his outrage and his frustration spring from very complex combinations of both these things, and clearly there are significant ways in which he and Nancy are helpless victims of circumstance. Jesus is injured, yet impotent to strike back at the white world he blames, rightly or wrongly, for his troubles. Yet why should he take all of his frustrations out on Nancy if he blames the white man, particularly since Nancy is no less a victim of those same forces? The answers are more psychological than sociological; he strikes out at the only thing he feels he possibly *can* strike out at, the woman he loves—but is that his only recourse? Nancy, for her part, strikes rather at herself—out of what combination of guilt or self-reproach or simple despair it is impossible to say—when she attempts suicide in the jail, and when she confronts Mr. Stovall in front of the bank, asking for her money: one can only assume that she gets exactly what she expected, perhaps wanted, from him. Surely she knew that under the circumstances he was more likely to beat her than pay her. Perhaps she thought her own pain, even her death, was a small price to pay for a public humiliation of Stovall. Or was she simply so high on drugs she didn't know what she was doing?

But the chemistry of our sympathy with her is seriously altered when we realize how dangerous it is for her to take the Compson children to her cabin with her for protection. If Jesus decides to kill her, as she believes he will, does she think he will spare the little ones? Even if she does think he will spare them, if she has thought about it at all, it is by no means responsible for her to try to hide behind them. Does she realize the danger, at any level? If Mr. Compson is the father of her child and so the author of her miseries, does Nancy deliberately, consciously or unconsciously, put them in harm's way to avenge herself on a white world, and a white man, that has wronged her?

I do not know the answers to these questions, and I do not believe that the story itself provides answers. But I insist that the story *asks* these and other questions, and that much of its power is directly related to the complexity of Nancy's characterization and to the complexities of the relationship between Jesus and Nancy. Faulkner's treatment of these two black characters is in many ways a direct, frontal assault upon racial stereotypes.

His white characters are likewise too often read as stereotypes. "Pantaloon in Black" is one of Faulkner's greatest stories. Critics have misunderstood "Pantaloon" not because of Faulkner's treatment of Rider, but because of their inability to see the deputy-narrator of the second part of that story as anything but a stereotypical Southern lawman. He is, of course, a redneck deputy, a Southerner identified by all the prejudices of his time and place and class. But if that is *all* he is, then "Pantaloon" seems to me an unsuccessful story that rather clumsily juxtaposes the moving story of Rider's love for Manny, his grief, his suicidal murder of the white man, and then his lynching, with the story of the redneck deputy and his crass, unloving wife.

Beyond those simplistic ironies is the story's real punchline. Why does the deputy continue to tell his wife the story of Rider's lynching, in complete detail, long after she has made it clear that she doesn't care about Rider or about the deputy either? The answer is that he isn't talking to her at all, but rather to himself. He has just experienced something, Rider's griefstricken and doomed humanness, which nothing in his background has prepared him for, and he is clumsily trying to talk it out, trying to explain to his own mind, using a completely inadequate redneck vocabulary and conceptual system, something it cannot quite grasp. Most have accepted that Faulkner wrote "Pantaloon" to force white readers to go behind the stereotype of a black man. He is also asking us to look behind the stereotype of the Southern lawman, even as Nub Gowrie's heartbreak forces Chick Mallison behind the stereotype of Beat Four rednecks: we who have eagerly seen Rider as a misunderstood human being have been unable to see the white man as equally human. The deputy is trying to make sense of his actual experience of Rider, which has made that magnificent black man something devastatingly different from the stereotype he has always presumed to think he knows: perhaps this deputy is also somebody devastatingly different from the redneck we have all presumed to know.

Thus that deputy is far more educable than the more highly educated and sophisticated lawyer, Gavin Stevens, whose presence at the end of *Go Down, Moses* has for five decades muddied the racial waters of that novel. For with all the best intentions to be helpful to demonstrate that he, at any rate, knows something of the civilized world, Stevens is completely alien to Molly's real humanity. Many have noticed this, of course, and thought Stevens's paternalism a weakness in the novel. But Faulkner deliberately sets Stevens in sharp opposition to the deputy of "Pantaloon." Both become privy to grief, to human passion, where they least expect it, in a Negro. The deputy tries to understand it; Stevens is arrogantly sure that he understands "The Negro" completely. Both have equal opportunities to test the cultural narrative about race against their actual experiences of racial otherness and then to rewrite the narrative. Both fail, but at least the deputy is aware of the narrative's distance from his experience, and seems shattered by the revelation; Stevens runs from Molly's grief, but in the story's final pages he calmly repositions her back into that narrative, where she is no longer a threat.

Perhaps there are no solutions to America's racial problems. None of Faulkner's fiction offers a solution, certainly, or much hope either, and it's worth noting how completely he simply gave up his public *engagement* with racial issues right after the Russell Howe interview, no doubt with a complete sense of having failed to provide solutions to the problems his fiction had so powerfully understood and dramatized. In life as in his fiction he met face to face the recalcitrance of the redneck, the intransigence of the best type of liberal Southerner, and the disbelief of black leaders. He found them all equally resistant, if for different reasons, to his brand of moderation, and he seems simply to have given up, retreated to his fiction, his grandchildren, and his privileged life among the foxhunters of Albemarle County.

No more than the deputy of "Pantaloon" could he have provided answers to America's racial problems, in his fiction or in his public agenda. But for a brief moment in a dangerous time he tried to get us to think about where our language and our policies were leading us. He tried to force us, like that deputy, at least to understand that we had not been asking the right questions.

Faulkner at Midcentury

For Jim Hinkle

There's a wonderful moment in the 1952 *Omnibus* television program about William Faulkner. Moon Mullins, Faulkner's old friend and the former editor of the Oxford *Eagle*, comes to Rowan Oak to tell Faulkner that he's won the Nobel Prize. The *Omnibus* camera stationed in the Rowan Oak living room watches from behind Faulkner as he answers Mullins' knock at the front door; Faulkner, neatly dressed in a coat and a tie, greets Mullins: "So you're the one the trouble begins with?" "Who did you want it to begin with?" Mullins responds, as they move together into the living room, sit down and chat. Faulkner says, "Look Phil. I don't see what my private life, the inside of my house, or my family have to do with my writing." Mullins insists that somebody will do the story, and he wants to be the one. "All right," Faulkner relents: "Do your story. But no pictures." Mullins remonstrates: "But you let the Oxford High School paper print your picture, by golly." Faulkner, smiling genially and with a sense of complicity, closes the conversation: "Yes, but my daughter was the editor of that paper, by golly." Cut, end of scene, move to Stockholm and the Nobel Prize.

The scene is cleverly written and staged, even pretty well acted. But I am always stopped short at the image of the smiling author, looking into the camera and saying "No Pictures." That smiling face, that beatific nimbus of graying hair, that well-cut coat, all reek of immortality: of wisdom, of comfort, contentment, serenity, and security. And not just of success, but of success hard won: hard won indeed, if you consider his struggles of the previous decade. Despite the defiant "No pictures," there's anything but defiance in his face;

no matter what sounds his mouth is making, his face says Welcome; I may be eccentric, but I am friendly. Thus the tableau is iconic. He's everybody's platonic image of Grandfather, if not of God, standing in the very sanctuary of the castle whose privacy he had become notorious for defending; he's looking into the TV camera that stands on the other side of that living room bastion, sitting comfortably in an easy chair throne, and saying: "No pictures" to the tens of thousands of people watching that very picture.

It's a delicious biographical moment, in a film whose very existence is an extended series of such moments. One wonders what ironies smirk behind those twinkling eyes, what congeries of satisfactions and secret pleasures gather there giggling or laughing out loud. One also wonders whether any sense of how terrifically the scene contradicts itself weighs, and how heavily, on his conscience or his soul.

There's a mildly dark underbelly to the film. Those who know anything about Faulkner's relationship with Phil Stone during this period may find their teeth set a bit on edge by Stone's performance in a later scene, just as those who know anything about the Faulkners' home life during the 1940s and 1950s will note jarring discrepancies between the biographical reality and the film's iconic depiction of Faulkner as home-centered family man, devoted husband and father, and as man about town. He is eccentric in the film, to be sure, but the center of the image is *Citoyen Faulkner*, a man who except for being a literary genius is not so different from you and me: husband, father, neighbor, responsible involved citizen. "Faulkner is a farmer," summarizes the narrator in the film's closing line, "who looks deep into the heart of life, and writes what he sees there."

The film is thus a pristine example of what Roland Barthes calls "the proletarianization of the writer" (Barthes 29). It wants to mainstream Faulkner, to normalize—i.e., neutralize—him, to make him acceptable to that very culture and world whose Chamber of Commerce values he had subjected to the intense scrutiny of his critical eye, a world he would continue to reject in his fiction and his personal life, even if not in his public pronouncements and postures. He's a farmer who looks deep into the heart of life, writes about it, and doesn't want his picture taken.

It is very much worth noting that in the film Faulkner seems to be enjoying himself immensely, and perhaps the most reasonable way to think about his participation in it is to assume that he's perfectly aware of what he's doing. We need not be judgmental, as we have traditionally been, and consider his cooperation in the making of this extraordinary film a betrayal of his previous high modernist indifference to and even repudiation of such commercial success—by God, we like our artists to *suffer*, not to be successful. Nor need we see his public life in the fifties as a simpleminded hypocritical pandering to the Great American Publicity Machine, which he used for his own benefit on the one hand, while on the other condemning it, as Louis J. Budd and others have suggested. Budd is correct, of course, to argue that the most interesting thing about the public and the private Faulkner of the 1950s is in the way we have reacted to the apparent disparities between them, and that as his readers we have mostly failed to confront the Faulkner of this period in all his complexity. In doing things so differently in the fifties, Faulkner may have been responding to the chastening experiences of his personal and professional hardships of the previous decade; he may simply have been bored, and seeking new avenues of expression. In thinking about his life during these very agonizing times, we should never forget that he continued a *very* active writing and publishing life, a highly visible literary life, an active and vigorous social life in Charlottesville and elsewhere, and a highly energetic engagement in the media with social and political issues of his day. Nor should we forget that he was still capable of being very funny, of discussing his work with students, and of taking great pleasure in his grandchildren. Finally, I don't believe we have to think of him as either duplicitous or simpleminded because we have no more right to expect a seamless, contradictionless life from him than we do from ourselves or, say, from Emerson, who very well contradicted himself. We have only to look at the photographs of Faulkner in the fifties to see that at some level he did indeed enjoy his celebrity, and we should not begrudge him pleasure in his success, whatever of consistency it costs us in thinking about it.

Nevertheless, the scene at Rowan Oak in the *Omnibus* film is the nub of a very complicated issue in Faulkner studies, out of which one can see spiralling in double helixes an increasingly complex series of biographical and critical issues. And I'd like to digress here for a moment to reflect on the ideological mainstreaming of Faulkner and upon the consequences of that mainstreaming for Faulkner as writer and for us as readers.

So far as I am aware, the Post Office did not give us a chance to vote on which image of Faulkner we wanted on our 22¢ stamp. But the terms of the debate about the Elvis stamp vote are very interesting indeed, and analogous to what might have occurred in a debate over the Faulkner stamp. Given a choice, which Faulkner—which *image* of Faulkner—would we have preferred on the stamp, which one enshrined in our official memories? the genial grandfatherly Faulkner of the *Omnibus* portrait, in less than a decade to become the Faulkner of the stamp, the wise and compassionate, the Successful, the certifiably Immortal Faulkner, Faulkner the visionary, the very nearly transcendant being so bathed in light as to seem to be the source of light itself, an author whose very few public statements about enduring and prevailing allow us not just to endure and prevail but also to believe in a reformed, a domesticated Faulkner, one congenial to our own moral and ethical systems, our own cultural and ideological codes?—a domesticated and *safe* Faulkner?

Or would we prefer the young, hard-gutted, demon-driven, frequently rude and arrogant Faulkner of the early years, the one who revolutionized American fiction; who wrote about decay, disaster, the horrific, who looked unflinchingly at all that is nightmarish and threatening in our lives and culture, all that we keep buried? This Faulkner's most well-known image is J. R. Cofield's photo, taken to publicize *Sanctuary*. This Faulkner is full of a different kind of self-confidence: his head is slightly tilted, his dark hair unkempt above deep dark eyes that stare straight at you, not even taking the trouble to be defiant; he is tieless, casual, in a tweed sport coat, his arms

Used by permission of
The Center for the Study
of Southern Culture,
University of Mississippi.
I am grateful to Tom
Rankin.

folded tightly across his chest; he's self-sufficient and complete, and his right hand, *his writing hand*, holds a lighted cigarette that could be a fuse. It's a closeup: Faulkner fills the frame, and the blurred forearm of that selfsame writing hand threatens to spill over the front edge; he's standing against a darkened curtain or wall that shuts out social context. He's young, lean, hard, anything but benign; the set of his mouth suggests he may be about to break out into laughter, but probably not at anything funny: as he wrote of Pete in *Requiem for a Nun*, you don't know what he's going to do, and you hope he's not going to do it this time. He's cocky, sinister, insolent, slightly menacing, almost threatening. Looked at abstractly, the portrait is a chiaroscuro of darkness and light, of shadows in which a large part of him always lurks, simmering and brooding, the better to see into the light. He's not saying "No pictures" to *this* camera, and he neither welcomes nor avoids its gaze: he's staring it down, daring it to do its worst. There's no fitter emblem for the works of that period, which are also youthful, cocky, insolent, and in some ways very threatening indeed, if we extrapolate from them (as we regularly do) a world view and a view of human nature that is almost unrelievedly bleak and problematic.

Like the Post Office, we have collectively chosen the older, benign Faulkner as our icon of the man and his career, while at the same time actually preferring the work of the lean, mean, writing machine. In certain important ways, we as a profession have grabbed and clung tenaciously to the rhetoric, fictional and nonfictional, of the "reformed" Faulkner's public statements, even though they form a very small part of his published work, and have made them central to our understanding of his life and work. Most curiously, and paradoxically, we don't generally care very much for the fiction of *this* Faulkner, precisely because we take it to be moralistic. So we can have it both ways: on the one hand we can be responsible, serious New Critical critics, and dismiss as inferior the fiction of the post-Nobel period because we know that moralizing fiction is bad fiction. At the same time, from the vantage of the benign author's pronouncements, we can look backward into the early fiction, which we *do* like, and find redeeming social and spiritual values that save those works from the nihilism and despair that *seemed* so inevitably lodged in them prior to the period of the late forties, when Faulkner's resurrection was getting a head of steam (Schwartz). As Cheryl Lester has demonstrated ("To Market"), in editing the *Portable Faulkner* in the mid-40s, Malcolm Cowley believed that Faulkner's strengths lay not in the individual stories and novels but in the larger pattern or design of the creation of Yoknapatawpha County. Cowley assumed that one could more readily see that design, and therefore more completely grasp Faulkner's claim on our attention, by emphasizing chronology. The result of this, Lester argues, is that chronology and location in north Mississippi became, willy-nilly, Cowley's principal critical agenda as, for years, following him, it became ours: fiction like *Pylon* or *The Wild Palms*, which did not fit a geographical or chronological grid, Cowley simply dismissed as inferior.

Likewise, we have permitted the two-Faulkner theory to control the way we read his fiction: we neuter the early and mostly dismiss the later, by reading the early through the filter of the later, and by using the early as a club to beat the later up with. The most deleterious ideological construct of the Faulkner field right now is that which has the notion of "the great books" or "the major phase" at the center. Over the years at the annual Faulkner and Yoknapatawpha Conference at the University of Mississippi, no matter what the topic—Faulkner and Race, Faulkner and Religion, Faulkner and Women—we seem not only to examine and to cite the same few "great" novels but to a large extent to cite and explicate the same passages within those same few books. To say this is by no means to criticize in any way the selection of papers for the conference; it is rather simply a description of Faulkner studies at the present, which is mostly structured around such a hierarchy of books and passages. We talk about Faulkner's "great books" in ways that make it unnecessary to take the late works, especially *A Fable*, seriously. I do it myself, in evangelizing for *Requiem for a Nun* and *A Fable*, when I argue that these novels too are "great" and *therefore* worth our attention, rather than that they are worth our attention because they are interesting and by an author whom we admire. Thus we tame those early, disturbing works, dismiss the later ones, and make them all serve the purposes of our own ideologies.

The question, *Which Faulkner?*, then, although I pose it whimsically, is not really an idle one, and the answer—the variety of possible answers—may allow us to think for a few moments about the ideology of Yoknapatawpha or, more generally, about what we bring to and take away from our reading of Faulkner: *why*, perhaps, we read literature, what expectations we have of the works themselves *as well as* what expectations we have of the authors whose works we read and admire, what expectations we perhaps have about any author's moral responsibilities to his or her works. That is, do we assume a direct and mutually validating relationship between an author's life and works, that the life must be in some measure the moral equivalent of the work's moralities? After all, at some level, most of us look to literature for some understanding of our lives, for some insight into our own behavior and that of others that will help us, in Walker Percy's phrase, to make it through a Thursday afternoon. What does it signify if an author's work is somehow at ideological or moral odds with her or his private life?

Faulkner's on-camera refusal to have his picture taken, then, invites some speculation about the extent to which in the film he publicly becomes a combatant in the Cold War, resolutely preaching the peculiarly American doctrines of individuality and privacy to the very camera that was invading his own privacy, and sharing his individuality with the large television audience. The scene stands there in Faulkner's life, memorialized on film, pristine in its paradoxicality; it is all the more paradoxical because Faulkner did not own a television, refusing to make one of the two-thirds of American households that by 1952 owned at least one (Sellers 402). Biographers have treated the episode of the film as part of a rather seamless series of incidents in Faulkner's life, one among many public gestures he made in the years following his investiture as a Knight of the Nobel Prize. But it strikes me as something of a pretty large rupture in the seam, even during this very volatile period of his life, when he teetered on the brink of the abyss far more unsteadily than in the years of his early struggle. So the scene, and the film, stand for me as something of an emblem of Faulkner's private and professional lives during the years following the prize and his public acclaim.

It is, at the very least, one of the most curious episodes in Faulkner's life, and from certain points of view it's one of the most astonishing—that he would have agreed to the program in the first place, much less to be *in* it. He had spent a lifetime generally protecting his right to be a private individual. Specifically, he had for over a year prior to the film steadfastly refused to cooperate with *Life Magazine* reporter Robert Coughlan who wanted to do a profile on him: he refused to cooperate and, when Coughlan published the piece anyway (in *Life* in September 1953) and later published it as a book (*The Private World of William Faulkner*), wrote an extended essay about the episode called "On Privacy" (written October 1954) as part of a planned series of essays under the general title "The American Dream: What Happened to It?" Less than a year later, when Random House asked him to cooperate with *Time* magazine for a story to publicize *A Fable*, he again refused, telling Bennett Cerf to calculate how much his refusal would cost the firm, and he would pay it rather than have anything to do with it (Blotner [1984] 586–87). Coughlan must have been bewildered.

Other contradictions rag and tatter at the edges of his life during this period. In April of 1952, for example, he wrote to Else Jonsson that he was going to accept the invitation of the French Government to participate in Paris's festival of 20th century works, but that he was not going as a "delegate": "the words 'delegate' and 'freedom' in the same sentence are, to me, not only incongruous," he wrote, "but terrifying too" (SL 330–31). But before the end of the lustrum he was travelling for the U. S. State Department around the world as a "delegate" for American values, though indeed these trips seem to have been problematized by some sort of internal resistance to what he was doing, so that he was constantly on the edge of shooting himself in the diplomatic foot. His local State Department hosts were constantly fearful that he would embarrass them and the United

States by his excessive drinking, but in all cases he finally did behave and perform admirably. He spent a good deal of time and energy in the mid-fifties speaking out against racial injustice in the South, but practically destroyed all his good efforts with one short statement— probably made while he was drinking, but almost certainly *made*—that if he had to kill Negroes in the street to defend Mississippi against federal intervention, he'd do it (ESPL 225; see Polk, "Man in the Middle"). In public speeches in Stockholm, Oxford, Pine Manor and, later, at the University of Virginia, he insisted that human beings had the capacity to endure, to prevail, to complete an incomplete world, to rid the world of tyrants by simply refusing to yield to the forces of oppression, by refusing to be afraid of the bomb, and by lifting their voices for justice and compassion. Privately, he expressed quite contrary opinions: "human beings are terrible," he wrote Else Jonsson in 1955. "One must believe well in man to endure him, wait out his folly and savagery and inhumanity" (SL 382). Early in the decade he wrote Joan Williams that she had to give up her enchainment to middleclass values in order to be a writer; by mid-decade, he was a cold-war warrior wittily proposing to other writers that one way to end the cold war was to bring 10,000 Communists a year to this country for a year, let them buy automobiles on the installment plan, get jobs in our plants and factories, experience collective bargaining, say what they wanted to say, and so see for themselves how good and satisfying a middleclass American life could be (SL 404); by 1957 he was dressing in jodhpurs and foxhunting with the haute bourgeoisie of Charlottesville. At the same time that he was railing against such depression issues as farm subsidies, he was travelling as a representative of the government that was giving the subsidies. At the same time he was delivering speeches extolling the value of home and family and *normalcy* (ESPL 135–42) he was perfectly aware of how far short of even normal, let alone ideal, his own family situation was.

Publicly, then, Faulkner was at the pinnacle of a career to be dreamed about; privately, his life was a singular hell, for reasons he couldn't seem to understand. He suffered excruciatingly from a bad back; he was in and out of hospitals here and abroad; he drank heavily and, in 1952, entered a New York hospital where he had psychiatric care and may have been administered electric shock treatments (Blotner [1984] 563–64). Even an amateur Freudian might want to see some form of self-punishment in his insistence on riding horses that frequently threw him and reinjured his back and in his refusal to have the operation that might have relieved some of his back pain. This was, then, a *highly* troubled period in Faulkner's life, a period characterized by a kind of restlessness that was entirely new to him (Gresset 70).

I don't want to trivialize the issues that I'm engaging here by suggesting that he, *even he*, was undergoing a belated midlife crisis, but in fact just about every one of his fictional and private utterances of the period is eye-ball deep in the symptoms of midlife crisis that find emptiness in the very success one has worked so hard to achieve, and I'll bet there's something very personal in Faulkner's portrait of Flem Snopes in *The Mansion*—the bank president, the pillar of the community, who after years of pursuing his own version of the American Dream finds less fulfillment at the peak of his success than at the beginning of his quest—sitting alone in his bigger house and chewing not even tobacco or gum but merely air. "I seem to have lost heart for working," Faulkner wrote his agent Harold Ober on August 20, 1952. "I cant find anything to work, write, *for*" (SL 339).

He wrote one of his most interesting and revealing letters to Joan Williams on April 29, 1953:

> And now, at last, I have some perspective on all I have done. I mean, the work apart from me, the work which I did, apart from what I am. . . . And now I realise for the first time what an amazing gift I had: uneducated in every formal sense, without even very literate, let alone literary, companions, yet to have made the things I made. I dont know where it came from. I dont know why God or gods or whoever it was, selected me to be the vessel. Believe me, this is not humility, false modesty: it is simply amazement. I wonder if you have ever had that thought about the work and the country man whom you know as Bill Faulkner—what little connection there seems to be between them. . . .
> (SL 348)

This letter rings with authenticity; it emerges ingenuously, from some amazed recognition of his gift, almost as an epiphany that produces a helpless sense of awe at how radically his gift had set him apart from ordinary people. There's no trace of megalomania, but just a bewildered astonishment at what he'd made of himself. It is as though he is looking at some such image of himself as we see in the *Omnibus* film, trying to find in the icon, the Nobel laureate, some semblance of himself that he can recognize.

This was by no means of course the first time he was conscious of the difference between himself and his background, of how paradoxical and outrageous he was. James Meriwether has long held that in his famous description of Eula Varner as a Frenchman's Bend product he was probably also talking about himself as a product of a "little lost village, nameless, without grace, forsaken, yet which wombed once by chance and accident one blind seed of the spendthrift Olympian ejaculation and did not even know it" (H 867). Faulkner had echoed this in a description of Oxford in a letter of August 3, 1951, to Bob Haas at Random House about his refusal to cooperate with *Life Magazine*: "I have deliberately buried myself in this little lost almost illiterate town, to keep out of the way so that news people wont notice and remember me" (SL 319). One of the characteristics of his work during this period is its tendency to incorporate his created world, and himself, into it. As Michel Gresset and others have shown, Faulkner's work throughout his career is full of autobiographical elements and of demonstrable self-portraits.

Three quasi-autobiographical pieces that he wrote within six weeks of each other in February and March of 1953, hard on the heels of the *Omnibus* filming in November and of its airing in December, and only a few weeks before that letter to Joan Williams, are very revealing. The slightest of these is "A Note on Sherwood Anderson," which he wrote as an introduction for a proposed edition of Anderson's letters that never happened. Published in the *Atlantic* in June 1953, it is a warm memoir of Anderson, whom Faulkner credits with having taught him that one place is as good as another to write about, that the single requirement of being a writer is to remember what you were, no matter where you start from: "You're a country boy," he says Anderson told him: "all you know is that little patch up there in Mississippi where you started from. But that's all right too. It's America too" (ESPL 8). To Anderson he attributes mentorship both in his example as a working writer and in his straightforward advice about the dishonesty of glibness: "You've got too much talent," Faulkner says Anderson told him: "You can do it too easy, in too many different ways. If you're not careful, you'll never write anything" (ESPL 7). While we may not doubt the sincerity of his affection for Anderson, it's fair to wonder whether Anderson did in fact say these things to Faulkner or whether Faulkner simply attributes them to Anderson in honor of the older writer's significance in his career— Anderson's looming giantism.

The memoir recounts their friendship, their life in New Orleans, and their falling out over the satire of Anderson's style in *Sherwood Anderson and Other Famous Creoles*, in terms that praise Anderson's hard work and his dedication to his craft, especially to his style—"the exactitude of purity or the purity of exactitude" (ESPL 6)—long after style was all he had left, and which Anderson in effect hid behind to protect the writer who knew that there was no content left. The essay resonates with so many things that seem to be on Faulkner's mind throughout this period that it is easy now to believe that he is mostly talking about himself, especially in the recognition of the virtuosity of his talent and of his responsibility to discipline that gift strictly. His fatigue and his difficulties completing *A Fable* certainly were major concerns that he expressed to others, privately, as a fear that he had scraped the bottom of the barrel, and had no more to write. He may also have been thinking of himself, even if not consciously or deliberately, when he described Anderson as "a giant in an earth populated to a great—too great—extent by pygmies" (ESPL 10).

The second piece is a short story that he sent to his agent Harold Ober on February 19, three days before he finished the appreciation of Anderson. "Mr. Acarius" is demonstrably autobiographical, at least in its origins in the time Faulkner spent in a private hospital in the Bronx, where he may or may not have had electric shock treat-

ments (Blotner [1984] 563–64), in December of 1952 during the in-
terim between the filming and the airing of the *Omnibus* feature. He
began working on "Mr Acarius" on January 16, while the details of
his stay there were fresh on his mind.

Briefly, Mr. Acarius is a wealthy man who is nevertheless very unhappy, whose money and Picassos and the other accoutrements of
success don't bring him any sense of permanence, any conviction that
there is any part of himself that, after the bomb, will have "left any
smudge or stain" (US 435) on the world. Mr. Acarius's curious name
is a form of a word designating a genus of "minute spider-like ani-
mals," a mite, one of the smallest of vermin, whose sole function
seems to be to cause skin disease. He wants to do something to give
his life meaning and he undertakes to "experience man, the human
race" (US 436) by getting drunk and debasing himself, even if not on
skid row but rather in an expensive alcoholic's hospital. His reason
for doing this is primarily to punish himself for being different, somehow to atone for that difference by finding a common sty to wallow
with humanity in:

> I'm not just no better than the people on skid row. I'm not even as
> good, for the reason that I'm richer. Because I'm richer, I not only
> don't have anything to escape from, driving me to try to escape from it,
> but as another cypher in the abacus of mankind, I am not even high
> enough in value to alter any equation by being subtracted from it. But
> at least I can go along for the ride, like the flyspeck on the handle of the
> computer, even if it can't change the addition. At least I can experience,
> participate in, the physical degradation of escaping . . . the surrender,
> the relinquishment to and into the opium of escaping, knowing in ad-
> vance the inevitable tomorrow's inevitable physical agony; to have lost
> nothing of anguish but instead only to have gained it; to have merely
> compounded yesterday's spirit's and soul's laceration with tomorrow's
> hangover. . . . Mankind. People. Man. I shall be one with man, victim
> of his own base appetites and now struggling to extricate himself from
> that debasement. Maybe it's even my fault that I'm incapable of any-
> thing but Scotch, and so our bullpen will be a Scotch one where for a
> little expense we can have peace, quiet for the lacerated and screaming

nerves, sympathy, understanding— . . . and maybe what my fellow in-
mates are trying to escape from—the too many mistresses or wives or
the too much money or responsibility or whatever else it is that drives
into escape the sort of people who can afford to pay fifty dollars a day
for the privilege of escaping—will not bear mention in the same breath
with that which drives one who can afford no better, even to canned
heat. But at least we will be together in having failed to escape and in
knowing that in the last analysis there is no escape, that you can never
escape and, whether you will or not, you must reenter the world and
bear yourself in it and its lacerations and all its anguish of breathing, to
support and comfort one another in that knowledge and that attempt.
(US 436–38)

It's not terribly difficult to hear Faulkner's voice in Mr. Acarius's
complaint (we can easily take his prose as a parody of Faulkner's style)
nor to see in Mr. Acarius's argument perhaps some of Faulkner's
explanations for or rationalizations of his similar behavior: his self-
lacerations and his sheer bewilderment at not knowing what he needs
to escape *from*. Doubtless Mr. Acarius's speech reflects Faulkner's
agony in trying to understand why he of all people should be so unhappy.

Mr. Acarius's desire to enter humanity is precisely Faust's desire,
stated almost in Faust's own language, in Goethe's great poem:

> Frenzy I choose, most agonizing lust,
> Enamored enmity, restorative disgust.
> Henceforth my soul, for knowledge sick no more,
> Against no kind of suffering shall be cautioned,
> And what to all of mankind is apportioned
> I mean to savor in my own self's core,
> Grasp with my mind both highest and most low,
> Weigh down my spirit with their weal and woe,
> And thus my selfhood to their own distend,
> And be, as they are, shattered in the end. (42)

This is not the Faustus of legend who sells his soul to the devil to
gain all knowledge and power, but rather that Faust who has already
gained all knowledge and power, has drunk its lees and found it want-

ing, and who asks Mephistopheles' dark powers to help rid himself of the burden of his superiority. Faulkner's evocation of Faust here is, I believe, conscious, and the autobiographical nature of the allusion speaks for itself.

Mr. Acarius doesn't find a humanity that he can share anything with. He is appalled at what he finds in the expensive hospital among the humanity who can afford to be there, much less what he would find in a Manhattan skid row gutter. They are shattered indeed, but he is not, and so returning home—unlike Faulkner, who goes home and writes about it—Mr. Acarius smashes all his bottles in the bathtub and swears off drink: "So you entered mankind, and found the place already occupied," his doctor taunts him. "Yes," Mr. Acarius says, cries, in an apparent non sequitur that echoes the runner's cry at the end of *A Fable*: "You can't beat him. You cannot. You never will. Never" (US 448).

"Mr. Acarius" and "A Note on Sherwood Anderson"—one fiction, one nonfiction—are, then, veiled autobiographical explorations of Faulkner's sense of his differences from other people. "Mississippi," which he wrote in March of 1953, is a *sui generis* combination of fiction and nonfiction, which he overlays with the deliberately autobiographical. In "Mississippi," Faulkner negotiates for his central autobiographical character a reconciliation with his native land and its citizens. He does not appear as a writer or artist but instead as a fully contextualized citizen, like the character in the *Omnibus* portrait. Unnamed, he could be Everymississippian: we know him only by his ages, as the boy, the young man, the middleaging, the gray-haired. In "Mississippi," Faulkner eloquently claims the full kinship, the commonality, with fellow human beings that he had sought in "Mr. Acarius" and "A Note on Sherwood Anderson."

I suppose I'm moving toward some agreement with Michael Grimwood that Faulkner became increasingly aware of the extreme distances between what he wrote and the capacity of the people he wrote about to understand anything he wrote, and so derive some benefit from it; Grimwood does not deal with the post-Nobel Faulkner who, for him, was so far gone in decline by 1942 that his career was virtually over. Nevertheless, from our vantage it is possible to see Faulkner's willingness to engage political and ideological issues publicly—to travel to universities in Oregon and Washington to deliver "On Privacy" as an address, to spend time at the University of Virginia discussing his work with students and faculty, his sustained efforts in behalf of racial justice in the mid-fifties, his numerous expeditions around the world in behalf of the State Department, and even his *Omnibus* portrait—as a necessary and inevitable extension of a growing conviction that artists don't have to be, don't even have a right to be, alien to or alienated from the world in which they have to live. This view would help us understand why he would accept commissions from such decidedly blue-collar publications as *Sports Illustrated* to do pieces on the Kentucky Derby and on an ice hockey game.

I certainly do not agree with critics of the late Faulkner who implicitly side with Phil Stone's comment that Faulkner got "Nobelitis in the head" (Blotner [1984] 562) and that his public life in the fifties is a direct expression of an inflated and preening sense of himself as having been certified Wise and so competent to speak on all things. There's simply too much pain and doubt in his life during these years to allow us to accept that. More to the point, there's simply too much disillusionment with the common run of humanity he has allied himself with. Like Mr. Acarius, he joins humanity not out of any sympathy with the masses, but simply to atone for his superiority; joining them, he finds not atonement but rather chaos, death, and more disillusionment (Carothers 105–06). More particularly like the runner in *A Fable*, he wants to join the ranks of the common soldier, to give up his pip, the sign of his superiority. The officer from whom he asks this boon assumes "[y]ou love man so well you must sleep in the same mud he sleeps in." The runner argues that it's not at all that he loves humanity, but quite the reverse: "It's just backward," he says. "I hate man so. Hear him? . . . Smell him, too":

> When I, knowing what I have been, and am now, and will continue to
> be . . . can, by the simple coincidence of wearing this little badge on

my coat, have not only the power, with a whole militarised government
to back me up, to tell vast herds of man what to do, but the impunitive
right to shoot him with my own hand when he doesn't do it, then I
realise how worthy of any fear and abhorrence and hatred he is. . . . So
I must get back into the muck with him. Then maybe I'll be free.

"Free of what?" his company commander asks, and he responds: "I
dont know either. Maybe of having to perform forever at inescapable
intervals that sort of masturbation about the human race people call
hoping. That would be enough" (F 721–22). For all his public testimony to humanity's capacity to renew itself, to endure and prevail,
there is no evidence to indicate that Faulkner really believed a word
of what he was saying, and quite a bit to suggest the opposite.

Thus whatever glaring contradictions one wants to find in Faulkner's career during the fifties, the ones that don't glare publicly are
the most problematic for him as a person and artist—and for us as
admirers—because there are not merely contradictions but an absolute schism between his public pronouncements and his private con-
victions; given that schism, there are certainly ways in which we can
call his appearance in the *Omnibus* film and his other public appear-
ances a gross hypocrisy at worst, at best a moral preening, a pandering
for attention.

But those who would criticise Faulkner for performing these cha-
rades might well think again. As Morse Peckham has pointed out,
the three speeches most often cited as *proving* Faulkner's new-found
celebration of human dignity—the Nobel Prize address, and his addresses to the Oxford High School graduates and the graduating class
at Pine Manor Junior College—were occasional utterances, written
for specific audiences, all three of which included his own daughter,
and were delivered under circumstances that made some form of op-
timism mandatory. What should the gloomy tragedian say to a group
of high school graduates on the verge of their lives?—*Congratulations
on making it this far. You've been lucky. I'm sorry to have to tell you now,
however, that life is all sound and fury, signifying nothing. Breathing is a
sight draft dated yesterday. Between grief and nothing always take grief, but*

don't count on much more. Go forth and await your doom. Thank you very much? Or how should he have addressed the younger aspirants to the Nobel Prize on the futility of it all when he, standing so successfully on that pinnacle in Stockholm, would himself have been the denial of his own nihilism? Could he discourage younger writers from their life's work by forecasting meaninglessness and doom? Manners, if nothing else, dictated that he could not (Polk, "Enduring" 115), and so he found himself participating in, acting out, literally and figuratively, the ideological rituals of his culture, formally endorsing them even though he himself did not find them fulfilling.

On its darkest side, one may find in this disturbing resonances with Arthur Koestler's novel of the Stalinist show trials of the thirties, *Darkness at Noon*, whose protagonist, completely innocent of the political crimes with which he is charged and for which he is going to die in any event, at first adamantly resists his counsellor's request that he confess publicly anyway and accept his punishment, and then, finally, accedes to the idea that the Party, the ideological structure, is more important than any of the individuals within the structure; he dies in the name of the structure. On the slightly less somber side, there are ways in which Faulkner resembles Miguel de Unamuno's memorable priest, "San Manuel Bueno, Martyr," who long after his own faith is gone continues to minister to his rural flock in the terms of that faith's rituals; he does so in order to sustain in them the hope of salvation (the hope of significance) that he himself has lost. In sustaining their faith, he asserts the value of the very ideology he has given up, sacrificing himself in its name but for their sake. In the Compson Appendix, Faulkner described Andrew Jackson's defense of his wife's honor as having nothing to do with her honor in and of itself but with "the principle that honor must be defended whether it was or not because defended it was whether or not" (330); like Jackson, Faulkner seems in the fifties to be defending certain values whether they are or not, and by doing so asserting their social and political and cultural value, if not their validity: hope, like grief, is better than nothing, certainly better than chaos.

Of course he could have refused to take part, he could have refused the Nobel Prize, as Jean-Paul Sartre did, on Sartre's grounds that he didn't want to accept the compromises that such recognition would necessarily entail. But Faulkner didn't refuse the recognition or the prizes, nor did he refuse the compromises, although he may have seen them not as compromises but as opportunities for expansion. In any case, act out those rituals he did, perhaps quite simply out of a refusal to extrapolate from his individual experience a universal declaration that success had to be empty for everybody, a refusal to believe that because he was not happy at home, nobody could be. Perhaps Unamuno's and Koestler's heroes are not so far apart in the practical effects of their sacrifices, but Koestler's hero sacrifices himself for the system, Unamuno's and Faulkner for the people within the system. San Manuel learned, as Faulkner would, how essential to people are the illusions that their ideologies provide.

Faulkner's mid-fifties *engagement*, then, was no simple-minded, knee-jerk response to the mantel of Sage that the Nobel Prize had invested him with, but rather a deeply felt attempt both to repatriate himself into a humanity from which his own giantism and despair had alienated him and to give that same humanity the capacity to face their individual lives without ideological illusion. He wanted, in effect, to give the masses a sign they could understand and respond to, in a language and in a medium they did have access to rather than in the language of his high art. He wanted to persuade them if not to individuality, then at least to their personal *and* collective best interests. For example, he argued the race question first on the moral grounds that racial inequality was wrong, then on the practical grounds that if Southerners didn't change the situation themselves, some other, outside, agency would force change upon them. Then as now, neither argument worked because of the mass mind that clung so tenaciously to the "mouthsounds" (ESPL 65) of their allegiance to the ringing rhetoric of liberty and justice for all while clinging equally tenaciously to racist and nationalist ideologies that denied equality, and would brook no suggestion that the mouthsounds flatly contradicted one another.

There is on occasion a kind of shrillness in Faulkner's ministry, that doubtless emerges from his increasing frustration with a humanity that insisted on acting in the mass, that acted out of mindless subservience to blatantly political ideological aggression and manipulation. His is, in short, a frustrated confrontation with humanity's refusal to be free, with its fear of freedom, and with its debilitating *need* to move en masse, in the ideological safety of numbers. His funniest and most trenchant treatment of this sort of behavior erupts—no: *explodes*—out of nowhere as the final paragraph of his January 24, 1955, *Sports Illustrated* piece called "An Innocent at Rinkside," in which he reported on his first visit to an ice hockey match:

> Only he . . . did wonder just what a professional hockey-match, whose purpose is to make a decent and reasonable profit for its owners, had to do with our National Anthem. What are we afraid of? Is it our national character of which we are so in doubt, so fearful that it might not hold up in the clutch, that we not only dare not open a professional athletic contest or a beauty-pageant or a real-estate auction, but we must even use a Chamber of Commerce race for Miss Sewage Disposal or a wildcat land-sale, to remind us that that liberty gained without honor and sacrifice and held without constant vigilance and undiminished honor and complete willingness to sacrifice again at need, was not worth having to begin with? Or, by blaring or chanting it at ourselves every time ten or twelve or eighteen or twenty-two young men engage formally for the possession of a puck or a ball, or just one young woman walks across a lighted platform in a bathing-suit, do we hope to so dull and eviscerate the words and tune with repetition, that when we do hear it we will not be disturbed from that dream-like state in which "honor" is a break and "truth" an angle? (ESPL 51)

Faulkner indeed became a cold war warrior, but he opposed Joe McCarthy and voted for Eisenhower in 1952 because he feared that another "liberal" president would lead to a backlash that would put a McCarthy in the White House (Blotner [1974] 1439). And, critical as he was of his own country, he did indeed support the notion that America, with all its problems, offered better alternatives for individual achievement than the Soviet Union. But he did not take the real problem to be a simple struggle between two contending powerful nations:

Because it makes a glib and simple picture, we like to think of the world situation today as a precarious and explosive balance of two ir-reconcilable ideologies confronting each other: which precarious bal-ance, once it totters, will drag the whole universe into the abyss along with it. That's not so. Only one of the opposed forces is an ideology. The other one is that simple fact of Man. . . . (ESPL 102)

The first paragraphs of "On Privacy" even more explicitly define the American Dream itself as a

sanctuary . . . for individual man: a condition in which he could be free not only of the old established closed-corporation hierarchies of arbitrary power which had oppressed him as a mass, but free of that mass into which the hierarchies of church and state had compressed and held him individually thralled and individually impotent. (ESPL 62)

The nations of the old world "existed as nations not on citizenship but subjectship, which endured only on the premise of size and docility of the subject mass" (ESPL 62).

Thus Faulkner conceived the ideological problem of the fifties not as a horizontal one, as Western and Eastern politicians would have had it, in which two contending economic and social philosophies vied for world dominance, but rather as a vertical one which in blood-chilling fact found Capitalism and Communism united with each other and standing in a deadly hierarchical opposition to the very people whom by their rhetoric Capitalism and Communism both claimed to serve. But the rhetoric made people servile by promising numerical security and hope: the precise condition of servitude that makes them contemptible to Mr. Acarius and to the runner of *A Fable*. What happened to the American Dream was not that it had to butt heads with temporal political and economic concerns, but rather that the dreamers, being human, always already preferred security to the freedom that the dream promised—indeed, threatened them with.

Throughout the period of the early fifties, Faulkner's continued work on *A Fable* forms a steady ground bass for all his other activities, public and private. It provides tempo and key for all the themes and variations at work in the upper and more visible registers and, like the ground bass, it is always at the root of the chord. Like Mr. Acarius, the runner in *A Fable* wants to leave the empyrean realms of officer-hood and rejoin the human race, to lose himself in that moiling mass, so that he can quit hoping *for them.* The runner is also at least partly an autobiographical—or autometaphorical, at any rate—figure, in some ways more specifically than Mr. Acarius is: when he leaves the front lines and returns to his old Paris neighborhood, to seek his lost dead youth, he seeks it by retracing "the perimeter of his dead life when he had not only hoped but believed" (802).

In Paris, he passes through the Luxembourg Gardens, past the stained queens, and down the rue Vaugirard, already "looking ahead to discern the narrow crevice which would be the rue Servandoni and the garret which he had called home (perhaps Monsieur and Madame Gargne, *patron* and *patronne*, would still be there to greet him)" (803). The rue Servandoni, of course, was the address of Faulkner's own little garret during his time in Paris in 1926, and I'd bet Luster a quarter that Monsieur and Madame Gargne were Faulkner's own landlord and landlady.

If in going to Paris to find his lost dead youth the runner is indeed an autometaphorical figure, he is also an artist figure, an artist like Faulkner, whose goal has become an impossibly romantic one—nothing less than to save the world through art—and who is ruthless in advancing his idealism. He believes that if he can just find the right secret sign, even if he has to steal one from the Masons, even if he doesn't fully understand its meaning, and even if he has to kill some-body in order to put himself in a position to show it, he can stop the battle, inspire the world toward pity and compassion, toward peace. He is searingly scarred in the attempt; and, at the end of the novel, for all his idealism, he remains always the needy child in a pietà, sucking at empowering and delimiting breast of the political institu-tion which alone can provide him nourishment and comfort, and screaming in echo of Mr. Acarius, "I'm not going to die. Never" (1072)—though he is of course here one of *us* instead of one of *them.*

In *A Fable*, a Christ-corporal leads opposing troops simply to stop fighting. The novel is about the efforts of the Allied military elite to work in concert with their German counterparts to prevent the soldiers from destroying the military—i.e., the world's political and ideological structures—which are essential to their lives: without those structures, without the symbolical walls of the city of Chaulnesmont to hold and contain them, they flow, shapeless and impotent, into the plains surrounding the city. The officers on opposing sides speak to each other in each other's language—that is, they speak to each other in ways the soldiers cannot; they have a common language not of nationality or geographical boundary, that the soldiers do not have, the language of class and power. The novel thus specifically evokes the class divisions of Jean Renoir's great 1937 film *Grand Illusion*, in which the officers of the opposing armies demonstrate their class solidarity by holding their most important conversations in English, which the French prisoners and the German guards cannot understand.

I'm not prepared to defend any proposition that the language of *A Fable* is as vivid or as rich in ecstatic or supple rhythms or in that vital allusive and implicative quality of the prose we generally understand, at its best, to be "Faulknerian," but I do claim that the prose is deliberate, as consciously a part of the novels' structure and meanings as it is in others of his novels. The prose in some ways presents actually fewer problems than others of Faulkner's novels: there is less of the de-stabilization of meaning caused by ambiguous pronominal references, for example, and fewer of the deliberate narrative gaps, as in *Absalom, Absalom!* or *Go Down, Moses*, or *The Hamlet*, where Faulkner frequently refuses to tell us *what happened*, preferring instead to allow narrator-characters to fill in those gaps themselves through their own reconstruction, reconstitution, and interpretation of the very few factual givens they have to work with—and, indeed, making of those attempts to reconstruct, reconstitute, and interpret the substance of the works, the essence of the fictional enterprise itself.

There are very few such gaps, even historical ones, in *A Fable*. What *happens* in *A Fable* is never at issue. Indeed, the entire military establishment is committed precisely to avoiding those historical and factual gaps: the military has a "metabolism which does everything to a man but lose him, which learns nothing and forgets nothing and loses nothing at all whatever and forever—no scrap of paper, no unfinished record or uncompleted memorandum no matter how inconsequential or trivial" (888). In fact, the completeness, the intactness of the record of Europe's past is very much a part of the "ponderable shadow" of the Roman citadel that looms over the martial headquarters city of Chaulnesmont, very much the "stone weight" of that citadel, of that specifically military history, which seems to "lean down and rest upon" (983) the actors in this drama. It is not, then, the corporal's reinterpretation of history or any effort to understand it, but simply his straightforward intervention in the people's blind and sheeplike allegiance to their history that rouses their ire, forcing the top-ranking generals of the Allies and those of their historical enemies, the Germans, to confederate, to heal the rupture the corporal has caused not just in the historical record but in the very structure of things, which is itself a product of that history.

If we accept John T. Matthews' formulation that central to Faulkner's understanding of language is the conviction that "any form of representation, any sequence of signifying gestures, behaves like a language" (Matthews, *Play* 17), we may be persuaded as well that whatever the effect of the prose of *A Fable*, that novel is no less concerned with language than any of his other novels, and that it accepts the idea of language as a "sequence of signifying gestures" perhaps more directly and deliberately than any of the other books do, and indeed makes of this idea one of the novel's major themes. Matthews suggests that Faulkner's novels "regularly center their crises on the capacity or failure of characters to interpret, explain, master—in a word, to articulate—the common predicaments of loss, change, or desire" (17). This does not hold strictly true for all the characters of *A Fable*, however; few of them seem to have problems with articulation, nor any experience of articulation as a crisis, though each of the main characters does indeed face the "common predicaments of loss, change, or desire" in varying degrees. Yet the book as a whole is very much concerned with problems of articulation, with the whole problem of fictional meaning and the ways in which fictional meaning is generated. In the most-often quoted passage from *A Fable*'s climactic interview between general father and corporal son, this powerful father defines for his idealistic son, and for the reader, precisely what the issues in their relationship are. They are not "two . . . peasants swapping a horse," he notes, but rather "two articulations" (988) — not "representatives" or "symbols," but specifically "articulations" — of two opposing but complexly related views of life: power, structure, pragmatics, disillusion if not cynicism on the one hand; weakness, idealism, hope, and need on the other. Put this way, the issues are the same we have seen constantly at work in his other fiction, but in reverse relief. The old general and the corporal are not, then, as the general reminds us, representations of ordinary, "real" people engaged in quotidien economic and social intercourse, and verisimilitude is no part of the problem: the old general admits, in ways I'm not sure occur elsewhere in Faulkner, that they are characters in a novel, signs, if you will, which are part of the language of fictional discourse. *A Fable* is a semiotician's dream.

They are, then, two "articulations": it is, for a number of reasons, a significant term, for if the corporal and the old general are equally articulations of their respective positions, they are by no means equally articulate of those positions. Indeed, though their confrontation has been compared to the dramatic discussion between Isaac and Cass in *Go Down, Moses*, theirs in fact in no way resembles a dialogue, since the old general does all the talking; the corporal hardly says anything at all, much less, like Isaac McCaslin, put forth anything resembling a coherent philosophical justification for what he does or thinks, here or anywhere else in the novel. There are sufficient reasons for this.

I have argued in another place at greater length that what Roland Barthes has to say about the nature of myth and of mythical language in his *Mythologies* seems to me particularly useful in thinking about *A Fable*, for *A Fable* is also precisely about the nature of myth, as Barthes defines it, and of its language. The two books are roughly contemporary—*A Fable* was published in 1954, but Faulkner had conceived and begun working on it in 1943; *Mythologies*, published in 1957, was written between 1954 and 1956—and both books are at least partly their authors' responses to the post-war ideological scramble in which the cold war, the mass media, and modern technology combined in ways that drove the wedge between the powerful and the powerless, the individual and the masses, the illusioned and the disillusioned, even more deeply than the war had. Though Faulkner doubtless would not have stated his own motives in the same way, a paragraph in Barthes' preface may well also stand as Faulkner's animus: the starting point of Barthes' reflections was usually a feeling of impatience at the sight of the

> "naturalness" with which newspapers, art and common sense constantly dress up a reality which, even though it is the one we live in, is undoubtedly determined by history. In short, in the account given of our contemporary circumstances, I resented seeing Nature and History confused at every turn, and I wanted to track down, in the decorative display of *what-goes-without-saying*, the ideological abuse which, in my view, is hidden there. (11)

In a general sense one may say that much of Faulkner's fiction has been devoted to finding a language for saying *what-goes-without-saying*. Many of the issues in his work may be seen as a confrontation between the *what is* and the *what ought to be* or *what might have been if things could have been different*. What separates *A Fable* from the rest of the canon most strikingly is that it is most concerned with the *what-is*: specifically, it is an analysis of the forces that create and perpetuate the *what-goes-without-saying*. All of Faulkner's other works are written from the point of view of the powerless, the have-nots, those who are disenfranchised in one way or another, who butt up against the *what-is* of culture, economy, society, family, tradition—all various names for the all-powerful father; who spend their lives and their voices trying, unsuccessfully, to articulate their estrangement from the historical processes that have created the terms of their ideological grasps of the world—their myths—and so to perhaps reconstitute themselves in history. Faulkner's work is filled with characters who confront the myths of their culture—Horace Benbow, for example, and the myth of justice; Quentin Compson and that of virginity; Thomas Sutpen and Flem Snopes and that of bourgeois power and respectability. In general, those who *act*, like Flem and Sutpen, make more of a mark on history, for good or, more likely, for ill, than those who merely talk. Horace and Quentin are destroyed by their inability to force reality to conform to their myths. But what Flem and Sutpen want most to do is not at all, like the corporal, to destroy or expose that myth, even though they die in the process, but rather to join forces with it, to become its willing, even self-sacrificial allies; whatever their degree of success, they are no less betrayed by those bourgeois myths than Horace and Quentin, than Levine, the Quartermaster General, and the priest—all of whom, like Koestler's and Unamuno's heroes, destroy themselves rather than admit the failure of the ideological structures they have invested in.

If the other novels can be said to be about the effects of the bourgeois myths on the characters, *A Fable* may be said to be about the established forces that perpetuate and maintain those myths, those who benefit by them, and those who know not only how to manipulate them to their own advantage but how to keep the swarming, incoherent, inarticulate masses believing that those myths operate in their own best interests. The old general and Flem Snopes understand, more perceptively than any of Faulkner's other characters, the ways that myths work in people's lives, and know how to exploit those myths to their own advantage: they know that people with illusions are ripe for exploitation. Unlike Flem, though, the old general has no illusions himself, except the major one that allows him to assume that he is where he is by virtue of who he is, instead of by virtue of the infinite numbers of accidents of history; at the top of the historical heap, he doesn't *need* illusion. Flem, starting from the opposite end of the political and social spectrum from the old general, believes that he can find happiness in the American Dream; the trilogy traces his rise from the obscurity of the Yoknapatawpha backwoods to become, in *The Mansion*, "a pillar, rock-fixed, of things as they are" (222)—

exactly what the old general is. The trilogy's human scale, its intimacy, make Flem's discovery of the emptiness of the bourgeois life,
and the passive form of suicide he commits a very personal thing, and
perhaps finally cathartic in its effect: few have felt pity or fear or
empathy in thinking about Flem, but I find him terrifying (Polk, "Idealism" 116–17).

A Fable's epic scale, the magnitude of the general's power over the
lives of all Western Europe, makes intimacy impossible, and we are
confronted on page after page with an old general who really believes
that he manipulates the belief systems of "the people" not for pernal
aggrandisement, either in the pleasure of exercising power or for any
kind of personal gain, but simply because *they need it*, because they
need some political or religous credo to provide coherence to their
lives. The novel's portrait of *the people*—they are sheep: helpless, inarticulate, contemptible, and barely able even to feed themselves without the military's help—seems to justify the old general's paternalism.
Indeed, one of the deeply disturbing aspects of the novel is how fran-
tically the masses run from the freedom the corporal offers. They love
the foul-mouthed cockney groom who cynically manipulates their fear
of death, who literally sells them a reason to live by betting that they
won't. They blindly follow to their deaths the runner who shows them
a sign, without once asking what the sign means or who is flashing it
or why. They are eager to be sheep, to live or die for something they
can believe in, though they die gloriously in the air or ingloriously in
the mud; they will eagerly die, babbling what the old general calls
"polysyllabic and verbless patriotic nonsense" (994). They are savagely angry at the corporal, their putative savior, because he forces
upon them a challenge to the Fatherland and Motherland totems of
their ideologies.

So the old general's—power's—absolutely inescapable bind is that
it *must* sustain the masses in one illusion or another simply to maintain
order, to keep them from trampling each other to death. In the
bleakest reaches of *A Fable*'s themes, there is no alternative to power's
ideological manipulation of "the people." The old general's pragmatic brilliance is precisely in co-opting the corporal's self-sacrifice,

in making of him a martyr who will confirm them again in their political myths, and soothe them back into a war which is destroying them,
but which they can, they think, understand: anything but freedom.
He can make of the corporal what the corporal cannot make of himself—a sign, the sign they would see and believe in. He can give them
what the corporal cannot: hope. The corporal can only give them
freedom, which they want no part of.

The old general believes that no ideological structures have validity, and that all of them have value only as they are co-opted and used
by a political/power system that itself has no illusions. The old general, who in his small size and the delicacy of his features makes
one with other Faulknerian selfportraits, has enough of character and
conscience, not to say enough of wealth and power, to be fully aware
of all these considerations and to entertain, without illusions about
them, a profound compassion for their moiling lives, their minimal
needs: their capacity to endure and prevail even when their only sus-
tenance is hope.

Having joined the human race in the ideological trenches, joining
the battle for their souls, and being beaten over and over by their
intractable and inexhaustible commitment to their ideological prisons,
Faulkner gave up. He tried his best to engage people on their own
terms, using the methods of logical argument and the media they
understood, to show them where their ideological commitments were
leading everybody, the nation and the world, and he failed to change
one damned thing. After 1956 there's a noticeable slowdown of his
public activities, a renewed and even mellow commitment to his fiction first and to a social life with Charlottesville family and friends
next.

And so in fact we may not have very much to choose between the
early Faulkner and the one of the mid-fifties: the differences may lie
more in the color of the hair and the set of the lip than in anything
going on under the surface, where there is great continuity between
that early tragic vision and what is arguably a profoundly darker vision
in the late work, especially in *A Fable*—a darkness more visible than
Milton's even, if we know how to see it, because it is systemic. It does

not derive from ambition, greed, or any of the psychic or criminal compulsions, as in Faulkner's early works, but from humanity's enslavement to its ideological illusions: who will not be free because they insist on hope.

Works Cited

Most citations of Faulkner's texts are from the following volumes:

William Faulkner: Novels 1930–1935. Ed. Joseph Blotner and Noel Polk. New York: Library of America, 1985.
William Faulkner: Novels 1936–1940. Ed. Joseph Blotner and Noel Polk. New York: Library of America, 1990.
William Faulkner: Novels 1942–1954. Ed. Joseph Blotner and Noel Polk. New York: Library of America, 1990.

Specific citations are as follows (the list is alphabetized according to the assigned abbreviation).

AA	*Absalom, Absalom!* (1936). *William Faulkner: Novels 1936–1940*, 5–315.
	"And Now What's To Do?" *A Faulkner Miscellany*, 145–48.
AILD	*As I Lay Dying* (1930). *William Faulkner: Novels 1930–1935*, 1–178.
	"Barn Burning." CS, 3–25.
CS	*Collected Stories*. New York: Random House, 1950.
E	*Elmer* (1925). Northport, Ala.: Seajay P, 1984; *Mississippi Quarterly* 36,3 (1983): 337–460.
ESPL	*Essays Speeches and Public Letters of William Faulkner*. Ed. James B. Meriwether. New York: Random House, 1966.
F	*A Fable* (1954). *William Faulkner: Novels 1942–1954*, 665–1072.
FA	*Father Abraham*. Ed. James B. Meriwether. New York: Random House, 1983.
FD	*Flags in the Dust*. Ed. Douglas Day. New York: Random House, 1974.
FU	*Faulkner in the University*. Ed. Joseph L. Blotner and Frederick L. Gwynn. New York: Vintage, 1965.

GDM   *Go Down, Moses* (1942). *William Faulkner: Novels 1942–1954*, 1–281.

H   *The Hamlet* (1940). *William Faulkner: Novels 1936–1940*, 727–1075.
"Hong Li." *A Faulkner Miscellany*, 143–44.

ID   *Intruder in the Dust* (1948). *William Faulkner: Novels 1942–1954*, 283–470.
"An Innocent at Rinkside." ESPL, 48–51.
"Introduction" to *The Sound and the Fury*. Ed. James B. Meriwether. *The Southern Review*, n.s. 8(1972): 705–10.

Jer   *If I Forget Thee, Jerusalem [The Wild Palms]* (1939). *William Faulkner: Novels 1936–1940*, 493–726.

LA   *Light in August* (1932). *Faulkner: Novels 1930–1935*, 399–774.

LG   *Lion in the Garden: Interviews with William Faulkner 1926–1962*. New York: Random House, 1968.

M   *The Mansion* (1959). New York: Random House, 1959.

May   *Mayday* (written 1926). Notre Dame: U of Notre Dame P, 1976.
"Mississippi." ESPL, 11–43.
"Miss Zilphia Gant." US, 368–81.
"Mr. Acarius." US, 435–48.
"A Note on Sherwood Anderson." ESPL, 3–10.
"On Fear." ESPL, 92–106.
"On Privacy (The American Dream: What Happened to It?)" ESPL, 62–75.

P   *Pylon* (1935). *William Faulkner: Novels 1930–1935*, 775–992.

RN   *Requiem for a Nun* (1951). *William Faulkner: Novels 1942–1954*, 471–664.

S   *Sanctuary* (1931). *Faulkner: Novels 1930–1935*, 179–398.

SF   *The Sound and the Fury. New, Corrected Text* (1929, 1981). New York: Modern Library, 1992. This text includes "Compson: Appendix: 1699–1945."

SL   *Selected Letters of William Faulkner*. Ed. Joseph Blotner. New York: Random House, 1977.

SO   *Sanctuary: The Original Text*. Ed. Noel Polk. New York: Random House, 1981.

T   *The Town*. New York: Random House, 1957.

"To the Graduating Class, Pine Manor Junior College."
ESPL, 135–42.

T13   *These 13* (1931). New York: Jonathan Cape and Harrison Smith, 1931.

U   *The Unvanquished* (1938). *William Faulkner: Novels 1936–1940*, 317–492.

US   *Uncollected Stories*. Ed. Joseph Blotner. New York: Random House, 1977.

WFMS   *William Faulkner Manuscripts*, 44 volumes reproducing facsimiles of manuscripts and typescripts at the University of Virginia and the New York Public Library. Ed. Joseph Blotner, Thomas L. McHaney, Michael Millgate, and Noel Polk.

WP   *The Wild Palms* (see *If I Forget Thee, Jerusalem*).

Secondary Works Cited

Abadie, Ann, and Doreen Fowler, ed. *Faulkner and Popular Culture*. Jackson: UP of Mississippi, 1990.

Barthes, Roland. *Mythologies*. Tr. Annette Lavers. New York: Hill and Wang, 1975.

Basset, John, ed. *William Faulkner: The Critical Heritage*. London: Routledge & Kegan Paul, 1975.

Bleikasten, André. *The Most Splendid Failure: Faulkner's* **The Sound and the Fury**. Bloomington: Indiana UP, 1976.

———. "Fathers in Faulkner." *The Fictional Father*. Ed. Robert Con Davis. Amherst: U of Massachusetts P, 1981, 115–46.

———. *William Faulkner's* **The Sound and the Fury**: *A Critical Casebook*. New York: Garland, 1982.

———. " 'Cet Affreux Gout d'Encre': Emma Bovary's Ghost in *Sanctuary*." *William Faulkner: Materials, Studies, Criticism* (Japan) 5 (May 1983): 1–25.

———. "Terror and Nausea: Bodies in *Sanctuary*." *The Faulkner Journal*. 1,1 (1985): 17–29.

———. *The Ink of Melancholy*. Bloomington: Indiana UP, 1990.

Blotner, Joseph. *Faulkner: A Biography*. 2 vols. New York, Random House, 1974. Revised, 1 vol. New York: Random House, 1984.

Bowden, Tom. "Functions of Leftness and 'Dam' in William Faulkner's *The Sound and the Fury*." *Notes on Mississippi Writers* 19 (1987): 81–83.

Bradford, M. E. "The Knight and the Artist: Tasso and Faulkner's 'Carcassonne,' " *South Central Bulletin* (Winter 1981): 88–90.

Brooks, Cleanth. *William Faulkner: The Yoknapatawpha Country*. New Haven: Yale UP, 1963.

———. *William Faulkner: Toward Yoknapatawpha and Beyond*. New Haven: Yale UP, 1978, 60–66.

Broughton, Panthea Reid. "Masculinity and Menfolk in *The Hamlet*." *Mississippi Quarterly* 22 (1968): 181–89.

Budd, Louis J. "Playing Hide and Seek with William Faulkner: The Publicly Private Artist." Abadie and Fowler [1990] 34–58.

Carothers, James B. *William Faulkner's Short Stories*. Ann Arbor: UMI Research P, 1985.

Carter, Hodding. *Where Main Street Meets the River*. New York: Rinehart, 1953.

———. *Southern Legacy*. Baton Rouge: Louisiana State UP, 1950.

Chodorow, Nancy. *The Reproduction of Mothering: Psychoanalysis and the Sociology of Gender*. Berkeley: U of California P, 1978.

Cohen, Philip. " 'A Cheap Idea . . . Deliberately Conceived to Make Money': The Biographical Context of William Faulkner's Introduction to *Sanctuary*." *The Faulkner Journal* 3,2 (1988): 54–66.

Cohn, David. *Where I Was Born and Raised*. Boston: Houghton Mifflin, 1948.

Collins, Carvel. "The Pairing of *The Sound and the Fury* and *As I Lay Dying*." *Princeton U Library Chronicle* 18 (1957): 123.

———. "The Interior Monologues of *The Sound and the Fury*." Alan S. Downer, ed., *English Institute Essays 1952*. New York: Columbia UP, 1954, 29–56. Reprint in James B. Meriwether, ed., *The Merrill Studies in* **The Sound and the Fury**. Columbus, Ohio: Charles E. Merrill, 1970, 59–79.

Coughlan, Robert. "The Private World of William Faulkner." *Life*, 18 September 1953. New York: Harper, 1954.

Cowley, Malcolm. *The Faulkner-Cowley File: Letters and Memories, 1944–1962*. New York: Viking, 1966.

Crane, John Kenny. "The Jefferson Courthouse: An *Axis Exsecrabilis Mundi*." *Twentieth Century Literature* 15 (April 1969): 19–23.

Crane, Stephen. *The Red Badge of Courage*. Ed. Henry Binder. New York: Norton, 1976.

Cruttwell, C. R. M. F. *A History of the Great War 1914–1918*, 2nd ed. Oxford: Clarendon P, 1936.

Davis, Thadious M. *Faulkner's "Negro": Art and the Southern Context*. Baton Rouge: Louisiana State UP, 1983.

Dreiser, Theodore. *Sister Carrie*. Ed. James L. W. West III. Philadelphia: U of Pennsylvania P, 1981.

Eliot, T. S. *Collected Poems, 1909–1962*. New York: Harcourt, Brace & World, 1963.

Ferrer, Daniel. "Editorial Changes in the Chronology of *Absalom, Absalom!*: A Matter of Life and Death?" *The Faulkner Journal* 5,1 (1989): 45–48.

Fowler, Doreen, and Ann J. Abadie, ed. *Fifty Years of Yoknapatawpha*, Jackson: UP of Mississippi, 1980.

———. *"A Cosmos of My Own."* Jackson: UP of Mississippi, 1981.

———. *New Directions in Faulkner Studies*. Jackson: UP of Mississippi, 1984.

———. *Faulkner and Women*. Jackson: UP of Mississippi, 1986.

———. *Faulkner and Race*. Jackson: UP of Mississippi, 1987.

Freud, Sigmund. *The Standard Edition of the Complete Psychological Works of Sigmund Freud*. Trans. and ed. James Strachey. London: The Hogarth Press and the Institute of Psycho-Analysis, 1955.

Girard, René. *Deceit, Desire, and the Novel: Self and Other in Literary Structure*. Tr. Yvonne Freccero. Baltimore: Johns Hopkins UP, 1965.

Godden, Richard. "Quentin Compson: Tyrrhenian Vase or Crucible of Race?" Polk, *New Essays*, 99–137.

Goethe, Wolfgang von. *Faust*. Trans. Walter Arndt, ed. Cyrus Hamlin. New York: Norton, 1976.

Greg, W. W. "The Rationale of Copy-Text." *Studies in Bibliography* 3 (1950–51): 19–36.

Gresset, Michel. "A Public Man's Private Voice: Faulkner's Letters to Else Jonsson." Gresset and Ohashi, 61–73.

———. *Fascination: Faulkner's Fiction, 1919–1936*. Durham: Duke UP, 1989.

——— and Kenzaburo Ohashi, ed. *Faulkner: After the Nobel Prize*. Tokyo: Yamaguchi Publishing House, 1987.

——— and Patrick Samway ed. *Faulkner and Idealism: Perspectives from Paris*. Jackson: UP of Mississippi, 1983.

——— and Noel Polk, ed. *Intertextuality in Faulkner*. Jackson: UP of Mississippi, 1985.

Grimwood, Michael. *Heart in Conflict: Faulkner's Struggles with Vocation*. Athens: U of Georgia P, 1987.

Housman, A. E. *The Collected Poems*. London: Jonathan Cape, 1960.

Hult, Sharon Smith. "William Faulkner's 'The Brooch': The Journey to the Riolama." *Mississippi Quarterly* 27,3 (1974): 291–305.

Irwin, John T. *Doubling and Incest/Repetition and Revenge: A Speculative Reading of Faulkner*. Baltimore: Johns Hopkins UP, 1976.

Jenkins, Lee. *Faulkner and Black-White Relations: A Psychoanalytic Approach*. New York: Columbia UP, 1981.

Kałuża, Irena. *The Functioning of Sentence Structure in the Stream-of-Consciousness Technique of William Faulkner's* **The Sound and the Fury**. Kraków: Nadladem Uniwersytetu Jagiellonskiego, 1967.

Kang, Hee. "A New Configuration of Faulkner's Feminine: Linda Snopes Kohl in *The Mansion*." *The Faulkner Journal* 8,1 (1992): 21–41.

Kartiganer, Donald. " 'Now I Can Write': Faulkner's Novel of Invention." Polk, *New Essays*, 71–97.

——— and Ann J. Abadie, ed. *Faulkner and Ideology*. Jackson: UP of Mississippi, 1996.

Kerr, Elizabeth. *William Faulkner's Gothic Domain*. Port Washington, NY: Kennikat, 1979.

Kloss, Robert J. "Faulkner's *As I Lay Dying*." *American Imago* 38 (1981): 429–44.

Knights, Pamela E. "The Cost of Single-Mindedness: Consciousness in *Sanctuary*." *The Faulkner Journal* 5,1 (1989): 3–10.

Kubie, Lawrence. "William Faulkner's *Sanctuary*: An Analysis," *Saturday Review of Literature* (20 October 1934), 218, 224–25. Reprinted in J. Douglas Canfield, ed., *Twentieth Century Interpretations of* **Sanctuary**: A Collection of Critical Essays. Englewood Cliffs, N.J.: Prentice-Hall, 1983, 25–31.

Kuyk, Dirk, Jr. *Sutpen's Design: Interpreting Faulkner's* **Absalom, Absalom!**. Charlottesville: UP of Virginia, 1990.

Lacan, Jacques. *The Four Fundamental Concepts of Psycho-analysis*. Ed. Jacques-Alain Miller. Tr. Alan Sheridan. New York: Norton, 1978.

Lester, Cheryl. "To Market, To Market: *The Portable Faulkner*." *Criticism* 29 (Summer 1987): 371–92.

———. "From Place to Place in *The Sound and the Fury*: The Syntax of Interrogation." *Modern Fiction Studies* 34,2 (1988): 141–55.

Lind, Ilsa Dusoir. "The Mutual Relevance of Faulkner Studies and Women's Studies: An Interdisciplinary Inquiry." Fowler and Abadie, 1986, 21–40.

Lockyer, Judith. *Ordered by Words: Language and Narration in the Novels of William Faulkner.* Carbondale: Southern Illinois UP, 1991.

Martin, Jay. " 'The Whole Burden of Man's History of His Impossible Heart's Desire': The Early Life of William Faulkner." *American Literature* 53 (January 1982): 607–29.

Matthews, John T. *The Play of Faulkner's Language.* Ithaca: Cornell UP, 1982.

———. "The Elliptical Nature of *Sanctuary.*" *Novel* 17 (1984): 246–65.

McHaney, Thomas L. "The Elmer Papers: Faulkner's Comic Portraits of the Artist." *Mississippi Quarterly* 26,3 (1973): 281–311.

McLemore, Richard Aubrey, ed. *A History of Mississippi*, 2 vols. Jackson: U and College P of Mississippi, 1973.

McMillen, Neil R., and Noel Polk. "Faulkner on Lynching." *The Faulkner Journal* 8,1 (1992): 3–14.

Meriwether, James B. *The Literary Career of William Faulkner.* Princeton: Princeton U Library, 1961.

———, ed. *A Faulkner Miscellany.* Jackson: UP of Mississippi, 1974.

———. "The Short Fiction of William Faulkner: A Bibliography." *Proof 1* (1971): 293–329.

———. "Faulkner's Correspondence with *Scribner's Magazine.*" *Proof 3* (1973): 253–82.

Millgate, Jane. "Quentin Compson as Poor Player: Verbal and Social Clichés in *The Sound and the Fury.*" *Revue des Langues Vivantes* 34 (1968): 40–49.

Millgate, Michael. *The Achievement of William Faulkner.* New York: Random House, 1966.

Minter, David. *William Faulkner: His Life and Work.* Baltimore: Johns Hopkins UP, 1980.

Morris, Wesley, with Barbara Alverson Morris. *Reading Faulkner.* Madison: U of Wisconsin P, 1989.

Muhlenfeld, Elisabeth. "Bewildered Witness: Temple Drake in *Sanctuary.*" *The Faulkner Journal* 1,2 (1986): 43–55.

Parker, Hershel. *Flawed Texts and Verbal Icons: Literary Authority in American Fiction.* Evanston: Northwestern UP, 1984.

———. "Regularizing Accidentals: The Latest Form of Infidelity." *Proof 1* (1973): 1–20.

——— and Brian Higgins. "Sober Second Thoughts: Fitzgerald's 'Final Version' of *Tender Is the Night.*" *Proof 4* (1975): 129–152.

Peckham, Morse. "The Place of Sex in the Work of William Faulkner." *Studies in the Twentieth Century* no. 14 (Fall 1974): 1–20.

Peters, Erskine. *William Faulkner: The Yoknapatawpha World and Black Being.* Darby, Pa.: Norwood, 1983.

Pitavy, François. "Through the Poet's Eye: A View of Quentin Compson." Bleikasten, *Casebook*, 79–99.

———. "The Gothicism of *Absalom, Absalom!*: Rosa Coldfield." Fowler and Abadie, 1981, 199–226.

Poe, Edgar Allan. *Poetry and Tales.* New York: Library of America, 1984.

Polk, Noel. " 'The Dungeon Was Mother Herself': William Faulkner: 1927–1931." Fowler and Abadie, 1984, 61–93.

———. *An Editorial Handbook for William Faulkner's* **The Sound and the Fury**. New York: Garland, 1985.

———. "Enduring *A Fable* and Prevailing." Gresset and Ohashi, 110–26.

———. "Faulkner at Midcentury." Donald M. Kartiganer and Ann J. Abadie, ed., *Faulkner and Ideology.* Jackson: UP of Mississippi, 1996, 297–328.

———. *Faulkner's* **Requiem for a Nun:** *A Critical Study.* Bloomington: Indiana UP, 1981.

———. " 'I Taken an Oath of Office Too'; Faulkner and the Law." Fowler and Abadie, 1980, 159–78.

———. "Idealism in *The Mansion*." Gresset and Samway, 112–26.

———. "Law in Faulkner's *Sanctuary*." *Mississippi College Law Review* 4,2 (1984): 227–43.

———. "Man in the Middle: Faulkner and the Southern White Moderate." Fowler and Abadie, 1987, 130–51.

———, ed. *New Essays on "The Sound and the Fury."* Cambridge: Cambridge UP, 1993.

———. "The Space Between *Sanctuary*." Gresset and Polk, 16–35.

———. "The Text of the Modern Library *A Curtain of Green*." *Eudora Welty Newsletter* 3, no. 1-A (Winter 1979): 6–9.

———. "Trying Not to Say: A Primer on the Language of *The Sound and the Fury*." Polk, *New Essays*, 139–75.

———. "Where the Comma Goes: Editing William Faulkner." George Bornstein, ed. *Representing Modernist Texts: Editing as Interpretation.* Ann Arbor: U of Michigan P, 1991, 241–58.

———. "Woman and the Feminine in *A Fable*." Fowler and Abadie, 1986, 180–204.

Putzel, Max. "Faulkner's Short Story Sending Schedule." *Publications of the Bibliographical Society of America* 71 (1977): 98–105.

Ross, Stephen M. *Fiction's Inexhaustible Voice: Speech and Writing in Faulkner.* Athens: U of Georgia P, 1989.

Roughton, Ralph. Letter to author, 21 July 1983. I am grateful to Dr. Roughton for permission to publish portions of his letter.

Samway, Patrick. "New Material for Faulkner's *Intruder in the Dust.*" Meriwether, *Miscellany*, 107–12.

Schoenberg, Estella. *Old Tales and Talking: Quentin Compson in William Faulkner's* **Absalom, Absalom** *and Related Works.* Jackson: UP of Mississippi, 1977.

Schwartz, Lawrence H. *Creating Faulkner's Reputation: The Politics of Modern Literary Criticism.* Knoxville: U of Tennessee P, 1988.

Sedgwick, Eve Kosofsky. *Between Men: English Literature and Male Homosocial Desire.* New York: Columbia UP, 1985.

Sellers, Charles, Henry May, and Neil R. McMillen. *A Synopsis of American History.* Seventh edition. Chicago: Dee, 1992.

Skei, Hans. *William Faulkner: The Short Story Career.* Oslo: Universitetsforlaget, 1981.

———. *Bold and Tragical and Austere: William Faulkner's "These 13."* Oslo: U of Oslo, 1977.

Strindberg, August. *A Dream Play.* Reprinted in *A Treasury of The American Theatre*, ed. John Gassner. New York: Simon and Schuster, 1965.

Sundquist, Eric J. *Faulkner: The House Divided.* Baltimore: Johns Hopkins UP, 1983.

Tanner, Tony. *Adultery in the Novel: Contract and Transgression.* Baltimore: Johns Hopkins UP, 1979.

Taylor, Walter. *Faulkner's Search for a South.* Urbana: U of Illinois P, 1983.

Trouard, Dawn. "Eula's Plot: An Irigararian Reading of Faulkner's Snopes Trilogy." *Mississippi Quarterly* 42,3 (1989): 281–97.

———. "Faulkner's Text Which Is Not One." Polk, *New Essays*, 23–69.

Vickery, Olga W. *The Novels of William Faulkner: A Critical Interpretation.* Baton Rouge: Louisiana State UP, 1959; rev. 1964.

Welty, Eudora. *A Curtain of Green.* New York: Doubleday, 1941.

———. *Collected Stories.* New York: Harcourt Brace Jovanovich, 1980.

———. *L'Homme Petrifié*, tr. Michel Gresset. Paris: Flammarion, 1986.

West, James L. W. III. "Editorial Theory and the Act of Submission." *Papers of the Bibliographical Society of America* 83 (1989): 169–85.

Wilde, Meta Carpenter, and Orrin Borsten. *A Loving Gentleman*. New York: Simon & Schuster, 1976.

Williams, Joan. "In Defense of Caroline Compson." Arthur Kinney, ed. *Critical Essays on William Faulkner: The Compson Family*. Boston: G. K. Hall, 1982, 402–07.

Wilson, Edmund. "William Faulkner's Reply to the Civil-Rights Program." *New Yorker* (23 October 1948). In John Bassett, ed. *William Faulkner: The Critical Heritage*. London: Routledge and Kegan Paul, 1975, 335–36.

Winter, William F. "New Directions in Politics, 1948–1956." In McLemore, 140–53.

Wittenberg, Judith Bryant. *Faulkner: The Transfiguration of Biography*. Lincoln: U of Nebraska P, 1979.

Wondra, Janet. " 'Play' within a Play: Gaming with Language in *Requiem for a Nun*." *The Faulkner Journal* 8,1 (1992): 43–59.

Index

Themes: autobiographical content of writings, 44–45, 253; castration, 120, 127f; childhood, xvi, 26–29, 43, 51ff, 142, 210ff; Christianity, 196–218 *passim;* cold war, 227, 249–72 *passim;* cuckoldry, 137–65, 184ff; domesticity, 169–95 *passim;* dreams (see also nightmare), 56, 214ff; family structures, 25–98; feminine, 196–218 *passim;* gender structures, 166–95 *passim;* homoeroticism, 113, 140–66 *passim*, 169–95 *passim*, 216; language, 99–136, 265–72; law, 26–28, 38, 60–71; lynching, 219f, 234ff; manuscripts, ix–xvi, 3–21; miscegenation, 137–44; nightmare, 45ff; Paris, France, 207–18 *passim;* race, xv, 137–44, 219–41; race as mask for gender, 137–44; sexuality, 147ff; virginity, 113, 178f, 213ff; women, attitudes toward, 147ff, 157ff. *See also* Freud, Sigmund

Works: *Absalom, Absalom!*, xi, xv, 5n, 7, 9, 13, 16–18, 24–25, 40, 72, 88–89, 137–44, 157, 177f, 198, 205, 221, 230, 233, 234, 237, 265; "And Now What's To Do?", 149ff; "Appendix: Compson: 1699–1945," 212, 260; "Artist at Home," 153–55, 157; *As I Lay Dying*, xi, 4, 5, 22, 35, 40, 147, 150, 198; "Barn Burning," 26–29, 96;